WISDOM
from ABOVE

DAILY ENCOURAGEMENT FOR LIFE
from THE PROVERBS

CHARLES F. STANLEY

HOWARD BOOKS
An Imprint of Simon and Schuster, Inc.
New York   Nashville   London   Toronto   Sydney   New Delhi

Howard Books
An Imprint of Simon & Schuster, Inc.
1230 Avenue of the Americas
New York, NY 10020

First Howard Books hardcover edition November 2016

HOWARD and colophon are trademarks of Simon & Schuster, Inc.

For information about special discounts for bulk purchases, please contact Simon & Schuster Special Sales at 1-866-506-1949 or business@simonandschuster.com.

The Simon & Schuster Speakers Bureau can bring authors to your live event. For more information or to book an event, contact the Simon & Schuster Speakers Bureau at 1-866-248-3049 or visit our website at www.simonspeakers.com.

Interior design by Davina Mock-Maniscalco

Manufactured in the United States of America

10 9 8

Library of Congress Cataloging-in-Publication Data is available.

ISBN 978-1-5011-3541-5
ISBN 978-1-5011-3542-2 (ebook)

Contents

Introduction

vii

JANUARY

Honoring God

1

FEBRUARY

Relationships

33

MARCH

Living Wisely

63

APRIL

Jesus

95

MAY

Emotions

127

v

JUNE

Temptation

159

JULY

Character

191

AUGUST

Communication

223

SEPTEMBER

Servant Leadership

255

OCTOBER

Stewardship

287

NOVEMBER

Blessings of Wisdom

319

DECEMBER

God with Us

351

Introduction

Do you believe that God wants you to succeed? Well, He does. In fact, He has greater dreams and aspirations for you than you probably realize. And when you walk in the center of His will, you have His presence, power, protection, promise, and provision to achieve the incredible goals He calls you to accomplish.

This is why it is so important that when you get up in the morning you get into God's Word and spend time with Him. Even spending just fifteen minutes with the Lord God of all creation will set the rudder of your day, will give you a sense of direction, and will energize you for whatever is ahead.

This devotional has been written to help you stay in Scripture— challenging you to read and meditate on God's Word every day. Each month moves through the whole book of Proverbs, which has thirty-one chapters total. The first day of the month features a verse from Proverbs chapter 1; the second day, from Proverbs chapter 2, and so on. A few pages in the back of the book have been reserved for your personal notes. As you walk through this book of wisdom, ask God to speak to your heart and fill you with His wisdom and guidance. Tell Him that you're committed to doing whatever He asks of you. Then watch as He directs your path in ways and to heights you never dreamed possible.

Honoring God

As you begin the new year,
set your heart on honoring and obeying God.
As you do, you will have more clarity
and purpose the whole year long.

Beginning

SCRIPTURE READING: PROVERBS 1; GENESIS 1:1; ISAIAH 43:19

The [reverent] fear of the Lord
[that is, worshipping Him
and regarding Him as truly awesome]
is the beginning and the preeminent part of knowledge
[its starting point and its essence].
PROVERBS 1:7 AMP

Today is the start of a new year, and along with it come fresh hopes and opportunities. A whole set of possibilities and uncertainties stand before you. The prospect of these new beginnings fills us with great awe, which is why many people make such an effort to commemorate this day—making resolutions and celebrating their arrival. The promise of a new beginning stirs hope in our souls.

But from the very first verse in Scripture—Genesis 1:1—we see that the most powerful beginnings come from God. And the very best, most fulfilling and fruitful commencements do not just *include* the Father but are initiated and guided by Him.

So as you start this year, the most important principle for you to embrace is that God formed you for a purpose and has been shaping you for the days and months ahead. He has a plan for you that is good, acceptable, and wise—and He promises to lead you well. Your responsibility is to always acknowledge Him as the living God, your Lord, and the sovereign Architect and Ruler of all creation.

If you wish to make this your very best year yet, allow God to begin it—every day of it—and trust Him to show you what He wants to accomplish in and through you. Look for Him to initiate the opportunities, healings, spiritual growth, and new areas of fruitfulness. For to do so, friend, is the very heart of wisdom.

Father, thank You for this new year and all the hope it brings.
Lead me, Lord, I revere You as my Savior and wise King,
and know that the best beginnings are from You.
Amen.

Seeking What He's Giving

SCRIPTURE READING: PROVERBS 2; MATTHEW 7:7

The LORD gives wisdom; from His mouth
come knowledge and understanding.
PROVERBS 2:6

Perhaps as the first days of this new year pass, certain questions are still on your mind that you just cannot shake. Issues that have long troubled you persist in causing your faith to waver. You wonder when or if God will ever help you.

You most likely have sought the Father before about these burdens, which is the very best thing you can do. But don't approach Him just to talk about the problems—He already understands all there is to know about them and doesn't benefit from your assessments. Instead, go before Him to *listen*. Remember that the fear of the Lord—the acknowledgment of Him as God—is the beginning of wisdom. And He freely gives knowledge and understanding to those who will wholeheartedly recognize that He holds the answers.

In fact, Jesus promised, "Keep on asking, and you will receive what you ask for. Keep on seeking, and you will find. Keep on knocking, and the door will be opened to you" (Matthew 7:7 NLT). This is a guarantee from God Himself: The Father *wants* to help you understand. He longs to show you what He is achieving through that situation, what He desires for you to learn from it, and how you can achieve the victory in it.

So the wisest thing you can do is continue getting on your face before Him in prayer—opening His Word and giving His Holy Spirit ample time to speak to you. Keep seeking and do not lose heart. The Lord will give you the wisdom you need to triumph in all you're facing.

Father, You know the questions that continue on my heart.
I come before You to listen, Lord, knowing You have the answer
to every need and the wisdom to guide me in every situation.
Amen.

Leaning on His Understanding

SCRIPTURE READING: PROVERBS 3; 1 CHRONICLES 29:11; LUKE 18:27

Trust in the LORD with all your heart
and do not lean on your own understanding.
PROVERBS 3:5

Do not lean on your own understanding. This is one of the most difficult commands to practice because it's far more natural for us to see a situation and make a judgment about it. It's what we've been taught to do from the time we are small children—we are instructed to assess situations and come to well-educated conclusions in order to make good decisions.

But leaning on our own understanding is often why we get so disheartened and fearful about the future. From our point of view, the adversity we face appears so overwhelmingly impossible that we cannot imagine how to overcome it. And we question why the Father would allow us to experience such difficulties.

But God does not look at the trials that come to you from the agonizing center of them like you do—but from beginning to end from His all-knowing, eternal perspective. In fact, before trouble touches your life, He has already charted the course and engineered your circumstances to build your faith and character, help you know Him better, and guide you to ultimate triumph. Knowing all of this, He calls you to trust Him—to refuse to rely on your assessment of the situation, but rather be confident that: "The things that are impossible with people are possible with God" (Luke 18:27).

So when trouble strikes, don't be disheartened by leaning on your limited, earthly understanding. Rather, be encouraged by focusing on the fact that the Father has your life in His wise, all-powerful hands and is working all things out for your good.

Father, thank You for seeing my situation clearly and for
leading me wisely in it. Help me to see life from Your
perspective and to trust You with all my heart.
Amen.

JANUARY 4

A Sure Road

SCRIPTURE READING: PROVERBS 4; 2 SAMUEL 22:36–37

When you walk, your steps will not be impeded;
and if you run, you will not stumble.
PROVERBS 4:12

God has a specific path for you to walk that is shaped by what He created you to become, so the decisions, struggles, and questions before you today are no surprise to Him. In fact, they are in your life for a purpose—to refine your faith and teach you how to walk with Him.

Of course, you may be wondering, *I thought these trials were in my life as a punishment because I've made so many mistakes. Maybe God is too angry or disappointed with me to bless me.* If these are the thoughts you are having, I want to encourage you: When Jesus is your Savior and you confess and turn away from your sins, God forgives you completely. He no longer holds your sins against you.

You may be facing the consequences of your mistakes, but God is not punishing you. On the contrary, the challenges you are facing are actively preparing you for the future so you can enjoy all the blessings He's planned for you. Your heavenly Father knows exactly what it is about you that causes you to choose the wrong path, and He loves you too much to continue allowing you to fall to the same temptations. So He will remove those inner stumbling blocks that hinder you through the adversity He allows to come into your life.

So analyze the decisions, struggles, and questions before you today. How are they an opportunity to choose differently from what you've chosen in the past? This is your chance to respond in a way that honors God. Because when you do, you'll find He makes your steps sure—just as He does your future.

Father, thank You for forgiving my sins and showing
me how to be completely free of them.
I praise You for making my way sure.
Amen.

All Your Paths

SCRIPTURE READING: PROVERBS 5; PSALM 139:16

The ways of a man are before the eyes of the LORD,
and He watches all his paths.
PROVERBS 5:21

Do you ever look at another person and think, "How in the world was that marvelous gift in you developed? How did you discover you could do that?" The wide variety of talents, abilities, and interests of people is astounding. And all of them have a story—a person who inspired them or an event that awakened their enthusiasm in a particular area.

When you think of all the possibilities, it may *seem* that a person's potential is endless, especially for those who have many earthly resources. And maybe that is somewhat disheartening to you today because your life feels limited by your background and burdens. You wonder if your circumstances had been different, if you could have been that award-winning athlete, performer, artist, or scientist. If life hadn't been so difficult, what could you have become?

But your situation is not as limited as it may seem. In fact, Scripture is clear that God has a *specific* plan for you (Psalm 139:16). He watches over every path that leads to your life—including the opportunities, influences, resources, and trials that affect you—in order to shape your character and gifts. Where you are is no mistake. On the contrary, it is all part of God developing you into all He created you to be. And His molding gives you far greater, eternal benefits than any earthly advantage could have.

So do not lose heart or look at others with envy. Rather, the wise course is to count on the Father to lead you step by step along His will for you—the only path that will lead to your full potential.

Father, thank You for guiding the circumstances that influence my life.
I trust that You're leading me in the best way possible.
Amen.

The Light of Your Life

SCRIPTURE READING: PROVERBS 6; PSALM 119:105

The commandment is a lamp and the teaching is light.
PROVERBS 6:23

Some days the path ahead may seem confusing because what you hear from the world and those around you is so vastly different from what God says in His Word. And because you and I are influenced by the sin nature, the world's way will always *appear* like the easier, more appealing course.

The problem is that if you respond according to the principles of this fallen world, you can expect more conflict, disappointment, disillusionment, and discontentment. And your path will grow even darker and more confusing. But if you choose to walk wisely—God's way—you can anticipate contentment when circumstances are difficult, courage in the midst of the storm, and confidence in the most fearful conditions.

Why? Because the Father's commands illuminate your way, giving you light even in the darkest situations. Psalm 119:105 affirms, "Your word is a lamp to my feet and a light to my path." Principles like forgiving your enemies, letting the Lord fight your battles, and being a giver rather than a receiver may all seem counterintuitive. But you can be certain that if God commands it, it is good, right, liberating, and true. His Word never fails to help you take advantage of opportunities, invest your time and resources wisely, and cultivate your relationships.

What you choose today will determine how the road looks tomorrow. So if the path ahead appears confusing, stop and make sure that the route you take has been mapped out by the Father. If you seek Him, He promises to direct you. So allow His commands to illumine the road before you and His teaching to be the light of your life.

Father, sometimes everything in me fights against Your commands.
But I will obey You in faith because Your light
faithfully delivers me from the darkness.
Amen.

Rule Your Heart

SCRIPTURE READING: PROVERBS 7; PSALM 25:10; JEREMIAH 17:9

Do not let your heart turn aside.
PROVERBS 7:25

You will have many choices today—steps you can take toward God and steps you can take away from Him. In fact, one or more of those choices may be on your mind right now.

These decisions are both small and large in scale, and raise questions such as: Will you exhibit faith in the challenges you are facing, or will you be ruled by your emotions? Will you courageously do what the Lord has directed you to do, or will you give in to your fears and self-interests? Will you trust the Father to fulfill your needs, or will you satisfy your desires in your own way?

You may be tempted to "follow your heart," but Scripture is clear: "The heart is more deceitful than all else and is desperately sick; who can understand it?" (Jeremiah 17:9). If you submit to what feels *natural*—what you would usually do out of habit or instinct—you will most likely find yourself in trouble. But "all the paths of the Lord are lovingkindness and truth" (Psalm 25:10). He will never fail to lead you in the best way.

Realize that whether the decisions you make today are minuscule or monumental, with them you travel farther down a road of your future. But you have a choice: You can allow God to rule your heart. You can deny the fallen nature in you and honor the Lord, trusting that His path leads to wisdom, greater character, eternal reward, and a deeper relationship with your Creator.

So make the choice with the important decisions you have today. Discipline your heart to follow God in faith. And have confidence that when you do, you've taken steps in the right direction.

Father, I choose You. Please give me the discernment and strength to follow You and keep my feet planted on the path of Your will.
Amen.

He Is with You

SCRIPTURE READING: PROVERBS 8; EXODUS 20:20

"I love those who love me; and those
who diligently seek me will find me."
PROVERBS 8:17

If you are feeling alone in your struggles today, take heart. There is a Person who pursues a deep and abiding relationship with you—One who lovingly walks with you, revealing the choices that will lead you to a spiritually rich and fruitful life. In Proverbs 8, this Person is characterized as Wisdom—for all knowledge and understanding come from Him. Yet wisdom is only part of all that your wonderful Companion is.

Of course, that Person is Jesus, who loves you and provides the very best for you. But perhaps with the discouragements you're facing today, you are doubtful if a relationship with Him is truly possible. After all, you cannot see or touch Him. Maybe you try to speak in faith, but when pressed about whether or not you genuinely believe the Lord will help you, the best you can say is, "I hope so." You're not completely sure He will respond. The messages keep playing in your mind: *These issues that break my heart are not really worthy of His attention.*

But friend, God never intended for you to approach Him with a "hope so" attitude. He wants you to be absolutely certain that He is right there for you. In fact, He may have even allowed the challenges in your life so that you will seek Him with more passion and devotion (Exodus 20:20).

Your loving heavenly Father wants to have a profound, intimate, moment-by-moment relationship with you—and all you have to do is turn to Him. The way He responds to you may not be what you expect, but He never fails to reply when you're willing to listen. So love Him and seek Him diligently, because you will certainly find Him.

Father, thank You for being there for me, walking with me
through every situation, and revealing the path
that leads me to a godly and fruitful life.
Amen.

Build Up

Wisdom has built her house.
PROVERBS 9:1

There are times you will feel weak, powerless to change the future or overcome the challenges ahead of you. In those moments, resist the temptation to entertain notions of defeat or to give in to despair, because with every negative thought, you are tearing down your life and faith.

You have a choice about how you respond to your low moments. And as you can see from today's verse, the person of wisdom makes a conscious effort to build up rather than destroy. In other words, you may feel weak, but you can make the choice to increase your strength.

How? Jesus said, "Everyone who hears these words of Mine and acts on them, may be compared to a wise man who built his house on the rock. And the rain fell, and the floods came, and the winds blew and slammed against that house; and yet it did not fall, for it had been founded on the rock" (Matthew 7:24–25). You grow resilient when you base your life on God's Word and obey it.

Friend, the storms *will* come. And if you want to be able to stand firm no matter how intensely the tempest blows, then a profound relationship with Jesus is the answer. Instead of dwelling on thoughts of defeat, you must turn your mind to the principles and promises of Scripture. Why? Because by doing so, you are reminded that your future is contingent not upon your strength but on the power and wisdom of God, who shapes and molds the days ahead.

Therefore, if you are feeling weak today, build yourself up by spending time in God's Word. Not only will the Lord help you through your difficulties, He also will use them to make you even stronger.

*Father, I feel weak, but I am so grateful You
are my future and my strength.
Build me up with Your Word so I may always honor You.
Amen.*

Perspective

SCRIPTURE READING: PROVERBS 10; HEBREWS 13:5

The way of the LORD is a stronghold to the upright.
PROVERBS 10:29

Regardless of what you have or who you are, circumstances will arise that make you feel insecure. Whether you experience physical, emotional, financial, or relational threats, they can strike at the very core of what you've built up as your safety and confidence. And if you measure those challenges against your own strengths, it's no wonder they make you so uneasy.

So right now, take a moment and look at those challenges from God's perspective. Are any of them beyond His wisdom to overcome or His power to conqueror? Of course not. The One who formed the heavens and the earth can do anything. Nothing is too difficult for Him.

But does the Lord love you enough to help you through your difficulties? Absolutely He does. One look at the cross and the life Jesus gave to save you and you know for certain He will do whatever it takes to support and sustain you. He will never abandon or forsake you (Hebrews 13:5).

What then is the real issue here? It all comes down to whether or not you trust God. Are you wisely accepting the Father's help by obeying Him, or have you foolishly walked away from His protection—demanding your own way rather than embracing His?

Friend, there is absolutely no safer place for you than the center of God's will. So if you've been obeying the Lord, rejoice because He is using these adverse circumstances to strengthen you. If you've drifted away from Him, thank Him for getting you back on track. Either way, trust Him. Because you never lose by wisely having faith in the Father, but you always suffer loss when you stray from His path.

Father, thank You that nothing I face is too difficult for You.
I trust You, Lord—lead me in the way I should go.
Amen.

Delighting Him

SCRIPTURE READING: PROVERBS 11; MICAH 6:8; HEBREWS 6:10

The blameless in their walk are [the Lord's] delight.
PROVERBS 11:20

You have the power to please God—to delight Him and fill His heart with joy. You may imagine this requires a full gamut of rules and regulations—that you must read your Bible and pray several hours a day, participate in an endless array of religious activities, and make absolutely sure you never make a mistake.

But the person who truly pleases God is the not one who is engaged in mindless rituals or tries to earn his own righteousness. On the contrary, the Lord treasures the believer who pursues a deeply personal relationship with Him out of gratefulness and who loves Him for who He is.

With this in mind, Micah 6:8 poses the question, "What does the Lord require of you but to do justice, to love kindness, and to walk humbly with your God?" In other words, the Father has shown throughout history that His highest desire is that you live in a manner that honors Him—with holiness, compassion, and obedience. And that you are motivated by faithfulness to Him.

And so what brings the most joy to your Father's heart is that you respectfully accept His instructions, exhibit the merciful character of Christ in all you do, and submit to His wisdom in every situation. Friend, God doesn't want you to practice religion. Rather, He wants you to be in relationship with Him. The sacrifices you make without love are ultimately meaningless. But He will never forget anything you do out of adoring devotion to Him (Hebrews 6:10). So seek Him, love Him, and follow Him today, and be a person who is a true delight to Him.

Father, how I long to please You. I love You, Lord!
May my life be an expression of worshipful devotion
to Your holy and precious name.
Amen.

The Favor You Need

SCRIPTURE READING: PROVERBS 12; EXODUS 7:3–5; JEREMIAH 31:3

A good man will obtain favor from the LORD.
PROVERBS 12:2

Perhaps as you arise today, there is someone on your mind who you wish would look upon you with grace and partiality. Maybe you wish to experience this person's approval, receive his or her encouragement, or obtain some gift or opportunity. It would mean the world to you to have his or her favor because then you would have the support and esteem you long for.

This was certainly true for Moses as he faced the daunting task of leading the people of Israel out of Egypt and into the Promised Land of Canaan. He desperately needed Pharaoh to agree to let God's people go.

But instead of softening Pharaoh's heart toward Moses, God did the opposite. The Lord said, "I will harden Pharaoh's heart that I may multiply My signs and My wonders in the land of Egypt" (Exodus 7:3). The Father did this so that Moses—and, in fact, all of Israel—would realize the support needed was not from someone with earthly and, therefore, limited wisdom, resources, and strength. No, he needed the counsel and favor of God Himself.

The same is true for you today as you think about the person whose approval you desire above everyone else's. Whether God turns that individual's heart toward you or away from you, realize it is the Father whom you really need and that only He gives you His very best. As a child of the Most High God, you have the support, grace, and favor you need to succeed in everything He gives you to do. So do not fear or fret if others reject you. Rather, rejoice that the only One who really counts loves you always (Jeremiah 31:3).

Father, thank You that because Jesus is my
Savior, I always have Your favor.
Thank You for providing everything I really need.
Amen.

Steady On

SCRIPTURE READING: PROVERBS 13; PSALM 73:13–14

Godliness guards the path of the blameless.
PROVERBS 13:6 NLT

Do you ever experience times when it seems like all you get for obeying God is heartache? Certainly, the psalmist Asaph felt this way. He said, "Surely in vain I have kept my heart pure and washed my hands in innocence; for I have been stricken all day long and chastened every morning" (Psalm 73:13–14). Sometimes it may appear that the only ones getting ahead in life are those who do evil, while your only consolation is that you have respected God.

But do not be discouraged. The Lord will certainly honor your faithfulness in ways you've never imagined. The Father calls you to be holy as He is holy—to live life as He would and to lead others to His salvation. This is not easy. In fact, it's *supposed to be* difficult. Why? Because that is how your character is established and how others see the mighty work of the living God in you. Thankfully, your loving heavenly Father gives you the Holy Spirit to guide you to victory.

So whenever you're tempted to despair because of the difficulty of your situation, ask yourself this question: What matters to me most— the Almighty God's opinion, or temporary earthly comfort? My fleshly desire to have ease, or someone else's salvation?

Always remember that when you remain steady in your walk with the Father, you will grow in your faith and in the fruit of the Spirit. And each time you honor God instead of giving in to hopelessness, you'll get stronger and wiser. You'll also have another testimony of having God's presence right there beside you when troubles come, which is of immeasurable value to your spirit—and may mean eternity to someone else's.

Father, I know You will never leave or forsake me—and You wouldn't
allow difficulty into my life without some good purpose.
Thank You, Father. I will trust in You.
Amen.

Your Fountain of Life

SCRIPTURE READING: PROVERBS 14; ISAIAH 40:29

The fear of the LORD is a fountain of life.
PROVERBS 14:27

As you read today's verse, you may be longing for that fountain of life to spring up and renew your energy and strength. There are so many burdens and obstacles that can drain you of the will to go on. But it may seem confusing that the *fear* of the Lord is the path to that life. After all, there is nothing that tires you like anxiety.

But understand, this verse does not mean you should be afraid of God. As a Christian, you have no reason to be frightened of your loving heavenly Father. Rather, the original Hebrew word for *fear* means that you should be reverent in the Lord's presence and respectful of His ways. God's awesome character should inspire you to take all He says very seriously. He is holy, righteous, and just—the only One worthy of your highest praise and worship. And recognizing that will help you realize how absolutely blessed you are to have His guidance, protection, and love.

So what today's verse really means is that when you have respect for God and obey what He says, you don't have to fear for your life because you know He will lead you in the best way possible. He will give you strength when you are weary and fill your life with His power (Isaiah 40:29).

Friend, if you do not have an adequate view of who the Father really is, you will be tempted to rely on yourself—and that will quickly drain all your energy and hope. But when your confidence is based on the matchless character of God, you can be joyful no matter what trial comes. So trust Him and experience the fountain of life He created you to enjoy.

Father, You alone are God and worthy of my praise.
May Your life flow through me.
Amen.

A Timely Word

SCRIPTURE READING: PROVERBS 15; ISAIAH 50:4–5

A man has joy in an apt answer,
and how delightful is a timely word!
PROVERBS 15:23

I hope that as you read this, you can recall a time when someone spoke into your life in a powerful way that you knew was straight from the Father. Perhaps it was a message of comfort during a difficult season. Or maybe someone gave you wise counsel at an important crossroad of your life. It may even be that at a crucial moment, you heard a word that helped you know God was with you.

The wonderful thing about the Father, however, is that He can make *you* into the person through whom He delivers those life-giving messages. Isaiah 50:4 NLT teaches, "The Sovereign LORD has given me His words of wisdom, so that I know how to comfort the weary." How does God do so? Isaiah goes on to say, "Morning by morning He wakens me and opens my understanding to His will. The Sovereign LORD has spoken to me, and I have listened. I have not rebelled or turned away" (vv. 4–5).

God takes responsibility for making you into the person who honors Him and encourages others. But did you notice your part in the process? The Father teaches you His ways, but it is absolutely crucial that you spend time with Him daily, listen to Him, and obey what He says.

So consider: Is there anyone who needs a word of encouragement? Is there someone who has been asking you for wise counsel or who would appreciate a reassuring note of friendship? The Lord will give you just the right message for him or her if you will turn your heart to Him and pay attention.

Father, I know just the individual You want me to reach out to.
Speak Your message of life through me so this person will be encouraged.
Amen.

Stepping Back to Go Forward

SCRIPTURE READING: PROVERBS 16; PSALM 27:13

The mind of man plans his way, but the LORD *directs his steps.*
PROVERBS 16:9

Perhaps you began life with joyful expectations and dreams of a great future. Maybe you even experienced a time when you were making so much progress, it seemed nothing could stand in your way. Yet now it seems that all your steps are backward.

Certainly this was the case for David. After being anointed to be the next king of Israel by the prophet Samuel, he enjoyed triumphs that set him apart as an important figure in the kingdom. He was King Saul's personal musician and armor bearer, he defeated the mighty Goliath, married the princess Michal, and was loved by all Israel. It seemed as if he was on the fast track to the throne.

But one day, David's life changed dramatically for the worse. King Saul became so jealous of David that he told "all his servants to put David to death" (1 Samuel 19:1). And just like that, David was an outcast, forced to flee the kingdom he'd been promised. For years, he struggled with devastating losses, assassination attempts, and demoralizing injustices. He seemed to have lost all hope.

Thankfully, we know that wasn't the end for David. In fact, all the challenges were God's indispensable training ground so David could become the great king of Israel he was created to be.

Likewise, it may seem as if you've taken steps backward in life. You're cut off from your dreams, circumstances look dire, and one heartbreak follows another. But do not despair. God isn't through with you yet. In fact, He is wisely preparing you a great future. So accept this difficult time as training for His eternal purposes and, like David, you will certainly see "the goodness of the Lord in the land of the living" (Psalm 27:13).

Father, thank You for training me for a great and hopeful future.
I will trust You and take heart.
Amen.

Refining Purpose

SCRIPTURE READING: PROVERBS 17; 2 TIMOTHY 4:18

The refining pot is for silver and the furnace
for gold, but the LORD tests hearts.
PROVERBS 17:3

One thing guaranteed in life is that the pressures and trials will come. And perhaps as you consider the day ahead, you already see difficult occupational, physical, relational, or financial circumstances on the horizon that cause you distress because of what they could cost you. You may be wondering if you need to give up on your goals and dreams because you feel like you will never reach or merit the good things you desire.

At such times, it is important for you to realize that through your difficulties, God is revealing what is in your heart—what you truly see as your significance, purpose, and security. He is showing you what you rely upon to prove that your life really matters.

But the truth is that your worth, identity, and protection have been established eternally by God and God alone (2 Timothy 4:18). He is the One who created you, formed you for His purposes, empowers you to achieve all He's planned for you to accomplish, and makes you into the best version of yourself possible. He knows you completely. He loves you unconditionally. And nothing—not even the losses you fear most—can take that away from you.

So instead of despairing about your circumstances, make the choice to cling to the only One who truly helps you overcome your challenges and gives you hope. The Lord has turned up the heat through these trials to refine you and teach you to depend upon Him moment by moment. And ultimately, He wants you to find your worth, purpose, and security in Him—trusting Him to make your life the finest it can be no matter what is going on.

Father, thank You for revealing what is in my heart.
Teach me to trust in You alone to make my life all it can be.
Amen.

Run to Him

SCRIPTURE READING: PROVERBS 18; PSALM 9:10; 23:4

The name of the Lord is a strong tower;
the righteous runs into it and is safe.
PROVERBS 18:10

You are not alone. Everyone experiences heartaches, disappointments, and doubts. We all face situations where we feel vulnerable, discontent, and helpless—when we wonder why our faith is so weak, and painful questions run rampant in our minds: *Has God forsaken me? Have I disappointed Him? Why has He allowed this?*

The truth is, if you're asking these questions, it means your heart is turned toward the Father—and that pleases Him (Psalm 9:10). When you run to Him, seek Him for answers, and cling to His wonderful character, you will always find a place of safety and acceptance.

You can take comfort from David's powerful testimony: "Even though I walk through the valley of the shadow of death, I fear no evil, for You are with me; Your rod and Your staff, they comfort me" (Psalm 23:4). David learned that the Father's protective presence was an undeniable, unchangeable fact, and you can too. No matter how hopeless or perilous your circumstances appear, the Lord will never leave you—not because of who you are or what you do, but because of who *He* is.

No, you're not alone. Every believer faces times of difficulty and doubt. And God *will* make it clear what He wants you to do. Whether you need to repent for some sin, take a step of faith, or simply wait on His perfect timing, be patient, because He will not fail to lead you in the way you should go. And just as He was with David and so many before you, your loving heavenly Father will be with you as well.

Father, thank You for being my strong tower—
my unshakable place of acceptance and safety.
Help me cling to You and obey You in every way.
Amen.

Contrary

SCRIPTURE READING: PROVERBS 19; JONAH 1–2

Many plans are in a man's heart,
but the counsel of the LORD will stand.
PROVERBS 19:21

Jonah was just like you and me—he had dreams and plans for his future. But when God revealed *His* objective for Jonah's life, it shook the prophet to the core: "Go to Nineveh, that great city, and cry out against it" (Jonah 1:2 NKJV). Jonah didn't like that assignment one bit. After all, the Assyrians were the sworn enemies of Israel, a brutal people who had no problem killing a meddling Hebrew prophet.

We all know the story. Jonah fled God's command on a ship to Tarshish, and the Lord sent a violent storm to prevent his progress. The situation became so dire that Jonah told the sailors to cast him overboard if they wanted to survive. So they did—they threw Jonah into the sea, and God sent a great fish to set him back on track. Eventually, Jonah repented and did as the Lord asked.

We may judge Jonah for running from God, but we often do the same thing. We flee from what the Father commands because we want to be in control of our lives and we want our lives to be comfortable. We may outright disobey God, or we may take a more subtle route—avoiding Him and claiming ignorance of what He wants. But understand, neither strategy releases us from the responsibility of obeying Him, which is why He sends contrary circumstances to get us back on the right path.

So take stock of your life. Does it seem that no matter how hard you strive, you're making no progress? Are you experiencing setback after setback, as if a strong hand were against you? Then it's possible God is trying to get your attention. Spend time in prayer and make sure you're obeying all He's called you to accomplish.

Lord, I want to obey You, no matter what.
Reveal Your will so I can work with You rather than against You.
Amen.

Spiritual Senses

SCRIPTURE READING: PROVERBS 20; MARK 8

The hearing ear and the seeing eye,
the LORD has made both of them.
PROVERBS 20:12

God gave us our senses to perceive the world around us. But as believers we have an additional privilege—the Father gave us spiritual eyes and ears to observe how He is working on our behalf and to learn His ways.

Unfortunately, we can get so caught up in our troubles that we miss God's activity. This was certainly true of the disciples. In Mark 8, Jesus miraculously fed four thousand people with seven loaves and a few fish. Even what was left over from the meal was several times more than what they'd started with. One would think that the disciples would learn that God was their great Provider.

But we read that not long after this miracle, the disciples forgot "to take bread . . . in the boat with them . . . They began to discuss with one another the fact that they had no bread" (vv. 14, 16). They had witnessed the miracle but had missed the point completely. So Jesus said to them, "Why do you discuss the fact that you have no bread? . . . Having eyes, do you not see? And having ears, do you not hear? . . . When I broke the seven for the four thousand, how many large baskets full of broken pieces did you pick up?" (vv. 17–20).

The disciples had seen what Jesus could do, but they didn't apply it to their lives. Do not make the same mistake. God is faithfully working around you, teaching you, and helping you. Don't be so focused on your problems that you miss His presence and provision. Watch for Him with spiritual eyes and ears, and you will observe the amazing ways He is already acting on your behalf.

Father, I want to learn from You. Give me spiritual
eyes and ears so I can perceive how You are at work
in miraculous ways in all of the details of my life.
Amen.

The Go To

SCRIPTURE READING: PROVERBS 21; I CORINTHIANS 14:33

There is no wisdom and no understanding
and no counsel against the Lord.
PROVERBS 21:30

As troubles arise in your life, what is your initial response? Do you analyze the problems from every angle or discuss them with loved ones? Or do you turn to the Lord? This is important because it shows where your confidence really comes from—whether you rely on yourself, others, or God. The Father is most likely trying to teach you something important through your trials, and you may unintentionally shut Him out of your life by handling them on your own or allowing others to influence your decisions.

When you try to overcome your challenges with your wisdom rather than God's, they usually appear far bigger than they really are. And the more you discuss your dilemmas with others, the more confused and overwhelmed you may become. Unfortunately, this is because human understanding generally tries to circumvent the path of faith the Lord wants you to take. And that never works.

This is why your first step should always be to turn to the Father. First Corinthians 14:33 promises, "God is not a God of confusion but of peace." The Lord is the only One who can lead you to the right course of action and will certainly do so if you seek Him. That's not to say you should never consult others. Rather, you should trust the Father to show you whom to speak to and when it is appropriate to do so.

So whatever you're facing today, develop the habit of going to the Father first with your problems. Let Him put your difficulties in perspective and direct you. Then you can discuss what He shows you with godly friends who will support you through prayer and encouragement.

Father, You know my troubles even better than I do.
Help me to go to You first. I trust You to lead me in the way I should go.
Amen.

Intimately Drawn

SCRIPTURE READING: PROVERBS 22; JEREMIAH 33:3

Incline your ear and hear the words of the wise,
and apply your mind to my knowledge . . .
So that your trust may be in the Lord.

PROVERBS 22:17, 19

Do you feel the unending tug on your soul—the one that makes you feel like something important is missing? That feeling is your heavenly Father drawing you to Himself. He wants you to spend time with Him and know Him intimately.

The Lord would love for you to get alone before Him, open His Word, and say, "Father, today I don't want anything but You. I long to know You better, understand Your ways, and experience Your divine presence. I yearn for a deeper relationship with You. So Father, I give myself fully to You. I'm listening. Show me who You are."

Why? Because God knows that it is in those intimate times of fellowship that you receive energy and wisdom for the challenges of life, where you find your purpose and experience His grace. It is during those moments that the Lord pours His life into you, filling what cannot be satisfied by earthly means and revealing "great and mighty things, which you do not know" (Jeremiah 33:3).

Of course, opening yourself up to an intimate relationship with the Father may appear somewhat daunting, but there's nothing in the world more worthwhile or wonderful than knowing Him and experiencing His love. So today, incline your ear to God and hear His words of wisdom. Apply your mind to knowing Him so that you can trust Him more. Allow Him to pour His love into your heart and His life into your spirit daily. Because then your soul will feel full and you will experience life at its very best.

God, here is my heart. I am vulnerable before You in every way—
I hold absolutely nothing back. I just want to know You, Father.
Open my ears to hear You.
Amen.

All You Need

SCRIPTURE READING: PROVERBS 23; ROMANS 15:4

Give me your heart, and let your eyes observe my ways.
PROVERBS 23:26 NKJV

You may not believe it as you consider all you have to face today, but your heavenly Father is truly all you need. In every area where you have a deficiency, He will be your supply. In every way you are too weak to prevail, He will be your strength and victory. The Lord God Almighty can be your unfailing Defender, wise and worthy Leader, constant Helper, and faithful Friend—just as He was to all the saints of old.

Do you realize that today? That you can experience God as powerfully and profoundly as anyone in Scripture has? You may look in the mirror and see all your faults and failings. But the Father looks at you with the same desire and ability to glorify Himself through you as He did Moses, David, and Paul.

In fact, Romans 15:4 tells us, "Whatever was written in earlier times was written for our instruction, so that through perseverance and the encouragement of the Scriptures we might have hope." In other words, what was possible for the biblical heroes is possible for you—not because of who you are, but because of the awesome God you serve.

You don't need anything extra to enjoy His love, wisdom, power, or provision—just an open heart that hungers to know Him, eyes that watch for Him, and a will set to obeying Him.

So consider, what is that that you really need today? Deep understanding and insight? Strength and guidance to help you triumph in your trials? Wisdom, power, and provision so you can succeed? There is One who longs to give you these things. So let Him. Give Jesus all you've got and He will become all you need.

Lord, I long for You to become all I need.
Teach me how to walk in such close fellowship with You.
Amen.

Get Up

SCRIPTURE READING: PROVERBS 24; PSALM 103:12;
ACTS 9:15; ROMANS 8:17; EPHESIANS 1:13–14

A righteous man falls seven times, and rises again.
PROVERBS 24:16

Have you messed up? Have you failed to achieve a goal or live up to expectations? Such incidents can be deeply discouraging, making us wonder if we can ever rise above our weaknesses and be worthwhile to others.

Yet there is a profound difference between being a failure and experiencing setbacks. You are not a failure. Your mistakes are only temporary defeats; they don't define who you are. In fact, Scripture is clear that once you trust Christ as your Savior, you are a new creation who has the extraordinary privilege of being imbued with His Spirit (Ephesians 1:13–14). *That* is your everlasting identity. You are an heir of God and coheir with Christ (Romans 8:17). Your failings are under the blood—removed from you for all eternity (Psalm 103:12).

The apostle Paul understood this well. No matter how many times he was rejected or imprisoned, he continued to look to Jesus to determine the truth about who he was—a chosen instrument of God, specially commissioned to proclaim the gospel (Acts 9:15).

You should do the same. When times of failure come, remind yourself of who Jesus created you to be. Your setbacks may delay you from reaching your goals, but they may also be the training necessary for you to reach them. So don't look at them as reasons to quit; rather, see them as opportunities for God to teach you important lessons. Then get up, dust yourself off, and get back to work. Because when you do, the Lord will honor your faith in Him. He will certainly give you the ability to persevere and stay the course until He shows you His victory.

Thank You for being my identity, Lord Jesus. I am not a failure.
I am a victor because of who You've made me to be.
Amen.

Submitting Our Understanding

SCRIPTURE READING: PROVERBS 25; ISAIAH 55:8–9; ROMANS 13:1

As the heavens for height and the earth for depth,
so the heart of kings is unsearchable.
PROVERBS 25:3

Romans 13:1 instructs, "Everyone must submit to governing author-ities" (NLT). We know that the challenge of this command occurs when our authority figures make decisions that we do not understand or agree with. We wonder if they had all the facts or if they had information that we weren't privy to.

The same is true for God—but in even greater measure. People have all kinds of ideas about what the Lord is really like apart from what Scripture reports about Him. Sadly, because of this, we may mistakenly invent an image of Him to suit our preferences rather than truly know-ing Him. These misconceptions often underestimate the surpassing greatness, wisdom, power, and love of our God.

But the Lord is clear: "My thoughts are not your thoughts, nor are your ways My ways . . . For as the heavens are higher than the earth, so are My ways higher than your ways and My thoughts than your thoughts" (Isaiah 55:8–9). Yes, God possesses information you do not have access to. In fact, His knowledge and wisdom are unsearchable—incomprehensibly beyond what you and I could ever hope to grasp. While He interacts with us in a close and personal way, He is still di-vine and far too grand to be defined according to our own human comprehension.

So submit to your heavenly Father. Even when you don't understand why He says yes or no to the cries of your heart, have faith that He truly is making the very best decision for you. You are not necessarily sup-posed to understand His "whys," but you can always trust the wisdom and love He shows on your behalf.

Father, I don't always understand You or Your ways, but I do trust You.
Help me to submit to You with faith and confidence.
Amen.

Better Wisdom

SCRIPTURE READING: PROVERBS 26; JOSHUA 6

Do you see a man wise in his own eyes?
There is more hope for a fool than for him.
PROVERBS 26:12

At times, the Father will direct you in ways you do not comprehend. Not only will He remain silent about things you wish to know, but He also will limit your view of the future to one small step at a time. And what God instructs you to do will require absolute faith in His wisdom and trust that He is leading you in the right way.

This was certainly the case for Joshua. As he led the Israelites into the Promised Land, the Lord didn't give him a complete battle plan outlining how to take possession of it. Rather, God led Joshua in a faith-stretching step-by-step manner, with tactics that would have been rejected by the usual general.

One has only to look at the attack plan against Jericho to see this illustrated. Instead of a scheme to infiltrate the city, the Lord instructed the Israelites to take it with seven days of marching and the blowing of trumpets (Joshua 6). Though the plan may have seemed irrational in Joshua's eyes, he chose to obey. Thankfully, it ultimately proved successful. But this is a principle we all must learn: The Father doesn't require us to understand His will, just to obey it, even if it seems unreasonable. His goal is to show us that our earthbound understanding falls short, but His heavenly wisdom always leads to victory.

If Joshua had believed himself wiser than God, the Israelites would never have taken the land. But because he trusted the Lord's direction, they triumphed. The same is true for you. The Lord may instruct you in ways that make no sense. But at such times, obey Him anyway. Victory is certainly ahead if you'll trust His wisdom above your own.

Father, I trust Your wisdom above my own.
I cannot see the way ahead, but it fills
me with comfort that You do.
Amen.

Just Don't

SCRIPTURE READING: PROVERBS 27; JEREMIAH 7:23

A prudent person foresees danger and takes precautions.
PROVERBS 27:12 NLT

Sometimes you may long to break free of God's restrictions and take advantage of the temptations before you. You imagine the pleasure you could enjoy, which stirs up your passions even more. Then you begin to wonder why the Lord would deny you the very blessings that would satisfy your soul so deeply.

Yet before moving forward, think about this: Does the force of gravity ever cease to exist simply because someone chooses to ignore it? Obviously, the answer is no. If a person jumps from a considerable height because he or she believes flying would give pleasure, the law of gravity will quickly prove inflexible. The result will not be the imagined outcome; it will be a painful fall.

The same is true of all God's commands. The One who created the universe understands how it works, and He has made His decrees known for our protection. He says, "Obey My voice, and I will be your God, and you will be My people; and you will walk in all the way which I command you, that it may be well with you" (Jeremiah 7:23).

God makes the dangers known to you through His commands so that you can live a good and fruitful life. A wise person understands that if something is treacherous enough for the Lord of all creation to point it out for our protection, then maybe we should avoid it.

Friend, if God warns you against taking part in something that appears to give you pleasure, it is because He sees beyond it to the pain it would cause your soul. Don't do it. Flee from sin. And be grateful for all the ways your heavenly Father protects you from falling.

Father, thank You for protecting me from dangers I cannot see
by warning me through Your Word. Help me to obey You.
Amen.

Battle Ready

SCRIPTURE READING: PROVERBS 28; EXODUS 14:14; ISAIAH 54:17

An arrogant man stirs up strife,
but he who trusts in the LORD will prosper.
PROVERBS 28:25

As conflicts arise in your life, it is understandable that you will wonder: *When do I engage? Jesus calls us to forgive, but when is it time to fight injustice? And how far should I go?* After all, not all skirmishes are mere setbacks that are easy to overlook. Sometimes you face an all-out war where there are no easy solutions and no way to avoid the onslaughts headed your way. The trial ahead may be life altering, distressing, and even affect those you love. So what can you do?

Of course, forgiveness is always necessary. But when God-sized battles arise, it is arrogant to think you can handle them by yourself with your own strength, political savvy, armaments, or diplomacy. But in fact, the Father may have allowed this war to teach you that these conflicts are never really your responsibility at all. Rather, they *always* belong to Him. So you don't have to come up with a plan—the Lord will fight your battles for you. He promises: "No weapon that is formed against you will prosper; and every tongue that accuses you in judgment you will condemn. This is the heritage of the servants of the Lord, and their vindication is from Me" (Isaiah 54:17).

So if you're facing a battle or unfair attacks today, put away your arrogance—your weapons, strategies, and earthly resources—as well as your right to engage the conflict on your terms. Rather, allow the Lord to be your Commander in Chief and obey Him without fear or flinching. No one can stand against your Defender, and surely, "The LORD will fight for you while you keep silent" (Exodus 14:14). And that, friend, will always be the uncontested road to victory.

Father, thank You for fighting for me.
Show me what to do and say as I await Your salvation.
Amen.

From Him

He who trusts in the LORD will be exalted.
PROVERBS 29:25

God Himself has chosen this for you. These obstacles in your path, these trials, these challenges—they are allowed in your life for His purposes. That may be a difficult word for you today. You may not be able to imagine why a *good* God would allow such trouble upon your already burdened soul. Haven't you sought His will? Haven't you followed Him as faithfully as you know how? And yet, all that's ahead of you appears dark and foreboding.

Understand that the Father has seen rare potential in you that must be developed, and the only way to set it free is to place you in situations that develop your trust in Him. He *has* to stretch your faith in order prepare you for His greater purposes.

No, it doesn't feel like something positive is happening. In fact, you most likely cannot see the way ahead, and the future may look quite hopeless. Perhaps you feel as if dream after dream has met its demise. Do not despair. This is what it takes to stop you from depending on yourself and train you to rely on God in greater measure. You are stripped down to nothing so He can be your everything.

So how should you respond? *First*, don't fight Him. Instead, ask the Father what He's teaching you. *Second*, realize the greatest obstacle to trusting God may be your emotions, but you don't have to live by them. Instead, take the Lord at His word and cling to His promises. *Finally*, whenever you are tempted to doubt, focus on God's eternally unchanging character and make the choice to have faith. The One who has proved Himself faithful throughout the generations will certainly not fail you or forsake you (Joshua 1:5). Trust Him.

Lord, I trust that these trials are from Your hand for Your purposes.
Help me to learn what You're teaching me.
Amen.

Right Direction

Scripture Reading: Proverbs 30; Psalm 16:7–8; 22:5

Every word of God is tested;
He is a shield to those who take refuge in Him.
PROVERBS 30:5

Perhaps you woke up today needing advice or a word of direction. You consider where to go—your friends, some authority figure, or even the Internet. Yet it occurs to you that those sources aren't always right and sometimes don't have the insight you require.

But there is One you can turn to who always has the counsel you need, regardless of what you're facing. That, of course, is the living God, whose wisdom is beyond understanding and whose Word has been proved true throughout the ages. In fact, countless believers throughout history have testified, "They trusted and were not disappointed" (Psalm 22:5). Like them, you'll never take a wrong turn when you seek God's wisdom for your life and obey Him. Certainly, the Lord will guide you with profound insight and unconditional love and lead you along paths of righteousness.

This is why David wrote: "I will bless the Lord who has counseled me, indeed my mind instructs me in the night. I have set the Lord continually before me; because He is at my right hand, I will not be shaken" (Psalm 16:7–8). David saw firsthand that the Father is trustworthy to lead us in the way we should go.

The Father's desire is for you to rely on His guidance at every turn in life—whether the decisions are large or small. So regardless of what counsel you need today, ask God to show you what to do. Open the Bible, bow before Him in prayer, and listen as He reveals Himself to you. Because nothing is wiser or safer than trusting in His Word. Certainly, you will not be disappointed.

Father, You know the questions on my heart today.
Thank You for Your Word. Lead me in the way I should go.
Amen.

True Worth

SCRIPTURE READING: PROVERBS 31; ZECHARIAH 4:6

Charm is deceitful and beauty is vain, but a
woman who fears the Lord, she shall be praised.
PROVERBS 31:30

Look in the mirror. Do you like the person you see? The negative thoughts can come in like a flood, enumerating all the reasons you do not deserve to be loved, respected, or blessed. All your faults, all the graces you lack, all your sins, all the mistakes of the past—why would God ever give you good gifts and the desires of your heart?

You may carry around a mental assessment of yourself that is very difficult to overcome. It will affect how you respond to circumstances and your relationships with God and others. For example, if you hate the way you look, doubt your skill, or question your intelligence, then you may operate with a lack of confidence and fail to pursue goals the Father has for you.

But God wants you to have a healthy self-esteem and a balanced attitude about yourself. He created you with unique features, talents, and abilities. But before you can truly put those to good use, you have to recognize and accept that He is the One who shines through you and decides your worth. He is your wisdom and strength. He is the One who makes you successful and makes your life count. As He said in Zechariah 4:6, "'Not by might nor by power, but by My Spirit,' says the LORD of hosts."

Friend, everything else you could possibly base your life on will ultimately fail. But the Lord will never disappoint or forsake you. So trust and commit to honoring Him with your life. Then look in the mirror and see the person God loves, empowers, and works through, and be glad.

Father, thank You that the fruit of my life
doesn't depend on me, but on You.
May Your Spirit triumph through me and may You be glorified.
Amen.

Relationships

*Relationship begins with God—who is three Persons in one.
The Lord is in perfect union with Himself; and as we imitate
Him, we also come into relationship with the three
Persons of the Godhead—Father, Son, and Holy Spirit.
What we learn from Him, we can apply
to our interactions with those around us.*

FEBRUARY 1

A Father to Us

SCRIPTURE READING: PROVERBS 1; MATTHEW 6:24–34;
HEBREWS 12:7–11; JAMES 1:17

Hear, my son, your father's instruction.
PROVERBS 1:8

The authority and wisdom of Jesus' teaching astounded the Jews of His day. His miracles of healing and control over nature's forces awed disciples and bystanders alike. But there was nothing more stunning to His audience than His constant reference to God as "Father." How could anyone claim such intimacy with the Lord?

Yet Jesus wanted us to understand an important aspect of the life He offers us. Being Christians means that we enjoy a special, eternal family relationship with the Creator of all that exists. Although once estranged from God by sin, when we accept Christ as Savior, we are adopted into His household and indwelt by the Holy Spirit so we can interact with our heavenly Father. No other religion offers this profoundly personal, transformative relationship. It's an astounding privilege.

Instead of being distant, unappeasable, or impersonal, your God works to have a relationship with you—one where you can experience growth, healing, unconditional love, and complete acceptance. When you pray, your Father hears you and delights in giving you good gifts (James 1:17). His objective is to lead you into a productive, meaningful life and to free you from distracting worry and draining fears (Matthew 6:24–34). And when you sin or make mistakes, He disciplines for your good so you can be free (Hebrews 12:7–11).

You are a child of the living God and have a heavenly Father who is completely trustworthy, wise, and able to lead you. So don't doubt Him if things turn rough. Accept that your heavenly Father is teaching you valuable lessons that will ultimately help you reach your full potential.

Lord, thank You for the astounding privilege of knowing You
as my Father. I praise You for raising me up as Your own.
Amen.

Prompted to Discern

SCRIPTURE READING: PROVERBS 2; PHILIPPIANS 1:9–10; HEBREWS 5:14

Wisdom will save you from evil people,
from those whose words are twisted.
PROVERBS 2:12 NLT

Have you ever walked into a place and felt an unpleasant tug in your spirit that immediately put you on guard? Have you ever spoken with someone and thought, *Something here isn't right?* If you are a believer, then most likely the Holy Spirit was prompting you to be on the alert. This is called *spiritual discernment*, and it is developed as you walk in wisdom with God.

The Father wants you to be able to discern when something is amiss with a person or a situation. So the Holy Spirit either reminds you of a principle in Scripture, reveals when something doesn't add up in a person's words, or gives you unease in your spirit to warn you against proceeding. Whichever way He communicates with you, if you will listen to Him, you will be equipped to avoid situations that could harm you.

So how can you grow in wisdom and spiritual discernment? *First*, become intimately familiar with the Word of God. The better you know Scripture, the better equipped you'll be to separate truth from fiction (Hebrews 5:14). *Second*, pay attention when the Holy Spirit speaks to you. God has placed His Spirit in you so you can have the most intimate relationship possible with Him. Do not ignore His promptings; instead, ask, "Lord what are You trying to show me?"

God gave you a discerning spirit because He wants to protect you (Philippians 1:9–10). So when you encounter people, messages, or circumstances that don't sit right in your spirit, stop and listen for His voice. Certainly, like a bright beacon on a dark night, He will illuminate the situation for you and show you whether or not to proceed.

Father, thank You for protecting me through Your Holy Spirit.
As I walk with You, please increase my wisdom and spiritual
discernment and help me always to listen to Your promptings.
Amen.

A Higher Standard

SCRIPTURE READING: PROVERBS 3; DEUTERONOMY 32:35; MATTHEW 5:39

Do not strive with a man without cause.
PROVERBS 3:30

It's amazing how even the briefest contact with certain individuals can set us on edge. It may be their personality that annoys us. Perhaps they have character flaws, areas of incompetence, or opinions that are offensive. Or maybe we see them as threatening, and we can't stand that they have the ability to hinder our lives in some way. Whatever it is, they're very effective at getting under our skin.

Too often, our initial response is to strike out at them—whether we do so with physical or verbal violence. We long to voice our frustrations and protect ourselves against them. This shouldn't actually surprise us—because of our fallen nature, we are not necessarily programmed for harmony with one another. However, Jesus calls us to a higher standard. He said, "Do not resist an evil person; but whoever slaps you on your right cheek, turn the other to him also" (Matthew 5:39). He calls us to forgive and live in peace with not only those who frustrate, scare, annoy, and offend us, but also those who outright hurt us.

This may seem like too much for Jesus to ask when you consider mankind's sinfulness. Yet He does so for your benefit and protection. And remember, God says, "Vengeance is Mine" (Deuteronomy 32:35). You can trust Him to set things right in His time.

So if you feel negatively toward someone today, remember that peace is not only possible—it's Christ's command. So ask the Holy Spirit to reveal why those individuals trigger such negative emotions in you and forgive them as Christ has forgiven you. And trust God to show you how to interact with those people in a manner that protects you and exalts Jesus.

Father, You know how I feel. Please reveal and heal the source
of my anger and help me to love and forgive as You would.
Amen.

Your Good Father

SCRIPTURE READING: PROVERBS 4; ROMANS 8:31–33;
12:5–11; 15:7; GALATIANS 3:26; HEBREWS 4:16; 13:5

Listen when your father corrects you.
Pay attention and learn good judgment.
PROVERBS 4:1 NLT

Galatians 3:26 teaches, "You are all sons of God through faith in Christ." This means that regardless of whether you had wonderful parents or less than optimal caretakers, the Lord wants to be your heavenly Father and walk with you through life in a profoundly intimate way. He wants to love, teach, and provide for you faithfully—for you to rely upon Him as a trusting child relies on his strong, wise, and godly dad.

Perhaps this is a strange idea to you. If so, you're not alone. Our first awareness of authority, love, provision, and security comes from our parents. It's only natural that their faults and limitations would influence our view of all relationships, including the one we have with God. Yet the Lord has gone to great lengths to provide an ongoing, intimate bond with us that transcends our earthly relationships (Romans 8:31–33). He knows that if we really get to know Him, we will love Him; and if we love Him, we'll obey Him—and that always works out for our good.

Our earthly dads may reject us and cause us pain, but not God. He always has time for us (Hebrews 4:16), will never fail or forsake us (Hebrews 13:5), disciplines us out of kindness for our good (Hebrews 12:5–11), and unfailingly accepts us (Romans 15:7). Though we may feel inadequate to have a relationship with the Father because of the past, remember: The One who saves you can teach you how to relate to Him. He will instruct you in how to walk with Him step by step, just like a truly wonderful and trustworthy dad would.

Lord, teach me to look to You as my Father and to heed Your instruction. Thank You for raising me up to walk worthy of You.
Amen.

A Blessing to Your Loved Ones

SCRIPTURE READING: PROVERBS 5

Let your fountain be blessed.
PROVERBS 5:18

In Proverbs 5, the "fountain" is symbolic of the family that flows from you. Since God is the Creator of the family and has given it to help you understand your relationship to Him, He desires that your family be strong and healthy.

Sadly, this isn't always the case. Because of this fallen world, families experience conflict, brokenness, and continual attacks from the enemy. Perhaps you know something about that today. Maybe as you read this, your family isn't all you wish it were. But take heart. No matter how dismal your situation may appear, there's hope, because the Lord has given guidelines for strengthening your relationships with your loved ones.

Deuteronomy 6:5–7 is God's foundation for a strong family: "Love the LORD your God with all your heart and with all your soul and with all your might. These words, which I am commanding you today, shall be on your heart. You shall teach them diligently." *First,* keep God central in your life. *Second,* teach His Word to those around you—not just in word but also by your consistent, loving example. It sounds simple, but it takes hard work.

You play a significant role in whether your loved ones are blessed. And even if you don't have kids, your children are grown, you're single, or your family is broken, it's never too late to start being a strong influence for good to others. So shine His light right where you are, and love those you've been given to love. Let God strengthen your relationships by honoring Him in everything you do. Because when your relationship with Him is your top priority, you'll affect not only those around you but also future generations. And your fountain will be blessed.

*Father, You know my hopes for my family. Help me to exalt You
so that my relationships will be strengthened and You'll be glorified.
Amen.*

Jealous?

SCRIPTURE READING: PROVERBS 6; JAMES 3:14–16

Jealousy enrages a man.
PROVERBS 6:34

It happens to every one of us—there's something we want with every fiber of our being. We pray, fast, and wait, but no matter how hard we struggle, we can't seem to attain the object we desire. To make matters worse, we know someone who receives what we want so badly but without the delays and heartaches we've experienced. From our point of view, that individual doesn't deserve the great blessing he or she has been given. Seeing that person with the gift we long for breaks our hearts, and we're convinced that if we were given the same opportunity, we'd handle it with much more wisdom and godliness.

The most painful part, of course, is that we wonder why God would reward someone else and yet seem to forget about us. We feel so abandoned, disheartened, and—if we're honest—angry, that we end up crying out, "What about me, Lord?"

Does any of this sound familiar? If so, then, friend, you have a jealousy problem, and you need to get your eyes back on God. You are on a destructive path, and the Father must free you from the devastating effects of jealousy before you can truly enjoy the blessings He has planned for you (James 3:14–16).

Jealousy runs deep, but you can shake free of it. *First*, resist asking, "What about me?" and start inquiring, "Lord, what is Your will?" *Second*, stop keeping track of what others have and what you believe you deserve, and praise the Lord for what He's actually given you. *Finally*, embrace the fact that God has unique plans perfectly suited to you. Fix your eyes on Him and thank Him for leading you to better blessings and a greater future than you've ever dreamed of.

Father, forgive me for my jealousy. I accept the wise
and wonderful plans You have for my life.
Amen.

The Truth About You

SCRIPTURE READING: PROVERBS 7; PSALM 139:14; ROMANS 5:8; 8:31–32

Call understanding your intimate friend.
PROVERBS 7:4

Do you feel like you fall short? Do you beat up on yourself, constantly telling yourself that you are not worthy? Are you critical of yourself even in areas where other people compliment you? Every one of us has a library in our mind of what we've been told and felt throughout our lives. Whether we realize it or not, these memories affect how we see ourselves and how we respond to the situations that arise.

So when you find yourself feeling worthless, it may be because of something that occurred in your youth that made a lasting impression. Therefore, consider: Did anything happen that made you feel shameful or undeserving? Did you feel embarrassed because of your looks, intelligence, or abilities? Did you fear that no one would ever love or respect you? Understanding the source of your feelings is the first step to healing, because then you can renew your mind with this undeniable truth: You are fully worthy to God.

The Savior sacrificed everything to have a relationship with you, including death on the cross at Calvary (Romans 8:31–32). Romans 5:8 confirms, "God demonstrates His own love toward us, in that while we were yet sinners, Christ died for us." Even when you were unable to do anything to please the Father, He loved you unconditionally. Therefore, He cares for you because of who you *are*—His child, whom He has redeemed—not what you *do*.

The Lord is the only One with an unrestricted view of who you are on the inside. In His sight, you are "fearfully and wonderfully made" (Psalm 139:14), absolutely worthy of love and respect. So cast aside the negative messages from your childhood and embrace this truth.

Father, thank You for making me worthy. When negative
feelings arise, give me understanding about their source
so I can counteract them with Your truth.
Amen.

Help in Master Work

SCRIPTURE READING: PROVERBS 8;
1 CORINTHIANS 3:10–11; EXODUS 3:1–11

*I was beside Him, as a master workman; and I was
daily His delight, rejoicing always before Him.*
PROVERBS 8:30

Every one of us wants to be the very best at something—a master workman who accomplishes exceptional objectives. In fact, you and I were created to achieve great, eternal goals (Ephesians 2:10); however, we cannot do so apart from God Himself. The apostle Paul wrote, "According to the grace of God which was given to me, like a wise master builder I laid a foundation . . . But each man must be careful how he builds on it. For no man can lay a foundation other than the one which is laid, which is Jesus Christ" (1 Corinthians 3:10–11).

Thankfully, from the time we accept Christ as our Savior, we are given a Helper who guides us—the Holy Spirit, who empowers us for the good works the Lord has planned for us to do. For example, the Holy Spirit enabled Bezalel to build the Old Testament tabernacle. In Exodus 31:3–5, the Lord says, "I have filled him with the Spirit of God in wisdom, in understanding, in knowledge, and in all kinds of craftsmanship, to make artistic designs for work in gold, in silver, and in bronze, and in the cutting of stones for settings, and in the carving of wood."

Likewise, when the Lord assigns you a task, the Holy Spirit equips you for it. Have you experienced the joy of becoming a master workman who achieves the good works the Father planned for you? Don't be afraid to step out in faith and do whatever He asks of you. Like Bezalel, the Holy Spirit will give you wisdom and understanding for whatever He asks you to accomplish.

*Holy Spirit, thank You for empowering me to be a master
workman—one who delights You and accomplishes
the eternal works You created me to do.
Amen.*

How Will You Respond?

SCRIPTURE READING: PROVERBS 9; JAMES 4:6–10

Do not reprove a scoffer, or he will hate you,
reprove a wise man and he will love you.
PROVERBS 9:8

It hurts when people criticize us, when they point out our flaws, mistakes, and shortcomings. Yet reproof is an acid test for our character. Are you a scoffer, or are you wise? Are you easily offended? Or are you strong enough to honestly assess negative words to see if there is any truth in them? Do you only see things from the human level? Or do you see everything that comes to you—even the rude words of others—as allowed by God's hand for your ultimate good?

Too often, we respond by immediately rising up in self-defense. Rather than humbly listening to what's been said about us and seeing if there's any truth in it, we may begin formulating excuses and thereby refuse to accept any responsibility for our actions or behavior. But this is because we respond out of anger based in fear. Subconsciously, we interpret the criticism as evidence that others don't respect us and find us unlovable.

But that is not what the Father intends for us as His children. Rather, the Lord calls us to be silent before our accusers, hear the criticism, ask Him for the discernment and strength to admit any personal fault, prayerfully consider what He may be asking us to change, and forgive those who may have wrongfully rebuked us (James 4:6–10).

Even though the process can be quite painful, it should be seen as an opportunity for spiritual growth, as well as an opportunity to strengthen relationships rather than destroy them. So when others criticize you, don't respond in anger or fear. Instead, say, "Thank you," and ask the Father to bring as much good from it as possible.

Father, I have been hurt so deeply by criticism. But I trust You to
reveal any truth in others' words, to heal my wounds, reveal my
blind spots, and give me wisdom through those experiences.
Amen.

Heed the Prompts

SCRIPTURE READING: PROVERBS 10; GALATIANS 5:25

He is on the path of life who heeds instruction.
PROVERBS 10:17

Do you ever find yourself at a loss as to what God wants? You long to follow, obey Him, and "walk by the Spirit" (Galatians 5:25), but you're not exactly sure how to do so. It seems so easy for some people, but somehow the practice escapes you.

It's not as difficult as you may think. You see, to walk in the Spirit simply means obeying His initial promptings. You do that by training yourself to be aware of God's presence with you at all times. As you feel Him tugging at your heart to take a course of action, you obey, even if you don't yet understand why He is doing so.

For example, you may feel convicted to drop a conversation, turn off a television program, or leave a place that is questionable. Most likely, the Spirit is warning you about a temptation to sin that you may be unable to resist unless you obey Him instantly. Or perhaps there's someone who comes to your mind during the day. You know he or she has been going through a difficult time and could use some support. The Spirit may want to minister to that person through you and is sure to give you the right words to encourage him or her.

Likewise, the Holy Spirit may guide you to pursue an opportunity that you never imagined you would take. The wisest thing to do is to submit to His plan regardless of whether it makes sense to you or not. The Spirit of the living God knows all things, including the future, and His direction is always for your benefit. You will not just be on the path to life, you'll experience it at its very best as well.

Holy Spirit, lead me. Make me conscious of Your
prompting and enable me to obey You in all things.
Amen.

Godly Friends

SCRIPTURE READING: PROVERBS 11; PSALM 55:22

Where there is no guidance the people fall,
but in abundance of counselors there is victory.
PROVERBS 11:14

You have not been called to "go it alone" in your walk of faith. In fact, no believer has ever been called to travel the road of the Christian life by himself or herself. This is one of the reasons why we are instructed to take part in the local church. When there are issues on your heart, it is good and right to first go to God about them. But the Father also wants you to talk to godly people whom you can trust and respect. The Lord may even show you whom to speak to.

The truth is that one of the greatest treasures in life is a Christ-centered, caring friend who will walk with you through the trying times and approach the throne of grace on your behalf. Of course, it is always wise to be cautious about whom you entrust with your concerns. You should make sure that your confidants are not only focused on God, but that they will be discreet about what you share with them as well. Likewise, as we said, it's important that you go to the Father *first* with your problems. As His child, you have the incredible privilege of seeking Him to alleviate your burdens (Psalm 55:22).

But once God puts your difficulties in perspective and directs you, feel free to discuss what He shows you with a friend who will support you with prayer and godly advice. That person may be going through a similar trial, and this may become an opportunity for you to encourage and support one another. You can help carry each other's burdens, and seeing God answer your prayers will certainly increase your faith.

Father, thank You for godly friends. Show me whom I can trust and bring
people into my life who will help me grow in my relationship with You.
Amen.

Bring Them In

SCRIPTURE READING: PROVERBS 12; ROMANS 10:14–15; 12:5

The righteous is a guide to his neighbor.
PROVERBS 12:26

If you've ever moved into a new neighborhood, enrolled in a new school, joined a new church, or started a new job, you know what it's like to be considered an "outsider." The process of building a fresh community of trust, support, and friendship can be long and frustrating, unless you have someone who will extend a welcoming hand to help you settle in and show you the ropes.

But consider the fact that those who don't have a relationship with Jesus as their Savior may feel like "outsiders" when it comes to church. This is because they are not yet "in Christ" and, therefore, not yet part of the family of God (Romans 12:5). You can imagine how difficult it must seem to them to fit in.

But hopefully, you can also see how you can make a difference in their lives if you will reach out to them and help them find what they are looking for. Ultimately, salvation occurs through the redemptive work of the Holy Spirit, but your loving witness can be an incredibly compelling influence that can motivate others to accept Christ as their Savior. Indeed, the Lord planned from the beginning to draw them to salvation through you (Romans 10:14–15).

So today, ask God to show you who could use a kind word, a helpful hand, or a spirit of service. Be accepting and supportive toward others and invite them to church. God will work through your acts of kindness to bring the lost into His family. And one day, they may truly become your brother or sister in Christ.

Father, give me a heart for the outsiders—especially for those who don't know Jesus as Savior. Show me people I can influence and help me lead others to know You and love You.
Amen.

FEBRUARY 13

Walk with the Wise

SCRIPTURE READING: PROVERBS 13; JAMES 1:5

He who walks with wise men will be wise.
PROVERBS 13:20

Sometimes you may become frustrated with yourself because you find yourself making the same mistakes over and over again. You're not growing in wisdom as you'd hoped you would. But much of that may be due to who or what is influencing your life. If you want to be wise, you must carefully examine whom you're allowing to speak into your decision-making process.

Think about the people whom you listen to the most—your friends and family members, for example. If they are spiritually minded and Christ-centered, then they will have a strong, positive impact on your life. However, if you spend all of your time with ungodly, worldly minded people, you will certainly be affected in a negative way. So consider: Do the people you associate with meditate on God's Word? Do they have a godly lifestyle? Do they have humble spirits and seek godly counsel? You may have to reexamine the time you spend with certain people and how they influence your decision-making process.

Moreover, you must be willing to examine your own life in order to determine if you are walking wisely. Do you meditate on God's Word, and do you live the kind of life that would bring another person closer to the Lord? Are you following the examples of the godly people around you, or do you constantly find yourself under conviction about how you fall short?

Friend, God wants you to be wise (James 1:5), and one way He trains you to become so is through other wise, godly people. So chose your influences carefully, and certainly you will grow in wisdom.

Father, help me to see who is wise so I may walk with
and learn from them. I want to honor You, Father.
Amen.

Unify to Build

Scripture Reading: Proverbs 14; Matthew 28:18–20;
1 Corinthians 2:2; 2 Timothy 2:14

The wise woman builds her house, but the
foolish tears it down with her own hands.
PROVERBS 14:1

Today's proverb draws the distinction between the wise woman (or man) who builds up and the foolish one who tears down. It seems silly that people would destroy their houses with their own hands, doesn't it? And yet that's what we unintentionally do when we get caught up in minor skirmishes in the church instead of working to carry out the Great Commission (Matthew 28:18–20).

The church's light shines brightest in our unbelieving world when we are unified in our faith and devoted to God, when our focus is the Savior and our motive is loving obedience to Him. Conversely, one of the greatest hindrances to our witness is division within the church family. Such dissension can occur over relatively inconsequential issues because of pride, competitiveness, and even personality-centered squabbles. Yet this discord can damage and demoralize the Body of Christ and—more important—turn unbelievers away from Jesus, which is why 2 Timothy 2:14 warns, "Stop fighting over words. Such arguments are useless, and they can ruin those who hear them."

In other words, we're tearing down the church with our battles rather than building it up by reaching and discipling the lost. How do we overcome this? The apostle Paul said, "I determined to know nothing among you except Jesus Christ, and Him crucified" (1 Corinthians 2:2). That's where our focus is to be as well. Our devotion, worship, and obedience belong to the One who has purchased our salvation through His shed blood. So build up the Kingdom of God by keeping your heart set on Him rather than on any of the peripheral issues.

Father, forgive me for getting caught up in the squabble.
Help me to stay focused on You and proclaiming Your Word.
Amen.

Gently Lead

SCRIPTURE READING: PROVERBS 15; 2 TIMOTHY 2:25

A gentle answer turns away wrath,
but a harsh word stirs up anger.
PROVERBS 15:1

Few things in life are more difficult than keeping a quiet spirit when conflicts arise. Our tendency in the heat of the battle is to vent what we're feeling. But God's Word instructs us to react with a Christ-like spirit: "Gently instruct those who oppose the truth. Perhaps God will change those people's hearts, and they will learn the truth" (2 Timothy 2:25 NLT).

What this tells us is that although self-preservation may be our initial reaction to conflict, we must control ourselves and choose a different response. We must follow Jesus' example. Although Christ constantly drew criticism from the religious leaders of His day, He did not lash out or defend Himself. Instead, He lovingly and patiently taught others. He disarmed opponents with mercy, wisdom, and compassion.

When our confidence is in God, we can likewise demonstrate a quiet, calm demeanor. We can express kindness and forgiveness knowing that ultimately justice belongs to God. Not that we compromise our convictions when conflict occurs—not at all. We must stand firm on the clear principles of Scripture. But we must also express genuine concern for those who disagree with us. A haughty, arrogant spirit is never justified, even when we think we're right, because we're sinners in need of God's grace just as they are.

Rather, we must be kind as Jesus was—concerned for the eternal condition of others and drawing them closer to the Savior through patience, love, and compassion. The ultimate goal is not to get others to agree with us but to be reconciled to God, who is certain to teach all of us how to walk with Him.

Father, I want to be a good witness for You. Help me to respond
to others with wisdom, patience, gentleness, and mercy as You would.
Amen.

Don't Follow the Bullies

SCRIPTURE READING: PROVERBS 16; DANIEL 3; ROMANS 13:1

Violent people mislead their companions,
leading them down a harmful path.
PROVERBS 16:29 NLT

At times there may be people who intimidate you. Perhaps they operate by coercion or seem to wield power that could crush you. So to get on their good side, you may be tempted to do what they say even when what they ask isn't right. But understand that what drives them isn't your well-being; rather, it's an ungodly need to control that won't be appeased. And ultimately, following them will lead you down a destructive road (Proverbs 14:12).

This was certainly true for King Nebuchadnezzar of Babylon, who had the greatest army on the planet and led the uncontested superpower at the time. Nebuchadnezzar issued a decree that everyone must bow before the immense gold statue he'd set up or be executed (Daniel 3). Three Hebrew men in the crowd—Shadrach, Meshach, and Abednego—understood that only God was to be worshipped. So they could either obey the Lord and be sentenced to the fiery furnace, or pay homage to Nebuchadnezzar and dishonor God.

Of course, those faithful men honored the Lord. Yes, they were thrown into the fire because of it, but God miraculously delivered them out of it. And because of their courage, Nebuchadnezzar acknowledged the God of Israel.

Although it's true you should always honor authority (Romans 13:1), you should never go out of your way to win favor with people at the cost of your relationship with God, especially when they ask you to do things contrary to His Word. Yes, standing strong against them may cause you trouble, but obey the Father and do not fear. Bullies come and go, but the Lord is eternal and He will always lead you on the right path.

Father, I will honor You. Thank You for leading me on the
path of life and protecting me from the ungodly.
Amen.

Be a Friend

SCRIPTURE READING: PROVERBS 17; 1 SAMUEL 16:1–13; 23:16–18

A friend loves at all times.
PROVERBS 17:17

It's normal to want deep friendship—the kind where we're unconditionally loved, supported, accepted, and respected by another person. Where we can be ourselves and be understood and never fear betrayal or disloyalty.

The Bible provides many illustrations of great friendships, with perhaps the most famous one being between Jonathan and David. First Samuel 18:1 tells us, "The soul of Jonathan was knit to the soul of David, and Jonathan loved him as himself." In other words, Jonathan took the initiative and cared for David deeply. As the son of King Saul and natural heir to the throne of Israel, Jonathan could have been jealous of the call God had placed on David's life to rule (1 Samuel 16:1–13). Instead, Jonathan honored the Lord and David above himself and showed true friendship—helping David become the man and ruler God created him to be (1 Samuel 23:16–18).

We usually experience friendship in proportion to our willingness to give it. It may be that as you read this today, you are lonely and have no close relationships because you are unwilling to risk being rejected. But one of the keys for unlocking the door to deep camaraderie with another is to make yourself vulnerable—giving of yourself even when you are fearful of being hurt.

Perhaps as you've read this devotion today, the Lord has brought someone to mind who could use a good, understanding friend. Take a bold step today and offer yourself in friendship. Freely give of yourself, and you may receive a wonderful blessing in return.

Father, thank You for bringing someone to mind.
Help me to reach out with wisdom and love.
Help me to be vulnerable where appropriate and love as You would.
Amen.

FEBRUARY 18

Your Support Network

SCRIPTURE READING: PROVERBS 18; HEBREWS 3:13; 10:24–25

He who separates himself seeks his own desire,
He quarrels against all sound wisdom.
PROVERBS 18:1

When you are under great pressure or emotional turmoil, do you isolate yourself from others? Do you retreat to a particular place or hide yourself in work or a hobby? Do you busy your mind with everything other than what actually concerns you?

Understand, God established the church for you to have a support network—to give you guidance and direction for your life; to provide strength, protection, and help in times of trial; and, of course, so you can be His representative to this lost world. And the truth of the matter is that eventually, a lack of encouragement and support from fellow believers will always take a toll on your spiritual life and will invariably lead you to feelings of despair that will be difficult to overcome alone (Hebrews 3:13; 10:24–25). Why? Because without other Christians, you'll find it difficult to counteract the ungodly messages of the world and will become an easy target for the enemy. This is why it's so incredibly important for you to invest in godly relationships with Christ-like friends and mentors who inspire you, hold you accountable, and challenge you spiritually.

God engineered it so that relationships with other believers is where you discover and fulfill His will for your life. And when you have godly, Spirit-filled people loving you, building you up, and ministering to you as you serve—well, that's when you're positioned perfectly to experience the fullness of the Father's grace, power, and plan. So when you're feeling depressed, don't hide yourself away. Instead, seek out godly friends. Because there's absolutely no telling what all God wants to do in and through your life or how another believer could help you get there.

Father, I do not want to isolate myself. Please lead me to
loving believers who can help me become all You created me to be.
Amen.

Real Friends

SCRIPTURE READING: PROVERBS 19; ROMANS 12:15

Wealth adds many friends,
but a poor man is separated from his friend.
PROVERBS 19:4

One of the most painful experiences in life is when you begin to doubt if your friends really love you for who you are. Do they care about you only because of what you do for them or give them? Or are they genuinely interested in you and the challenges you face? This, of course, may lead you to consider how you attracted those friends in the first place. Unfortunately, when you lack discernment in your relationships or try to win people over based on what they do for you or how they make you feel, you're headed for hurt.

The best way to guard against this, of course, is to first go to Jesus for your identity, worth, and security. When you understand who you are in Christ—loved, accepted, respected, and wanted—you'll be more discerning about what people seek when they approach you. Likewise, you'll learn to be a friend who invests in others' spiritual growth, motivated by the love of God. After all, you teach people how to treat you. If you want a friend who genuinely loves you for who you are, then you must begin by caring for them—as Jesus cares for you. That means you "rejoice with those who rejoice, and weep with those who weep" (Romans 12:15).

The truth of the matter is that it is better to have one true, loyal friend who encourages, helps, and lifts you up in times of trouble than to be popular with many disingenuous people. Ask God to teach you how to be a good friend and to lead you to friends who'll be true. And then love whomever He gives you to care for.

Lord Jesus, I know You are a real friend to me. Teach me to love others
as You would and lead me to people I can trust to love me in return.
Amen.

Influence

SCRIPTURE READING: PROVERBS 20; 2 CORINTHIANS 3:5–6

A righteous man who walks in his integrity—
how blessed are his sons after him.
PROVERBS 20:7

We are influenced by so many things in life: whom we meet, the information we consume, the places we go, and the things that happen to us. But have you ever considered the effect *you* have—or could have—on every person you meet?

People need good, godly examples, and you can offer that to them. Regardless of whether they are your natural children or your spiritual offspring, people will look to you to model the continual love, support, and wisdom of Christ. This is a challenge, of course, and perhaps you don't really feel up to it. You know your mistakes and failures. Why would anyone listen to you?

Yet understand, even the apostle Paul didn't feel adequate for that important work, which is why he wrote, "It is not that we think we are qualified to do anything on our own. Our qualification comes from God. He has enabled us to be ministers of his new covenant" (2 Corinthians 3:5–6 NLT). He realized that we are not doing the important work of convicting and transforming; rather, it is the Holy Spirit in us who does so. Our responsibility is to submit to His leading.

So today consider, are you willing to be the kind of parent, relative, teacher, mentor, or friend who will stand up and influence others to be godly? I certainly hope so, because you can make an incredible difference in the world. Countless people could be blessed by how God shines through you, so pray for His help in leading the people in your life toward a deeper relationship with Him.

Lord, I don't feel too confident about my influence over others.
But Father, I recognize You are my adequacy.
Encourage, lead, and transform people through me.
Amen.

Important Work

SCRIPTURE READING: PROVERBS 21; JEREMIAH 45:5;
MATTHEW 19:30; JOHN 15:18–22; JAMES 4:10

He who pursues righteousness and loyalty
finds life, righteousness and honor.
PROVERBS 21:21

There are times when people will make you feel unimportant, un-needed, and unwanted—as if you're below their notice. This can be at work, in your relationships, and even at church. But God never sees you that way. He has placed you in the Body of Christ for a purpose, an eternal reason that will influence how others respond to the Savior.

You are most definitely important. However, when you're obeying God, it may often mean that you'll turn away from what this world considers prominence and power in order to do the crucial tasks He calls you to. In fact, Jesus said, "Many who are first will be last, and the last, first" (Matthew 19:30). This is because His kingdom is not about promoting yourself; it's about glorifying Him. And He is calling for servants who will obey His everlasting purposes instead of seeking great things for themselves (Jeremiah 45:5).

This is counterintuitive and convicting to the world, which is why people may overlook, dislike, or even persecute you when you're doing significant work for God (John 15:18–22). They may disparage you, but don't despair. You're in good company. Jesus was crucified between two thieves when He was saving the world. Paul was in prison when he wrote the epistles that make up the majority of the New Testament. Your work is likewise no less exalted because it's done in humble circumstances.

So don't fret when other people don't applaud you or recognize your worth. And don't grow disheartened when they demean you. Instead, "Humble yourselves in the presence of the Lord, and He will exalt you" (James 4:10). You play an important part in the Body of Christ. Keep serving Him as He shows you, and He will lift you up.

Lord, thank You that my worth and eternal purposes come from You.
Help me to follow Your lead in doing Your work.
Amen.

The Miracle of Giving

He who is generous will be blessed,
for he gives some of his food to the poor.
PROVERBS 22:9

We know that "God loves a cheerful giver" (2 Corinthians 9:7) and that He blesses those who obey Him. But sometimes the Father does so in ways we'd never imagine. Take the Shunammite woman, for example. One day she observed that the prophet Elijah often passed through her town, so she began preparing meals for him. Later, she and her husband added an upstairs room where he could rest when he was weary. Elijah was so overcome by her generosity that when he saw that the desire of her heart was to have a child, he asked God to provide her with a son (2 Kings 4:8–17).

You may be thinking, *That's sweet. She helped the prophet and he blessed her.* Yet that's not the end of the story. You see, when her son was grown, he died suddenly. Immediately, the Shunammite woman turned to Elijah, and before she knew it, the Lord raised her son from the dead through the prophet (2 Kings 4:18–37). With her own two eyes, she saw her boy resurrected. She gave what little she had and received back a miracle—experiencing the power of the living God in a way few ever will.

You may be a giver but not see much fruit from your generosity. But understand, when you participate in a lifestyle of selfless giving like the Shunammite woman, you're inviting God to work in your life in extraordinary ways. So be sensitive to the needs of others and obey when the Lord prompts you to give. Then be patient and keep watch. Because the Father will certainly surprise you with how He rewards your faithful obedience.

Father, show me the needs You desire me to meet
and help me always to honor You.
I trust You to provide in ways beyond my imagination.
Amen.

Don't Be Foolish

SCRIPTURE READING: PROVERBS 23; PSALM 14:1

Don't waste your breath on fools,
for they will despise the wisest advice.
PROVERBS 23:9 NLT

Many people believe a fool is a person who is silly or frivolous. But understand the unwise mind as Scripture describes it: A fool is a person who arrogantly and persistently chooses his or her own way over God's. Foolish people push the Father out of their lives by refusing the direction that Scripture offers. This is why Psalm 14:1 presents this description: "The fool has said in his heart, 'There is no God.'" In other words, that individual is convinced he possesses the ultimate understanding.

It seems clear-cut: People who suppose they are smarter than the Lord are fools. However, it's amazing how many people *say* they believe God's Word is right, good, and true, but deny Him by their deeds. They consistently second-guess the Father and go their own way. Usually, they wouldn't admit that they think their comprehension surpasses His, but they say such things as, "God wouldn't care about my insignificant problems." In this way, they give themselves an excuse to choose their own way, without truly seeking God's full wisdom.

So consider your own heart. Are you fully convinced that God's way is best? Do you live out that belief by seeking Him in every situation? Do you trust that the One who created the heavens, established the foundations of the earth, and knit you together knows best? The Father cares about every detail of your life and wants to walk with you step-by-step. So don't be foolish by going your own way or leaning on your limited understanding. Seek the Lord first, for His is *always* the wisest counsel, regardless of what you may face.

Father, I want to be wise. Show me the areas of my life
where I am leaning on my own understanding
and teach me to walk in all Your ways.
Amen.

Forgive for Your Own Good

SCRIPTURE READING: PROVERBS 24; MATTHEW 5:44–45

Do not rejoice when your enemy falls,
and do not let your heart be glad when he stumbles.
PROVERBS 24:17

The Lord understands how difficult it is to deal with suffering that other people have caused you, and He realizes that the wounds they've cause you can run deep. But He also sees that when you refuse to forgive others or wish them harm, you're only hurting yourself. You give that person power over you that will deepen your woundedness and eventually drive you to sin.

This is why Jesus teaches, "Love your enemies and pray for those who persecute you, so that you may be sons of your Father who is in heaven" (Matthew 5:44–45). This may sound unreasonable at first, but the Lord understands that it's only when you see your enemies through His eyes of mercy and allow His unconditional love to flow through you that you can forgive them and be free of what they've done.

So intercede for those who oppose you, and actively invite God's compassion for them into your heart. As you do, you'll begin to understand the difficulties they've faced and the wounds they carry. You may discover that the people who hurt you have actually endured a great deal of suffering in their own lives—troubles that explain why they respond as they do. And before you know it, God's grace will flow through your heart, and you'll find yourself wanting to forgive them as Christ forgave you. And instead of plotting how you'll avenge yourself for what they've done, you'll be asking the Father to heal your offender. And when you do so, you'll not only protect your heart from sin, but you'll also become His ambassador of reconciliation to others who need Him.

Father, help me to forgive. Give me compassion for those who
hurt me and help me be a minister of Your grace to them.
Amen.

Breaking Free from Gossip

SCRIPTURE READING: PROVERBS 25;
ROMANS 1:29–30; 2 CORINTHIANS 12:20

Do not reveal the secret of another.
PROVERBS 25:9

Can others trust you? Are you known for your discretion and honorable character? Or do you regularly reveal things about others in order to fit in? Gossip is not a popular subject, but unfortunately it is a widespread activity in the church among both women and men. Many people spend a great deal of time participating in disparaging talk about others, betraying confidences and making hurtful judgments—usually with the intention of promoting themselves or winning favor in some way.

But Scripture lists the practice of gossip among sins like deceit, malice, murder, slander, and arrogance (Romans 1:29–30; 2 Corinthians 12:20). Why? Because gossip is deceptive and destructive—and not only to the person being spoken of. People who participate in it may do so in order to feel superior over someone they envy or to feel accepted by others. However, what it really does is undermine their credibility, hinder the intimacy they desire, inspire anxiety, and destroy the unity of the church.

Friend, gossip doesn't fit who you are as God's child. Just as you can't have poison and pure water pouring from the same stream, you cannot have both God-honoring talk and scandalous chatter coming from the same person. If you are given to gossip, it's indicative that something is off in your heart. Thankfully, God can help you overcome the bondage that the sin of gossip has trapped you in. It's never too late. Start today. The Father will not only teach you a different way to communicate, but He will also show you how to get your needs met in a way that builds people up rather than tearing them down.

Father, please forgive me for the times I've gossiped.
I want to be loved and respected. Show me how to relate to people
in a positive way that builds them up instead of tearing them down.
Amen.

Stay Out of It

SCRIPTURE READING: PROVERBS 26

Like one who grabs a stray dog by the ears, is someone
who rushes into a quarrel not their own.
PROVERBS 26:17 NIV

It is extremely difficult to watch someone you love be wronged and hurt by others. You may want to jump into the fray, take sides, plead his or her case, and add your input about the situation—safeguarding your friend or family member from further distress. However, be warned, the Lord may have an important purpose for the conflict that you are not aware of.

This proverb likens rushing into someone else's quarrel to grabbing a stray dog by the ears. When you do so, you're aggravating an unfamiliar canine without reason. You do not know the history of the dog or how it responds to stressors, so it's likely you'll get hurt in the process.

Likewise, the Lord may have allowed this trial in your loved one's life for an unseen but crucial purpose. And when you wade into the battle without understanding what is going on, you may unintentionally hinder His work in them, provoking Him to take action against you. Then you won't be fighting those who are hurting your loved one—you'll be waging war against God Himself. And that never turns out well.

Ultimately, the Lord is a greater, more powerful and wise Defender than you are, so be assured that your loved ones are safe in His hands. You don't have to shield them from quarrels or conflicts and you should never try to fight for them. Instead, faithfully pray for and support them, always spurring them on to godly conduct and faith in the Lord. By doing so, you're sure to observe God's interests as well as theirs.

Lord, this conflict in my loved one's life grieves me.
But I trust You to safeguard and teach them through this.
Please show me how to encourage them to stay faithful to You.
Amen.

Impact

SCRIPTURE READING: PROVERBS 27; MATTHEW 5:16; 28:19

Iron sharpens iron, so one man sharpens another.
PROVERBS 27:17

Do you want to *impress* people, or do you want to *impact* their lives—allowing God to work through you to transform them? Many people do everything they can so that others will like them. They spend a great deal of money, dress a certain way, drive expensive cars, and live in exclusive neighborhoods. It's obvious to everyone around them that their main goal is to impress.

However, Jesus taught that we have a responsibility to *influence* those around us, not simply get them to like us. He wants to impact them through you, working through what you say, how you live, and your very presence to inspire them to rethink their lives, prompting them to change—like "iron sharpens iron." This will require a dynamic in your relationships with others that may not be easy or comfortable, but will mean a difference in eternity.

It is God's will for all believers to live in such a way that we lead the people around us to Him (Matthew 5:16). One of the big mistakes we make as the Body of Christ is that we sing, pray, and read the Bible together, but we often do not put what we learn into practice in a concrete way. We think that if we fulfill our role as the church within the walls of the building, that is enough. However, Jesus was clear. He said, "Go therefore and make disciples of all the nations" (Matthew 28:19). Coming to church is excellent—and we should all do it—but it is not enough. The Savior also calls us to *go*. The people we talk to, listen to, and work with should see a difference in our lives—we should be sharing all that God teaches us with them.

Father, I don't want to impress others—I want to impact
their lives for the sake of Your kingdom. Work
through me to draw others to Jesus.
Amen.

Playing Favorites

SCRIPTURE READING: PROVERBS 28; JEREMIAH 7:23;
ROMANS 2:11; 2 PETER 3:9

*To have regard for one person over another
and to show favoritism is not good.*
PROVERBS 28:21 AMP

Have you ever felt the sting of favoritism, when others are preferred above you because of some unknown or superficial reason? It doesn't matter how hard you work, how loving you try to be, or how devotedly you walk with God. You still don't fit in. You're still not accepted. Certainly, it is painful. You continually get the feeling that you lack something important—perhaps wealth, upbringing, beauty, social standing, or some other quality that you just can't help. You think, *If they could just see who I really am, maybe then they could love me.*

Thankfully, God does see you—*all* of you. And He loves you deeply and unconditionally. In fact, the Father says that you *belong* to His family eternally. He doesn't show favoritism the way people do (Romans 2:11), but He does enjoy a special closeness with those who are especially devoted to Him (Jeremiah 7:23).

So why has Father allowed you, His beloved child, to face rejection from a person or group of people who are so important to you? It may be because He wants you to stop focusing on them and start ministering to others. Because the Father is not partial but desires that all people be saved (2 Peter 3:9), as a believer you are to have the same desire.

So consider: Have *you* been showing partiality? Is there a person or a group that you've been ignoring because you feel they are somehow beneath your notice? If so, consider how you can reach out to and serve them with God's love. Don't repeat the mistakes of those who hurt you. Instead, be an example through your kindness.

*Father, I don't want to be guilty of partiality or
favoritism because I know how much it hurts.
So make me an envoy of Your love to others.
Amen.*

Living Wisely

There is no greater, more fruitful, or more blessed life than the one based on God's wisdom. You exchange your earthly perspective for His omniscient understanding of all things and enjoy the incredible blessing of walking in His ways.

Intimate Communication

SCRIPTURE READING: PROVERBS 1; PSALM 140:13

A wise man will hear and increase in learning,
and a man of understanding will acquire wise counsel.
PROVERBS 1:5

How much time in any twenty-four-hour period does God have your undivided attention? Are you truly spending time listening to and fellowshipping with the Father? Or are you only making your requests and then hurrying on your way?

The truth is, Jesus wants you all to Himself daily. He wants to spend time with you when there's no one else around, when you can be unhurried, uninterrupted, and completely unimpeded in your focus.

Think about two young people who are falling in love. They don't avoid each other when they have decisions to make or face challenges. They make time to interact; discuss their ideas, beliefs, and struggles; and demonstrate their support and care. And it is in those moments of undistracted intimacy that they learn the most profound truths about each other and find their way through life together.

The same is true in your relationship with God (Psalm 140:13). For you to know Him and enjoy His wisdom for your life, you need to take time out from everything that is going on and seek His wonderful presence. Tell Him about your struggles, listen for His comfort and direction, and learn about His matchless ways and unshakable character.

Because that is how you will take hold of the power, joy, and hope of having the Father in your life and walking in the path of His wisdom. And when you do, you'll find yourself longing for constant communion with God because you will experience what an immense privilege knowing Him truly is.

Father, I want to hear You, learn Your ways, and acquire Your
wise counsel. Thank You for teaching me how to live a life of
wisdom and intimate communion with You.
Amen.

The Example of Others

SCRIPTURE READING: PROVERBS 2; MATTHEW 7:7–8

You will walk in the way of good men
and keep to the paths of the righteous.
PROVERBS 2:20

Are you desperate for God's answer today? Do you wonder if He will talk to you and come through for you in time? What you're experiencing is not a new dilemma. Godly people throughout history have come to the same crisis of faith. And as He did for them, if you're truly seeking God and are willing to obey Him, He will move heaven and earth to show you His will.

I recall a particularly difficult season during my senior year in college. At one point, the pressure grew so great that I said, "Father, I've got to be absolutely sure what Your will is for me. Please show me what to do." The Lord comforted me with a memory of my grandfather. He'd gone through a similar time in his life when he was seeking God's guidance. He said, "Lord, if You're calling me to preach the gospel, let me see two falling stars." Sure enough, he looked up and saw two bright lights streaming across the night sky. I thought, *If Granddad asked for something that specific and the Lord answered, maybe He'll do the same for me.* So I prayed, and a couple of evenings later, I saw two brilliant meteors shooting across the night sky at the same time. It was as if the Lord said to me, "You asked, and I've answered."

So if some trial, temptation, or challenge is tearing you asunder, don't give up. Even if you have been pursuing God's direction for a while, keep seeking, asking, and knocking (Matthew 7:7–8). Other believers before you have been where you are, and they all found Him faithful. You will too. The Father will not fail to show you His plans and lead you in the way you should go.

Father, thank You for the testimonies of those who have gone
before me. I trust You to answer my prayers as You did for them.
Amen.

MARCH 3

In God's Arms

SCRIPTURE READING: PROVERBS 3; PSALM 46:10; ISAIAH 40:11

In all your ways acknowledge Him,
and He will make your paths straight.
PROVERBS 3:6

There are trials so profoundly difficult and that pierce you so deeply that they leave you stunned and unable to proceed. Perhaps it is an emotional loss that drains every bit of energy you have. Or it could be a physical infirmity that leaves you completely without strength. You feel so profoundly helpless and defeated that you do not have the where-withal to go on.

In those seasons, there is only one thing the Lord asks of you: "Cease striving and know that I am God" (Psalm 46:10). Be still. Stop fighting. Fret not. End the constant churning of your mind as you try to solve the problem with your limited sources and capacity. Instead, consider what it means that your heavenly Father is the everlasting, al-mighty, wise Creator of all that exists. Think about what it means to have all of His resources posed to rush to your aid.

Your God understands the despair you are facing and is tender to-ward you. Isaiah 40:11 describes Him as the Good Shepherd, who "will carry the lambs in his arms, holding them close to his heart" (NLT). Yes, He will stretch your faith to the breaking point, but He never intends to harm you. On the contrary, His goal is to see you triumphant and full of joy.

So whatever you are facing today, rest in the arms of your Savior with full confidence, listen to His heartbeat, and allow Him to carry you through. Know that He is God and He will not fail or forsake you. And be assured that when you do, He will lead you in the way you should go.

Father, You alone know how deeply this trial affects me.
All I can do is lean on You and trust. Thank You for carrying me,
ministering to my heart, and making my path straight.
Amen.

Prepared and Protected

SCRIPTURE READING: PROVERBS 4; MATTHEW 25:1–13

Do not forsake wisdom, and she will protect you;
love her, and she will watch over you.
PROVERBS 4:6 NIV

Have you ever suffered from an ailment, problem, or tragedy that could easily have been prevented? It's normal to look back on such situations and wish you had done things differently. Of course, that isn't possible in all the challenges and trials you face, but many times you can—by prayer and preparation—prevent negative problems from arising.

Consider the story of the ten virgins of Matthew 25:1–13. Five of the young ladies prepared their lamps for the arrival of the bridegroom and five of them failed to do so. When the bridegroom called for them, only the five who were ready were able to go with him and enjoy the celebration. The other five were shut out. Of course, Jesus told this parable to illustrate the importance of being prepared for His return. But this parable also demonstrated how crucial it is for us to maintain a consistent, daily relationship with Him—having a constant supply of the oil of His presence to light our path.

Often, we wait to cry out to Him until we are in the middle of an emergency. Although it's good to remember the Lord while you are hurting, how much better is it to walk with Him *before* disaster strikes—strengthened for whatever comes and possibly even averting adversity altogether? It's incredible how much heartache you could avoid if you would listen to and obey Him daily.

So don't wait to call upon Him. Spend time with the Father today and let Him guide and strengthen you for the path ahead. He will lead you safely past the pitfalls, and when you do face a trial, you won't need to fear because you'll know for certain He is with you.

Father, thank You for protecting and preparing me.
Instruct and strengthen me daily for the road ahead.
Amen.

Don't Wander—Follow

SCRIPTURE READING: PROVERBS 5; PSALM 23:1;
PROVERBS 16:25; MATTHEW 6:13; 9:36; ROMANS 7:5

She doesn't consider the path of life;
she doesn't know that her ways are unstable.
PROVERBS 5:6 HCSB

Sheep are infamous for aimlessly wandering, which inadvertently puts them in danger of all kinds of hazards—predators, poachers, and polluted waters that make them sick. Unaware of the threats, they need wise, watchful shepherds to lead them away from hazards, protect them from predators, and tenderly care for their needs.

Interestingly, Scripture compares us to sheep without a shepherd (Matthew 9:36)—like lambs unintentionally wandering into dangerous terrain. Proverbs 16:25 teaches, "There is a way which seems right to a man, but its end is the way of death." In other words, when we operate out of our natural instincts without God's guidance, we unwittingly choose a path of destruction (Romans 7:5). Perhaps this is the reason we get into such trouble and face such confusion when making decisions.

Yet Jesus offers to be our Good Shepherd, promising to give us what is best and to protect us from harm. He pledges to guide, protect, and care for each of us—leading us not into temptation, but delivering us from evil (Matthew 6:13). This is why Psalm 23:1 proclaims: "The Lord is *my* shepherd." Because of Christ's matchless character, we can follow Him with confidence.

As you read this, you may question whether God grasps the pressure you're under today and the need you have for His direction, comfort, and wisdom. Yes, He does. God cares for you intimately and individually—every detail of your life is in His sovereign care. You can trust Him for the decisions you have to make. So stop wandering and start following Him. And be assured that He will not fail you.

Lord, You know the questions on my mind and how fearful
I am of making a bad decision. Thank You for leading me
and for guiding me to choose the best path.
Amen.

The Ant Approach

SCRIPTURE READING: PROVERBS 6; EPHESIANS 2:10; PHILIPPIANS 3:14

Go to the ant . . . observe her ways and be wise.
PROVERBS 6:6

Important lessons can be learned from even the smallest teachers. Such is the case with the common ant, which exhibits the inspiring qualities of *initiative*, *cooperation*, and *diligence*. Proverbs 6:7–8 tells us, "Having no chief, officer or ruler, [the ant] prepares her food in the summer and gathers her provision in the harvest." In other words, ants accept the tasks ahead and get to work—often carrying objects many times their own weight. Operating in unison with other ants, these amazing creatures take on specific roles and are able to build, clean, provide for, and defend their homes. And together they complete astounding endeavors. In fact, *Guinness World Records* reports that the largest ant colony in the world stretches approximately thirty-seven hundred miles.

Think of something so small achieving such comparatively grand exploits. Yet we are often shortsighted about what we can accomplish—even though we are endowed with the power of the living God, who enables all our labors. Instead of preparing for the future and being industrious, we focus on our problems and how we feel about them—effectively short-circuiting our efforts. But the Lord calls us to do our best every day and to continue striving toward what He's called us to, regardless of the challenges (Ephesians 2:10; Philippians 3:14).

So today, instead of focusing on the trials, think about the ant and ask the Father what He wants you to do. And like that tiny but wondrous creature, take the initiative in what God calls you to accomplish, look for ways to cooperate with those around you, and be diligent. You'll never see all the Lord could do through you until you get moving.

Father, I want to believe You can accomplish great things through me. Help me to take the initiative, cooperate with others, be diligent, and focus on You.
Amen.

Dying to Live

SCRIPTURE READING: PROVERBS 7;
MATTHEW 6:19–21; 16:24–26; JAMES 4:14

He was like a bird flying into a snare,
little knowing it would cost him his life.
PROVERBS 7:23

Jesus is clear. He says, "If anyone wishes to come after Me, he must deny himself, and take up his cross and follow Me. For whoever wishes to save his life will lose it; but whoever loses his life for My sake will find it. For what will it profit a man if he gains the whole world and forfeits his soul?" (Matthew 16:24–26). Real life—the kind of life that moves mountains and overflows with God's power—is the life that has been buried in Christ.

Unfortunately, the snare of this life is that this is all there is. We are trapped into thinking we must assert and protect our rights here and now, because if we don't, we'll die without living. And we fret over all of the earthly blessings we do not yet have—a spouse, children, wealth, prominence, physical pleasures, and possessions. Yet the truth of the matter is that this life is but a breath (James 4:14), and what we invest here doesn't last. But as believers, we have eternal life to prepare for, which is why we are called to store up our treasures in heaven (Matthew 6:19–21).

So search your heart. Do you feel dissatisfaction today? Does it hurt that your life isn't what *you* want it to be? Then it is possible that you haven't given your life fully to Jesus. And if you haven't, then, friend, you aren't truly living. Don't fall into the trap. Don't let your search for a satisfying earthly life cost you the supremely superior blessings of a life built on Christ. Give yourself over to Him fully today.

Lord Jesus, I confess that I haven't turned everything over to You—
but I want to. I belong to You, Lord Jesus. Lead me.
Amen.

Crossroads

SCRIPTURE READING: PROVERBS 8; ISAIAH 11:2

On top of the heights beside the way,
where the paths meet, she takes her stand.
PROVERBS 8:2

A re you at a crossroad today? Do you have two options stretched out before you—each with its positives and negatives? Are you at a loss about what to do because of the uncertainties that line each way? It is unsettling when you don't know what to do or where to go. After all, we are accustomed to street signs, maps, and clearly marked roadways. The path of life, however, is not so conveniently equipped with such signs.

Thankfully, God has given you three spiritual maps to follow that will help you make decisions. The *first*, of course, is the Bible. In its pages is guidance for nearly every situation you will ever encounter. *Second*, God has provided wise teachers to help you grow in understanding. *Finally*, you have been given a priceless inner compass through the indwelling presence of the Holy Spirit.

Isaiah 11:2 describes the qualities of the Holy Spirit as they would appear in the Person of Jesus. "The Spirit of the Lord will rest on Him, the spirit of wisdom and understanding, the spirit of counsel and strength, the spirit of knowledge and the fear of the Lord." The wonderful news is that all of those qualities of the Holy Spirit are available to you today. And as you open God's Word and pray or as you listen to godly counsel, the Holy Spirit will reveal the way you're to go.

The wise direction will make itself known as you follow the Father's three spiritual road maps. So when you feel lost, open God's Word and listen for the Holy Spirit's promptings. In Him you'll find the direction and assurance you long for.

Lord God, thank You for Your Holy Spirit, Your Word,
and Your people. Father, please show me what way to go.
I trust You to lead me on the best path possible.
Amen.

The Main Benefit

SCRIPTURE READING: PROVERBS 9; MATTHEW 6:33

If you become wise, you will be the one to benefit.
If you scorn wisdom, you will be the one to suffer.
PROVERBS 9:12 NLT

The greatest advantage that pursuing wisdom gives us is the opportunity to know God better. After all, wisdom is defined as reverence for the Lord. So as we strive to be wise each day through the decisions we make and the challenges we face, what we're really doing is learning God's ways, seeking His thoughts, and reflecting His character.

Unfortunately, we too easily revert to our human wisdom, focusing more on our problems than on the One who helps us. This, of course, makes our troubles bigger than they actually are. But this is why the Father instructs us to be still and know Him—to stop striving and consider who our God really is. He is the Lord of the universe, and He has eternal wisdom and understanding. Nothing is impossible for Him.

Additionally, you have been given the astounding promise, "Seek first His kingdom and His righteousness, and all these things"—all that you need to live—"will be added to you" (Matthew 6:33). Therefore, with wisdom comes a sense of confidence, assurance, and security. Fear, doubt, and insecurity are replaced with His promises and the joy of His presence. You realize that there is no need to worry about the future because God loves you and has a plan—not only for your life but also for every problem you face.

Therefore, today, take time today to pursue wisdom by renewing your trust in God. He is the goal, after all. So focus on Him and enjoy all the benefits of knowing Him.

Father, You are the Lord of all creation who helps me
in every situation. Help me to honor You as God and to obey Your
commands so I may experience the blessing of knowing You.
Amen.

Unshakable

The righteous will never be shaken.
PROVERBS 10:30

Today's verse may seem unreasonable and impossible: *The righteous will never be shaken.* After all, your life may seem to be a continual onslaught of problems that unsettle you to the core. Yet there is a way to stay steady during troubles. For example, Paul's letter to the Philippians was written during a long and unjust imprisonment; however, the short epistle is full of rejoicing. So how was the apostle Paul able to stay firm and faithful despite his circumstances?

Most people would blame others for their problems, complain, and search for a way out of the situation—making things far worse in the process. But not Paul. He understood that in order to live above his circumstances and gain victory in them, he had to shift his focus. So instead of endlessly analyzing his problems and whining about them, he looked to the Father and thanked Him for being his strength in the midst of adversity. Paul wrote, "[God] has said to me, 'My grace is sufficient for you, for power is perfected in weakness.' Most gladly, therefore, I will rather boast about my weaknesses, so that the power of Christ may dwell in me" (2 Corinthians 12:9).

You can do them same. Yes, God wants you to be honest with Him about your trials, but He also wants you to trust Him to see you through them. So today, don't wallow in self-pity or complain. Rather, look to Jesus and learn to live the unshakable Christian life. Acknowledge that Almighty God is in control of your situation and will guide you every step of the way to victory.

Father, You know that my trials are truly unsettling.
But I will steady myself by trusting in You. Thank You for
this opportunity for the power of Christ to dwell in me.
Amen.

The Hopelessness of Pride

SCRIPTURE READING: PROVERBS 11; DEUTERONOMY 14:22–25

When pride comes, then comes dishonor,
but with the humble is wisdom.
PROVERBS 11:2

Hopelessness will often arise when you imagine that you are the one in control. This is why adversity sometimes comes in the areas where you believe yourself most faithful or talented. You begin to develop pride in yourself rather than relying on the lovingkindness of God.

For example, perhaps you trust the Father sufficiently to tithe and you do so faithfully. But then a financial problem comes along that causes you a great deal of pain and confusion. You may think to yourself, *I don't deserve this. I tithe. I've earned the right to be rewarded rather than face such financial pressures.*

This whole line of thought implies a prideful attitude of self-sufficiency, not faith. In fact, the very purpose of tithing is to acknowledge that God is your Provider and the Lord over all that you have (Deuteronomy 14:22–25). You don't tithe Him to pay Him off. You do so to honor the One who has given you all things.

Do you see the difference? Sadly, a prideful attitude sets you up for desperation and disillusionment when things go awry. Your focus is on what you deserve or have earned rather than on how the Lord is revealing Himself to you.

But take heart, God is in your situation and will not fail you. Humble yourself before Him and acknowledge that even the good things you do are only because of His Holy Spirit's guidance and grace. And when those feelings of hopelessness arise, evaluate your life and make sure that all your trust is in the Father and all control remains firmly in His hands.

Lord, I confess that I have tried to take control of my circumstances
and now feel hopeless. Forgive me of my pride, Father.
I trust You to lead, provide for, and deliver me.
Amen.

A Question of Belief

SCRIPTURE READING: PROVERBS 12; JEREMIAH 32:27

The root of the righteous will not be moved.
PROVERBS 12:3

The Lord God is *omnipotent*—all-powerful and capable of helping you. He is *omniscient*—He knows everything, including every detail that concerns you. He is *omnipresent*—He never leaves you. And the Father loves you unconditionally, which means He will always act in your best interest.

Though you may intellectually accept these facts about God, the important thing is to apply them to your circumstances. Whenever you face times of trial, you must ask yourself: *Do I truly trust that God is able and willing to handle any problem I experience?* If you do, then you won't be shaken. But if you don't, then the difficulties that arise will move you to fear and despair.

The truth of the matter is that the Father never wrings His hands when you go to Him with a challenging situation. He is capable of leading you to victory regardless of what you face.

In fact, He asks the rhetorical question, "I am the Lord, the God of all flesh; is anything too difficult for Me?" (Jeremiah 32:27). Absolutely not. He was able to create all of humankind from dust—with our immensely intricate biological systems, distinctive physical attributes, unique personality traits, and different spiritual gifts. The God who can do that can take care of any issue that concerns you.

Though your struggles may appear insurmountable or unending today, to the Lord they are simply an opportunity to draw you closer to Himself and to teach you to rely upon Him more. The question is: "Can you stop trying to manage your situation and invite Him to handle it? Can you let go of control, allowing Him to do as He intends?" The answer to that will reveal what you really believe.

Father, I really want to trust that You are omnipotent, omniscient,
omnipresent, and that You love me unconditionally.
I believe, Lord, help my unbelief.
Amen.

The Message of Your Mouth

SCRIPTURE READING: PROVERBS 13; ACTS 16:16–34;
PHILIPPIANS 4:13; JAMES 3:6

The one who guards his mouth preserves his life;
the one who opens wide his lips comes to ruin.
PROVERBS 13:3

Do you realize that what you say affects every facet of your life? Your words don't just influence those who listen to you; they also have an impact on your own well-being—sometimes negatively. The apostle James wrote, "The tongue is set among our members as that which defiles the entire body, and sets on fire the course of our life" (3:6). James also gives two other examples of the tongue's power to set our direction: the power of a bit over a horse and the power of a small rudder over a large ship. In other words, when you speak, you are alerting your body to respond accordingly—in some way you're choosing your path.

Thankfully, the apostle Paul taught us another side of this principle, and that is the power of positive confession. For example, Paul proclaimed, "I can do all things through Him who strengthens me" (Philippians 4:13)—a proclamation he made from the confines of a jail cell. On another occasion when he was unjustly imprisoned, he sang hymns of praise to the Lord (Acts 16:16–34). Why? Because he understood that these testimonies of Christ's power reinforced his faith. He had been through all types of suffering, and he'd experienced the benefits of speaking out God's truth despite his circumstances.

In our culture, it has become normal to say everything we feel without restraint, but that does not reflect the wisdom of God and is the path to sure ruin. Instead, guard your mouth and make sure that what proceeds from it exalts the Lord. Make a commitment to confess the Word of God. The choice is yours. Your life can be transformed by changing what comes out of your mouth.

Father, I praise You! May what proceeds from my mouth exalt
You in every situation so that You may be glorified
and my faith may be strengthened.
Amen.

The Wisdom of Waiting

SCRIPTURE READING: PROVERBS 14; PSALM 27:14;
ISAIAH 64:4; HEBREWS 11:1

A patient person shows great understanding.
PROVERBS 14:29 HCSB

No one likes delays. And if you are experiencing a season of waiting today, you may feel frustrated, anxious, and even as though your hopes are dying within you. It is exasperating to feel as if you lack control over your circumstances or that your progress is being impeded. You may fear that the Lord has forgotten you or that He's found you undeserving of the desires of your heart.

But understand, every time of waiting is just your heavenly Father working in the unseen for your ultimate good. As Isaiah 64:4 says, "God . . . acts in behalf of the one who waits for Him." You may not perceive Him, and you may not be able to imagine how He is engineering your circumstances for your benefit. In fact, the Father has allowed this season in your life by design so you will honor Him as God and abandon yourself to His care. Your responsibility is to set your heart on Him and trust that your life is safe in His all-powerful, wise, and loving hands.

This is the wisdom of the patient person: He or she understands that God is actively orchestrating the details of his or her situation and will intervene at just the right moment, even when there is no evidence of His activity (Hebrews 11:1).

So today, be wise. Don't make your own way or run ahead of the Lord's plan. Instead, be patient and remain in your present circumstances until you receive further instructions. Because God *will* intervene. Therefore, "wait for the Lord; be strong and let your heart take courage; yes, wait for the Lord" (Psalm 27:14).

Father, I want to have faith and wisdom, but this is a difficult situation.
Please help me to trust that You are working everything out
on my behalf even though I cannot see You.
Amen.

Wait for Direction

SCRIPTURE READING: PROVERBS 15; PSALM 119:105

The heart of the righteous ponders how to answer.
PROVERBS 15:28

Do you feel pressure regarding a decision you must make? This is not unusual. The stress you experience may be coming from others who wish to push you in a certain direction. It can also originate from your own insecurity because of the weight of the choice or because you are so desperate for a change. But regardless of the source of the pressure you feel, don't make a move until you hear from God. If you don't have clarity from the Lord, it is always best to wait.

Instead of making choices that may be in conflict with His will, follow these simple principles to ensure you're relying on His wisdom and receiving His guidance. *First*, remove all obstacles to hearing Him by repenting of sinful attitudes and behaviors. *Second*, make sure you can honestly say that you want God's will to be done more than your own. *Third*, exercise patience by submitting to the Father's timing. *Fourth*, evaluate your situation from God's perspective—what does Scripture say about the decision you're about to make? *Fifth*, persist in prayer, trusting that the Father will answer in His perfect time. *Sixth*, rest in God's promises, allowing them to be a lamp to your feet and a light to your path (Psalm 119:105). *Finally*, wait for His peace, which is the evidence that you are following His path. When you have the Lord's direction, His calm assurance will comfort your heart and mind.

Friend, the Lord isn't trying to keep His will secret—He wants you to make the best decision in every situation. Just because you haven't yet received an answer from Him doesn't mean He isn't listening or leading you. He is. So wait on Him. Acknowledge that He alone has the right to direct your choices, and know that He will give you wisdom.

Father, I will wait on You, regardless of the pressure.
I trust You to lead me always.
Amen.

Purpose in Everything

SCRIPTURE READING: PROVERBS 16; 2 CHRONICLES 36:15–21

The LORD has made everything for its own purpose,
even the wicked for the day of evil.
PROVERBS 16:4

We know God is good and loving. And so it seems counterintuitive to think that our compassionate heavenly Father would work through something evil, as today's Proverb suggests. But throughout Scripture we see that He allowed wicked nations to rise up in order to discipline the Jewish people so that they would repent of their sins and return to Him. This was certainly the case when the Babylonians took the people of Judah into captivity for seventy years (2 Chronicles 36:15–21).

Being so far from home in Babylon was both difficult and heartbreaking for God's people. But the Father did not abandon them—nor would He ever. In fact, because of the adversity, many of the Jews were cleansed of the idolatry that had plagued them. They renewed their commitment to the Lord and taught their children to seek Him. They also gathered and protected the manuscripts that would become the Old Testament canon. And because they were so far from the holy temple, they established centers known as *synagogues*, where they could assemble for prayer and study Scripture—a development that would later become vitally important to the first Christians.

In other words, God accomplished incredible things through Judah's time of captivity. Likewise, you may not understand why the Lord has allowed some evil people and circumstances to arise in your life. But understand that He has permitted them for His purposes to cleanse you of sin, stretch your faith, build your character, and deepen your relationship with Him. So don't despair, no matter how bad things look. Trust that God is still in control and that one day you will see His goodness shine through all that currently plagues you.

Father, I confess that sometimes my heart wavers in unbelief
because of the evil I see. But I trust that You are still
in control and that You will never leave or abandon me.
Amen.

The Blessing of Accountability

SCRIPTURE READING: PROVERBS 17; HEBREWS 10:24–25

*A rebuke goes deeper into one who has understanding
than a hundred blows into a fool.*
PROVERBS 17:10

Do you have people around you who can speak truth into your life, who can confront the strongholds and blind spots you bear? A wise person understands how important it is to have mentors and accountability partners. So what should you look for when seeking out an accountability partner or mentor? Look for someone who is:

- *Christ-centered*—walking in the Spirit and offering you biblical principles rather than personal opinion.
- *Inspiring*—stimulating you to seek God more through his or her example.
- *Edifying*—building you up and encouraging you to be and do your best in every area.
- *Courageous*—lovingly confronting you with the truth, even when it hurts or it's difficult.
- *Forgiving*—allowing you to be yourself—mistakes and all— and being patient with you as you grow in Christ's likeness.
- *Trustworthy*—keeping everything you reveal in the strictest confidence.

Friend, you can benefit from having someone in your life who is able to say what you need to hear without making you feel threatened. Yes, the rebukes may sometimes sting, but if you've chosen the person wisely, you'll know that what he or she says is ultimately for your good. If you don't already have an accountability partner, pray that God will provide one for you today.

*Lord, please lead me to a mentor or accountability partner
who will be Christ-centered, inspiring, edifying, courageous,
forgiving, and trustworthy—always speaking Your truth into my life.
Amen.*

Are You Listening?

SCRIPTURE READING: PROVERBS 18; LUKE 1:37

To answer before listening—that is folly and shame.
PROVERBS 18:13 NIV

Does prayer ever feel like you're just talking to yourself? When you pray, do you have your own limitations in mind rather than God's limitless power? Although you may acknowledge that the Lord exists and go to Him regularly with your petitions, it is possible that you're still trying to resolve difficulties yourself rather than entrusting them to Him. This is why from your narrow, earthbound point of view, you may see no hope in your situation or end to your suffering.

Instead, when you approach God, you must embrace the fact that you are interacting with the Almighty, your Lord, Maker, King, Mighty Warrior, and Redeemer. After all, trusting God means looking beyond what you can see to what He sees and can accomplish. And there is absolutely nothing too challenging for Him to overcome (Luke 1:37). But your problem may be that you don't stop talking long enough to listen. The Father can communicate with you all day long, giving you His comfort, guidance, and wisdom, but if you're not willing to hear and act on what He is saying, then it will make no difference in your life.

Friend, your God is the God of all Creation, the Wise Counselor who sees every detail of your life more clearly than you ever could, and He is willing and eager to lead you. But you may be ignoring His counsel. You may be trying to lead your own life without sincerely seeking His will. Don't make that terrible mistake. Rather, go before the Father in prayer and open His Word, which contains His principles for living. Spending time in Scripture will familiarize you with who God is and how He communicates His will to you. This will train you to hear His voice. So today, listen to the Father by being silent before Him, embracing His leadership, and studying His Word.

Lord God, I will open Your Word. Speak to me,
Father. I am listening and will obey.
Amen.

Accept His Schedule

SCRIPTURE READING: PROVERBS 19; PSALM 37:4

He who hurries his footsteps errs.
PROVERBS 19:2

Psalm 37:4 declares, "Delight yourself in the Lord; and He will give you the desires of your heart." You may wonder about that promise as you serve God faithfully yet see no fulfillment of the longings that fill you. However, you need to understand that when you are walking in His will, what you desire may very well be what the Lord has purposed to provide for you, but the timing is not yet right for Him to bless you with it.

As is often said, timing is everything—and even more so, God's timing. As you wait, key puzzle pieces are falling into place. The Father is changing hearts and engineering circumstances you have no idea even exist. Therefore, the delays you face are not a denial of His promises; rather, they are an integral part of His strategy to arrange all the details and get you positioned for His excellent plan.

So today, don't be discouraged if you have not yet received the desires of your heart. Use this opportunity to make sure that you are in the center of His will. And when the pressure is on and everything around you is pushing you to move, move, move, and God says, "Don't even think about budging"—listen to Him. Stay where you are and trust Him to work on your behalf. Do so with the understanding that when you run ahead of Him—taking matters into your own hands or forcing your way into opportunities you have no business partaking of—you undermine and even destroy the good things He's designed for you. But when you accept His schedule, you know for certain you will receive His very best blessings.

Father, thank You for the good things You've planned
for me. Keep me in the center of Your will.
I will trust Your timing and wait on Your provision.
Amen.

The Good Side of Adversity

SCRIPTURE READING: PROVERBS 20; ROMANS 5:3–5; 8:28

Stripes that wound scour away evil,
and strokes reach the innermost parts.
PROVERBS 20:30

One of the most important lessons the Father has taught me is to see all adversity as coming from Him for my good. Through our trials, He draws us closer to Himself, conforms us to the character of Christ, prepares us for ministry, reveals our sin, heals our wounds, and strengthens our faith. Understanding this truth—that the adversity He allows is actually for our benefit—protects us from bitterness, resentment, and hostility toward those who wrong us. It also prevents us from becoming disheartened when trials assail us.

Romans 8:28 affirms, "We know that God causes all things to work together for good to those who love God, to those who are called according to His purpose." For example, you and I may experience earthly losses during a battle, but if the struggle brings us to the point of total surrender to the Lord, we can consider it a spiritual victory.

Likewise, other promises throughout Scripture, such as the one in Romans 5:3–5, demonstrate the purifying and edifying effects of adversity: "We also exult in our tribulations, knowing that tribulation brings about perseverance; and perseverance, proven character; and proven character, hope; and hope does not disappoint, because the love of God has been poured out within our hearts through the Holy Spirit who was given to us."

Therefore, friend, if the Father allows suffering in your life, you can be certain it is ultimately for your good and His glory. So whenever you face a tough time, ask, "God, what is Your goal for allowing this to happen?" Before you know it, you will be praising Him for the very difficulties that once caused you such grief.

Lord, thank You that nothing is lost—every trial
that touches my life is for my good. I will trust You,
Father. Teach me what You want me to learn.
Amen.

Already Won

SCRIPTURE READING: PROVERBS 21;
2 KINGS 6:15–17; 1 CORINTHIANS 15:57

The horse is prepared for the day of battle,
but victory belongs to the Lord.
PROVERBS 21:31

When the enormous Aramean army surrounded the city of Dothan, the prophet Elisha was surprisingly unaffected by their show of force. His servant, Gehazi, on the other hand, saw that multitude of soldiers, horses, and chariots and was absolutely terrified—as any normal person would be. He cried out, "Alas, my master! What shall we do?" (2 Kings 6:15).

Elisha remained calm and replied, "'Do not fear, for those who are with us are more than those who are with them.' Then Elisha prayed and said, 'O Lord, I pray, open his eyes that he may see.' And the Lord opened the servant's eyes and he saw; and behold, the mountain was full of horses and chariots of fire all around Elisha" (vv. 16–17).

While Gehazi saw the enemy encamped around the city, Elisha perceived the greater spiritual reality: *that God was already fighting and winning the battle for them.* This was how the prophet was able to remain confident and secure despite the threats of the enemy—he understood that the Lord had it all under control.

This biblical account can and should be instructive to you today. There is an unseen reality—the spiritual perspective of the situation you are facing that is far different from what you perceive with the human eye. You may see so many problems lined up against you that you feel absolutely hopeless. But that's not how God views your situation. He's just waiting on you to acknowledge His victory in faith. So do it—obey Him and trust Him to prevail. Because with Him fighting for you, the triumph is always assured (1 Corinthians 15:57).

Father, open my spiritual eyes and show me how You're fighting
on my behalf. I trust that You've already won these battles
for me and are leading me to victory.
Amen.

The Source

SCRIPTURE READING: PROVERBS 22; PHILIPPIANS 2:13;
4:13; COLOSSIANS 3:23–24

Do you see a man skilled in his work?
He will stand before kings.
PROVERBS 22:29

Have you ever been made to feel inadequate or useless? Have you ever been prevented from pursuing a goal because you were told you could not possibly succeed? Then it's important for you to memorize this verse and remind yourself of its promise every day: "I can do all things through Him who strengthens me" (Philippians 4:13). The Lord promises to help you succeed in whatever task He gives you, and He takes full responsibility for providing all the skill, wisdom, and power you require as you obey Him.

How does God enable you to do all the things He calls you to achieve? When you accept Jesus as your Savior, His Holy Spirit comes to dwell within you. He is the One who qualifies, equips, and empowers you to complete the assignments the Lord has planned for your life—even the ones that appear far beyond you.

Yes, you should always strive to do your best and work with all your heart in everything God gives you to do (Colossians 3:23–24). But ultimately, the omnipotent, omniscient, omnipresent Lord of creation is the One who enables you to do remarkable things. As Paul wrote: "It is God who is at work in you, both to will and to work for His good pleasure" (Philippians 2:13). So no matter what challenges, obstacles, or assignments arise in life, you can be confident of your success because the Lord is with you. All you have to do is obey God daily with diligence and leave the consequences to Him. And be assured that He will never steer you wrong, but will elevate you to heights you never thought possible—even raising you up to stand before the superiors you most respect.

Father, thank You for enabling me to do all You have planned for me.
Because of You, I know my life can be a greater success
than I'd ever imagined! Lead me in the way I should go.
Amen.

The Wings of Wealth

SCRIPTURE READING: PROVERBS 23; MATTHEW 14:13–21

Wealth certainly makes itself wings like
an eagle that flies toward the heavens.
PROVERBS 23:5

Where does your money go? Certainly at times the proverb above seems all too true. No matter what you do, it seems your resources sprout wings and take flight through the costly expenditures that arise. What happened to all you've worked so hard to gather?

This is why many verses in the Bible have to do with money and speak to how we can be good stewards of what God has placed at our disposal. Sadly, two of the most common ways we violate these biblical principles are through waste and debt. We squander what God has entrusted to us, unwilling to wait for Him to provide what we really need.

Yet just the opposite can be true as well. Consider what the Lord did with five loaves and two fish at the feeding of the five thousand (Matthew 14:13–21). When we submit what we have to Him, He can take our meager resources and stretch them far beyond imagination. He gives them a different kind of wings—ones that raise us up to the throne of heaven and give us His heavenly perspective of our true wealth.

So today consider how you handle your finances. Do you ask the Lord to guide you and give you wisdom, or do you make decisions based on what you think is wise? Realize that when you violate the principles of Scripture concerning your finances, you are inviting trouble, suffering, and sometimes disaster. But when you honor God's Word and submit what you have to Him, you will be blessed with greater treasure than you can imagine.

Father, I submit all my resources to You. Teach
me how to be a wise steward who exalts You with
everything I have. You are my truest treasure.
Amen.

Trusting in God's Power

SCRIPTURE READING: PROVERBS 24; NEHEMIAH 2

A wise man is strong, and a man
of knowledge increases power.
PROVERBS 24:5

Nehemiah had no reason to believe the Jewish people would accept him as a leader. He was merely the cupbearer to the Persian king—what right did he have to ask the people to follow him? But no one had been able to fully rebuild the walls of Jerusalem in the 140 years since the Babylonians had destroyed them. And Nehemiah knew God had called him to fix the situation.

So as Nehemiah entered Jerusalem, he quietly surveyed the situation, trusting that the Father would give him the right words to convince the Jews to work with him to raise the city's defenses. And that's exactly what happened. Nehemiah told the people, "You see the bad situation we are in, that Jerusalem is desolate and its gates burned by fire. Come, let us rebuild the wall of Jerusalem so that we will no longer be a reproach" (Nehemiah 2:17).

It wasn't the cleverness of Nehemiah's message that gave it power—it was the Spirit of the living God in it. Nehemiah simply told the people of Jerusalem what the Father was calling them to accomplish, and they immediately responded to His invitation (Nehemiah 2:17). Only the Father could have moved their hearts to bring about such agreement for such a great endeavor.

The same is true for you. Your success isn't based on what you know, what you can do, or who you are. Rather, God takes full responsibility for your needs when you obey Him. Your wisdom comes in trusting His power. So don't be afraid to step forward in faith and do as He calls you, even if you feel completely unqualified. Simply obey Him and He will take care of the rest.

Father, I feel so inadequate for the tasks You've given
me to accomplish. But like Nehemiah, I will depend
on You. You are my wisdom, power, and joy.
Amen.

Spiritual Control

SCRIPTURE READING: PROVERBS 25; 2
CORINTHIANS 10:5; EPHESIANS 6:12

*Like a city that is broken into and without walls
is a man who has no control over his spirit.*
PROVERBS 25:28

There will be times in your life when you experience negative feelings that you cannot explain. Yes, you may be facing some trying circumstances, but they don't warrant the emotions you're experiencing. But no matter how hard you try, you cannot pinpoint the source of your despair or why ungodly thoughts are flooding your mind. All you really know is that something is wrong. It feels as if you're under attack from some invisible enemy, covertly convincing you to give up.

Friend, take heart. You are indeed engaged in an unseen spiritual battle. Ephesians 6:12 explains, "Our struggle is not against flesh and blood, but against . . . the spiritual forces of wickedness in the heavenly places." These foes wage war against your spirit by contradicting the truth of God and the hope He offers you. Slowly they chip away at what you know to be true in order to drive you to your downfall.

This is why today's proverb teaches that a person who fails to control his or her spirit is like a city without defenses. You have a choice over what you will believe—over what you allow to influence your spirit. But if you refuse to take a stand, you will continually face defeat. So what can you do to claim victory? Second Corinthians 10:5 admonishes, "Demolish arguments and every pretension that sets itself up against the knowledge of God, and . . . take captive every thought to make it obedient to Christ." In other words, take control of this spiritual battle by affirming the truth of Scripture and applying godly wisdom. Success is yours. Claim it today in Jesus' name.

*Father, protect me with Your truth. Tear down the lies of the enemy
and lead me to Scripture with which to fight this battle.
Thank You that I am more than a conqueror through Christ.
Amen.*

MARCH 26

Ensnared by Gossip

SCRIPTURE READING: PROVERBS 26

The words of a whisperer are like dainty morsels,
and they go down into the innermost parts of the body.
PROVERBS 26:22

Be careful of whom you listen to. There are people who are experts in appearing to have an inside track on the latest news. They make it seem as if they're privy to the information you want access to and are happy to share it with you. This may make you feel loved, privileged, and maybe even secure; however, what they're really doing is ensnaring you in the deceptive practice of gossip. And as today's proverb suggests, it is bondage that reaches down to the core of who you are.

Why? Because like any other sin, when you engage in gossip you're meeting your needs in a destructive manner rather than God's way. For example, perhaps you receive a sense of security from what you're hearing—that by being "in the know" you can prevent bad things from happening to you. But gossip is actually known to increase anxiety. After all, most chatter is merely speculation, which invites the imagination to run wild—and that can be truly fearsome. Gossiping may feed your drive to feel loved or important, but you must recognize that nothing about it gives you any true worth. In fact, if you become known as a busybody, it will destroy your reputation.

Friend, don't fall prey to the sin of gossip—it isn't worth it. One day we will each give an account to the Lord for how we've lived, including the words we've said. Now is the time to use your voice for good—edifying others instead of tearing them down and proclaiming the truth of the gospel instead of other people's secrets. So use wisdom regarding whom you listen to and how they may be ensnaring you by what they say.

Father, please free me from the bondage of gossip
and protect me from those who would ensnare me with it.
Amen.

The Wounds of a Friend

SCRIPTURE READING: PROVERBS 27; PSALM 141:5

Faithful are the wounds of a friend.
PROVERBS 27:6

When a friend confronts us about something in our lives or is less than supportive about our goals, it can be devastating. We may feel blindsided and lonely. We may immediately begin listing their faults and replaying their words in our minds in order to refute them. What may particularly hurt is how much we trusted them, have done for them, and have believed in them. Why would they intentionally hurt us this way?

Yet at such moments it is necessary for you to take a deep breath and step back from the situation. Is your friend really trying to wound you, or is he or she alerting you to a blind spot in your life? That person knows you well—sees mistakes you're making in a way that you can't. Especially if your friend is a particularly godly and trustworthy person, it's possible that he or she is actually speaking in your best interests, even if it doesn't appear that way (Psalm 141:5).

Granted, the way your friend confronted you may not have been optimal. Even so, forgive him or her, thank God for your friend, and ask Him to give you the proper perspective about the encounter. Ask the Lord if there was any truth in what your friend said. If the Father identifies something that needs to change in your life, obey however He leads you to proceed. Likewise, if you responded badly to your friend, ask for forgiveness and request his or her help in overcoming your shortcomings. But the point is, don't give up on a person who loves you enough to tell the truth. You may find that person is actually the truest friend you have beside Jesus.

Father, don't let me be hard-hearted. I want to honor You,
so help me to see when You're speaking through my friends.
Amen.

Yes, He Cares

SCRIPTURE READING: PROVERBS 28; PSALM 62:8; MATTHEW 10:30

He who walks blamelessly will be delivered.
PROVERBS 28:18

Your Savior is working it out. It may seem like He is absent from your situation at this moment, but He isn't. As a child of the living God, your Father is always interested in helping you overcome anything that is defeating, discouraging, or depressing you. He wants you to talk to Him about the things that concern you. And He desires you to seek His counsel and guidance, regardless of how small the issue may seem to you.

Of course, from a theological perspective, you may know that God cares for you. But at times your difficulties may make you feel insignificant, inadequate, and unworthy—so much so that you begin to feel you are below the Father's notice. After all, He has the entire world to care for—why should He spend time on the challenges that distress you? And the truth of the matter is that you've gone to Him with your troubles so many times before that you wonder if He is tired of listening to you.

However, Jesus said, "The very hairs of your head are all numbered" (Matthew 10:30). That means the Father cares about each detail of your life, and He wants you to experience deep fellowship with Him about everything that concerns you. He never grows weary of hearing your heart and He hasn't abandoned you. Just because you don't perceive His activity at a specific moment doesn't mean anything.

So as you endeavor to walk wisely with God, never say, "God doesn't care about *that.*" He does. If it concerns you, it matters to Him. Your Savior is working it out. Therefore, as Psalm 62:8 instructs, "Trust in Him at all times, O people; pour out your heart before Him; God is a refuge for us."

Father, thank You for caring about everything that concerns me.
I don't always perceive Your activity, but I praise You anyway,
trusting You are working all things for my good and Your glory.
Amen.

Ultimate Authority

SCRIPTURE READING: PROVERBS 29; JOHN 19:10–11

Many seek the ruler's favor, but
justice for man comes from the Lord.
PROVERBS 29:26

It is amazing how often our future appears to be dependent upon the decisions made by others. Will we receive that promotion? Will the insurance accept our claims? Will that company consent to our proposal? Will that judge rule on our behalf? It seems at times as if other people have too much influence on whether we succeed or fail.

But I write "appears to be" and "seems" because the truth is that your life is in God's hands. He opens and closes all the doors you encounter for eternal purposes. And if He allows you to experience some trial, you know that it is ultimately for your good and His glory.

Nowhere was this more evident than at the cross. From an earthly viewpoint, Pilate, the Jewish leaders, and the crowds seemed to have the power to either send Jesus to His death or stay the execution. Pilate even said, "Do You not know that I have authority to release You, and I have authority to crucify You?" (John 19:10). Yet Jesus explained, "You would have no authority over Me, unless it had been given you from above" (v. 11). And we understand that God authorized the crucifixion for our salvation.

Likewise, the Father permits the circumstances you are experiencing for His greater purposes as well. This is not about the person making the decision, even though so much may seem to depend on what he or she chooses. Rather, this is about you trusting God in the midst of this situation and allowing Him to work in and through you. So have faith in the Father and know that your ultimate justice will come from Him.

Father, I am grateful that my life is in Your hands.
Thank You for leading me, increasing my faith, refining
my character, and protecting me in all things.
Amen.

The Name of Jesus

SCRIPTURE READING: PROVERBS 30; ACTS 4:12; ROMANS 7:7;
HEBREWS 4:16; PHILIPPIANS 2:10–11; JUDE 24

Who has established all the ends of the earth?
What is His name or His son's name? Surely you know!
PROVERBS 30:4

As the One who established the earth and the laws governing nature and humanity, God saw fit to require a blood offering to forgive sin. Then in His compassion, the Lord announced how imperfect people could be cleansed—the priests would offer an animal sacrifice to cover their iniquities. However, that system was imperfect, merely an alert to the problem of sin (Romans 7:7). But at the cross, God accepted a final shedding of blood as the onetime payment for all iniquities—past, present, and future. Jesus Christ's sacrifice paid for all our transgressions so that we could be reconciled to the Father.

This is why the name of *Jesus*—which means *God saves*—is so important. His name has been appointed as the key to every blessing of heaven. He has paved the way for you to have access to the Father and enjoy His will. Anyone who has received Him as personal Savior can approach the throne of Almighty God with confidence for help in time of need (Hebrews 4:16). Jesus is the One "able to keep you from stumbling, and to make you stand in the presence of His glory blameless with great joy" (Jude 24). Truly, there is power in the name of Jesus!

So today, call upon the name of Jesus and proclaim it far and wide. "For there is no other name under heaven that has been given among men by which we must be saved" (Acts 4:12). And one day, "at the name of Jesus every knee will bow . . . and every tongue will confess that Jesus Christ is Lord" (Philippians 2:10–11).

Jesus, Yours is the most beautiful name! Thank You for reconciling me
to the Father and for showering me with the blessings of heaven.
To You belong all honor, glory, power, and praise.
Amen.

Making a Defense

Open your mouth for the speechless, in the
cause of all who are appointed to die.
PROVERBS 31:8 NKJV

Matthew 27 reports the incredible detail that as Pilate questioned Jesus and the Jewish leaders accused Him wrongly, He did not open His mouth. Jesus "did not answer [Pilate] with regard to even a single charge, so the governor was quite amazed" (v. 14). However, it is important for us to understand *why* Christ didn't defend Himself: It was because He had a much more important battle to fight, and He was not about to be distracted. In fact, He was about to engage in the war of the ages—the ultimate confrontation between sin and the holiness of God, between death and eternal life.

Hebrews 12:2 says, "For the joy set before Him, [Jesus] endured the cross, despising the shame." In other words, He ignored the empty words of His accusers because He was focused on obeying the Father and saving you—that was His ultimate joy. It was far more important to Him to reconcile you to God than to vindicate Himself. Likewise, the Savior understood that just three days later, the Father would make the ultimate statement by raising Him from the grave. Not only would the resurrection silence Pilate and the religious leaders for good, but it would herald His everlasting victory over sin and death.

Now here's the question for you today: Can you keep your mouth shut over insignificant things in order to glorify your Savior? Can you maintain what He loves as your foremost goal—redeeming the lost and obeying the Father? Because when you open your mouth, you either draw people to God or drive them away from Him. Choose wisely, as He did.

Jesus, thank You for choosing me over defending Yourself.
I recognize that my words have consequences.
Help me to always glorify You with what I say.
Amen.

April

Jesus

The cross shows the ultimate difference between the wisdom of God and that of mankind. God's wisdom is redemptive rather than destructive, sacrificial instead of self-serving, and eternal rather than momentary or fleeting. The resurrection is proof that what the Lord says will be established—not even sin and death can stop Him from accomplishing His every good purpose.

No Good

SCRIPTURE READING: PROVERBS 1; ROMANS 5:8;
EPHESIANS 2:8–9; 1 JOHN 1:9

Their feet rush into evil.
PROVERBS 1:16 NIV

When we look to the cross, we see the starkest illustration of human nature ever displayed in history. The Son of the living God—God Himself—was nailed violently and mercilessly to those splintered boards of wood. And what did mankind do? Because of sin, we spurned His holiness, lied about Him, and sentenced Him to death. We wanted no part of Him.

Thankfully, the Father understood that because of our fallen nature, we did not have the capacity to seek Him. So, "God demonstrates His own love toward us, in that while we were yet sinners"—and completely unable to love Him—"Christ died for us" (Romans 5:8).

What this shows us is that salvation is entirely a gift of the Father—not something we can ever attain ourselves. We should never believe that there is good in us that can earn our way to God (Ephesians 2:8–9). He must come to us; He must provide it Himself. But because of that fact—because salvation is something Christ gives us freely and not a blessing we could ever merit—we can likewise never lose it. Nothing we do can disqualify us from the salvation Jesus offers us once we've accepted it by faith.

Your feet may have rushed into evil today, and you may feel as if God could never forgive you for what you've done. But take heart. Christ's shoulders already bore your guilt on the cross. He will not reject you. Turn back to Him and trust that He loves you enough to forgive you—always (1 John 1:9).

Jesus, I confess my sins to You. Thank You for forgiving me
and for cleansing me of all unrighteousness. Help me to turn
from any behaviors or thoughts that displease You.
Amen.

A Guarantee from the Resurrection

SCRIPTURE READING: PROVERBS 2; EPHESIANS 1:19–20

He preserves the way of His godly ones.
PROVERBS 2:8

The message of the resurrection is a powerful one for you today—Jesus triumphed in the battle He fought on the cross. How do we know He was victorious? Because He is alive! He broke the shackles of sin, and He brought forth life from death. This is extremely important in an eternal sense, of course. But it should encourage you in your daily life as well. After all, you will certainly face situations where all hope seems gone, buried in the grave of devastating circumstances.

Yet there is, indeed, hope for you. As long as you have Jesus, you can always have the joyful expectation of better days ahead. Why? Because He is the One who has conquered your most insurmountable foes: sin and death. Could your situation possibly need more power than the resurrection, where Jesus—after bearing the penalty of sin for *every* person throughout *all* history—was bodily raised to everlasting life? Of course not. And yet this is the power promised to you! This is why Paul admonishes, "Understand the incredible greatness of God's power for us who believe Him. This is the same mighty power that raised Christ from the dead and seated Him in the place of honor at God's right hand in the heavenly realms" (Ephesians 1:19–20 NLT).

The Father employs His wisdom, influence, authority, and strength when defending you, and He promises to always preserve the way of His godly ones. Friend, the challenges before you today are no match for the Lord. So rejoice in this fact, and be assured that He will faithfully help you, regardless of what you face.

Jesus, thank You for the hope that the resurrection gives me.
Nothing is impossible for You! You give me purpose in every trial
and breathe life into me when I think I can't go on. Thank You, Lord!
Amen.

Your Great Physician

SCRIPTURE READING: PROVERBS 3; PROVERBS 20:27; MALACHI 4:2

*It will be healing to your body
and refreshment to your bones.*
PROVERBS 3:8

It is the unseen wounds within you that continually cause the pain you feel and cause you to respond in destructive ways. Of course, these injuries were caused by sin—both those you've committed and those perpetrated against you. There is only One who is able to reach deep within your soul and repair them—the Great Physician, the Lord your God. He is your one hope for recovery.

Yet Malachi 4:2 promises, "To you who fear My name The Sun of Righteousness shall arise with healing in His wings" (NKJV). We now know exactly what the prophet meant. Jesus came into the world so you could be healed—in your relationship with God, from the penalty of sin, and from those deep emotional hurts within you. In fact, the moment you accept Christ as your Savior, you are indwelt by the Holy Spirit. And as we know from Proverbs 20:27, "The spirit of man is the lamp of the Lord, searching all the innermost parts of his being." It is the Holy Spirit who seeks out and formulates the treatment plan for every wound within you.

Perhaps today you are frustrated by the old hurts that continually plague you—the rejections, betrayals, and failures that have shaped your life for so long. Friend, take heart. God is working to heal you. At times He does so through the trials and challenges you face, but do not despair. He knows exactly what He's doing as He surfaces the problems and uproots them completely. It may take some time, but be absolutely assured—your Great Physician will not fail you.

*Lord Jesus, thank You for being my Great Physician—
saving me from my sins and healing my inmost
wounds. I will trust You to lead me.
Amen.*

Light for the Path

SCRIPTURE READING: PROVERBS 4; ISAIAH 42:16;
DANIEL 12:3; ROMANS 8:24

*The path of the righteous is like the light of dawn,
that shines brighter and brighter until the full day.*
PROVERBS 4:18

Some days can appear very dark indeed. You cannot see the way ahead. All you can do is put your hand in God's and trust that your heavenly Father is leading you in the right direction. This is the essence of faith. The Lord asks you to trust though you do not see. As Romans 8:24 says, "Hope that is seen is not hope; for who hopes for what he already sees?"

And so the Father bids you to follow blindly down an unfamiliar path. He makes sure you cannot handle it in your strength and wisdom, because if you could, it wouldn't be a step of faith for you and would carry no potential for revealing His character, love, power, and wisdom. Of course, during such times, you may wish to overcome the uncertainty you feel by finding your own way. But understand that only God can offer you true light. When you fight the dark with more darkness, all you get is trouble and despair.

But the good news is that the Father promises to illuminate the path. He says, "I will make darkness into light before them" (Isaiah 42:16). That's not just the road ahead but also the profound spiritual realities that affect your life. And even better, He will make you a light to others. As Daniel 12:3 says, "Those who have insight will shine brightly like the brightness of the expanse of heaven."

Friend, the Father is leading you brilliantly. So when the dark feels overwhelming, hold His hand tightly. He will be your light and you will have nothing to dread.

*Lord, You do all things well. I know I can only see step-by-
step before me because You are stretching my faith. Help
me to honor and trust You regardless of what happens.
Amen.*

Changing Direction Through Jesus

SCRIPTURE READING: PROVERBS 5; ROMANS 3:10;
5:10–11; 10:9; EPHESIANS 2:8–9

Her feet go down to death, her steps lay hold of hell.
PROVERBS 5:5 NKJV

Are you worried that you don't measure up in your relationship with God? That you're not really getting it right? Before Christ, faithful Jews tried to please the Lord by adhering to the Law He'd given Moses. Day after day, they made sacrifices in accordance with that Law, hoping it would be sufficient to earn His favor and prevent the alternative—an eternity in hell. However, it was never enough. Each day brought new temptations and violations of God's holy standards. It seemed hopeless that anyone could really have a relationship with Him. And truly, it *was* absolutely impossible because "THERE IS NONE RIGHTEOUS, NOT EVEN ONE" (Romans 3:10).

But take heart, it was unattainable only until Jesus died on the cross and rose from the grave, reconciling us to God once and for all (Romans 5:10–11). When you trust Jesus as your Savior, He makes you holy—fully acceptable and capable of experiencing God's loving presence. Jesus does it all for you because He knows you cannot do it for yourself (Ephesians 2:8–9). You're right, you can't get it right. Like the ungodly woman of Proverbs 5, your feet were going down to death and you were on a one-way road to hell. But Jesus changed your course through His great sacrifice. All that was left for you to do was accept His gift of salvation by faith (Romans 10:9).

Today, think about that and rejoice in the great gift your Savior has given you. You don't have to toil, fret, or be perfect in your relationship with God. He saves you freely. So don't try to earn His favor; just accept you have it. Stop struggling and start enjoying Him. And live your life as an expression of gratefulness to Him. Because truly, He deserves your praise.

Lord Jesus, I praise You! Thank You for making me acceptable
and restoring my relationship with the Father.
Amen.

APRIL 6

Time to Reach Out

SCRIPTURE READING: PROVERBS 6; MATTHEW 5:14;
EPHESIANS 2:4; 1 TIMOTHY 2:3–4

Calamity will come suddenly.
PROVERBS 6:15

Adversity is unpredictable. It strikes us swiftly, often without warning. Our ability to prevent it is limited indeed. And if you've had a
loved one pass away suddenly, you know how frightening and disheartening this can be.

As believers, we are not called to live in constant fear. However, understanding how fleeting life is should prompt us to warn those without
Christ that time is short. We know firsthand the precariousness of the
situation. There is nothing any of us can do to motivate God to save us.
There is nothing we could do that would pay the sin debt we owe.

Yet we also know that "God our Savior . . . desires all men to be
saved and to come to the knowledge of the truth" (1 Timothy 2:3–4).
Our loving heavenly Father chooses to redeem us through Christ's sacrifice on the cross because He loves us (Ephesians 2:4). And as beneficia-
ries of the Lord's work of deliverance from eternal death and His gift of
everlasting life, we should be motivated to reach out and share the Good
News of salvation with others. We are charged with shining His light
here on earth so that others may see the goodness of God, give Him
glory, and accept His gift (Matthew 5:14).

It is not the will of our heavenly Father that anyone be lost. And life
is short. Calamity comes suddenly. This is why God is constantly reaching out to humanity and inviting people into a love relationship with
Him. So let us join Him in that important work and make the most of
the moments we're given.

Jesus, thank You for the salvation You've provided to me.
Help me make the most of every opportunity
and be Your ambassador to the lost.
Amen.

APRIL 7

Warnings for Good

SCRIPTURE READING: PROVERBS 7; JOHN 10:10;
1 CORINTHIANS 6:12; GALATIANS 5:1

Keep my commandments and live,
and my teaching as the apple of your eye.
PROVERBS 7:2

If Jesus' death on the cross forgave our sin past, present, and future, why should you and I continue to live by God's commands? Why is it important? To answer, I would direct you to the words of the apostle Paul, "It was for freedom that Christ set us free; therefore keep standing firm and do not be subject again to a yoke of slavery" (Galatians 5:1). Remember, sin is bondage. Jesus didn't die on the cross so you would continue being enslaved to the very things that were destroying you. He freed you so you could experience abundant life! (John 10:10).

This is why we experience the internal pressure of conviction when we disobey the Lord. There are even things that we may be at liberty to do that would actually lead us back into emotional, spiritual, and physical bondage. So God warns us against them for our safety and benefit. The apostle Paul explains, "All things are lawful for me, but not all things are profitable. All things are lawful for me, but I will not be mastered by anything" (1 Corinthians 6:12). The Father is looking out for you and wants to protect you from any destructive consequences.

Friend, if the Holy Spirit is convicting you of sin, do not wait any longer. Confess it to God and allow Him to free you from it. You can always be certain that your heavenly Father speaks for your benefit, to keep you free, safe, and joyful. Therefore, if He alerts you to danger, don't proceed on the path to destruction—run the other way.

Father, I know that You lead me on the path to life at its best.
I will obey Your commands and trust You always.
Amen.

Who Helps You

SCRIPTURE READING: PROVERBS 8; MARK 9:23; ROMANS 8:32

From everlasting I was established, from the beginning,
from the earliest times of the earth.
PROVERBS 8:23

The trials and burdens you face today will seem overwhelming as long as you attempt to handle them in your own strength. But when you look at them in terms of what the Sovereign Lord can do, nothing will seem impossible to you. This is because you're assured that the One who established wisdom from the foundation of the earth lovingly helps you. So regardless of what happens today, keep these two facts in mind:

First, the Lord loves you unconditionally and wants the best for you. The apostle Paul asks, "He who did not spare His own Son, but delivered Him over for us all, how will He not also with Him freely give us all things?" (Romans 8:32). Do you believe the Lord would willingly sacrifice so much for you and then leave you helpless? Of course He wouldn't. Therefore, you don't have to wonder if the Father has your best interests at heart. He absolutely does and will help you no matter what you face.

Second, the Lord has both the wisdom and power to help you. Not only is the Father willing to assist you; He is capable of doing so in ways you could never imagine. God is *omnipotent* (all-powerful), *omniscient* (all-knowing), and *omnipresent* (simultaneously existing everywhere at once), which is possible because He is outside of time and the limitations of this world. There's nothing you could face that requires more strength or knowledge than He possesses.

With such an awesome Defender available to you, do you really ever have any cause for fear? Certainly you don't. Allow the immense support and provision that's available for you as a believer to fill you with faith, courage, and confidence.

Father, truly, "All things are possible to him who believes" (Mark 9:23).
Thank You, Lord, for helping me in everything I face!
Amen.

Whom Are You Talking To?

SCRIPTURE READING: PROVERBS 9; HEBREWS 11:6

The fear of the LORD is the beginning of wisdom,
and the knowledge of the Holy One is understanding.
PROVERBS 9:10

Do you really know God? Do you trust His character? How you see Him is incredibly important when it comes to your prayer life. For example, your opinion of the Lord influences your attitude in talking to Him. If you have a low view of the Father—thinking He's not actively engaged in your life or even that He's cruel—then you won't want to interact with Him. However, if you love and respect Him as God Almighty—realizing the great privilege you have in being able to converse with Him—then you'll want to approach His throne with humility and expectancy.

Also, your view of the Lord will affect the nature of your prayers. What you express during your time alone with the Lord says a great deal about what you think of Him. If you're consistently focused on yourself during times with the Lord, then your attention is misplaced. You're missing out on one of the greatest blessings a soul can experience—the love and power of being in the awesome presence of the living God.

Finally, your perception of the Father will impact whether or not you expect Him to answer you. Do you trust that the Lord is working on your behalf? Are you confident that He hears your petitions and is leading you in the best way possible? Hebrews 11:6 is clear: "Without faith it is impossible to please Him, for he who comes to God must believe that He is and that He is a rewarder of those who seek Him."

How you see God will shape your prayer life. So seek Him out and know Him. Find out Whom you're talking to and discover what a truly wonderful privilege you've been given in prayer.

Father, I want to know You!
Reveal Yourself to me in a powerful way.
Amen.

Stepping Away

SCRIPTURE READING: PROVERBS 10; MATTHEW 6:24;
ROMANS 8:38–39; 1 JOHN 1:9

Love covers all transgressions.
PROVERBS 10:12

Once you trust the Lord Jesus for salvation, nothing can eternally divide you from God ever again. Don't ever worry about that. There isn't anything in all creation that can separate you from His love (Romans 8:38–39). However, your sins can *impede* your relationship with Him. This is because God is holy, and everything He commands you to do is consistent with His righteous character. So when you disobey Him, you step away from His perfect path and hinder His purifying work in your life. Notice: You reject Him—not the other way around.

In fact, every time you sin, you're actually declaring that you want to be the lord of your life rather than God. Jesus warned against this, saying, "No one can serve two masters; for either he will hate the one and love the other, or he will be devoted to one and despise the other" (Matthew 6:24). In other words, you're devoted to either your will or to His. Think about that. Consider who might have the better plans: You with your limitations? Or the omnipotent, omniscient Lord of creation, who can ensure that His purposes come to pass?

Friend, if you desire God's best for your life, you must acknowledge that He is the only One truly equipped to lead you. Thankfully, "if [you] confess [your] sins, He is faithful and righteous to forgive [your] sins and to cleanse [you] from all unrighteousness" (1 John 1:9). Once you agree that you want the Lord to rule, you can trust Him to welcome you back with open arms. Therefore, if you've sinned, pray for forgiveness and don't allow anything to impede you relationship with your Savior. He will certainly cover your transgressions and lead you back to the path of life.

Father, I confess that I've put my will above Yours. Please forgive me.
You have the very best plans for my life.
Help me walk in the center of Your will.
Amen.

Heavenly Rewards

SCRIPTURE READING: PROVERBS 11;
1 CORINTHIANS 3:11–14; HEBREWS 6:10; JAMES 1:12

He who sows righteousness gets a true reward.
PROVERBS 11:18

Have you ever thought about the rewards you'll receive when you get to heaven? Throughout Scripture, you're promised that when you obey the Lord with godly conduct, He will honor you with blessings. For example, James 1:12 tells us, "Blessed is a man who perseveres under trial; for once he has been approved, he will receive the crown of life which the Lord has promised to those who love Him." Therefore, you know there is a crown of life awaiting you when you honor God as you endure suffering.

Why is this important? Because when you are serving the Lord faithfully here on earth and everything seems to be going wrong, you have to remember there is an eternal reality at work. Representing Him to a lost world isn't always easy, and at times you will face persecution because of your faith. But don't hold back. Remember that God will reward you on the basis of three criteria: how much light of truth you knew, what opportunities He gave you to express that truth, and if you were faithful to obey Him with those opportunities.

No, you may not be rewarded here on earth. However, the Lord assures you that nothing you do in obedience to Him will ever be overlooked (Hebrews 6:10). On the contrary, the Lord is watching every detail. And on that great day when your eyes finally behold your Savior, you are assured that your rewards will match your deeds and the Father will rejoice over everything you've done in obedience to Him (1 Corinthians 3:11–14). So keep serving Him, because everything you do to honor Him now will certainly be celebrated in heaven for eternity.

*Father, thank You for reminding me that there are
eternal awards awaiting me that will never pass away.
Help me to honor You with everything I do.
Amen.*

True Life

SCRIPTURE READING: PROVERBS 12; 2 CORINTHIANS 1:8–9

In the way of righteousness is life,
and in its pathway there is no death.
PROVERBS 12:28

Do you realize that the Father wants you to possess the abundant life—and works tirelessly to see it born out in you? This may be difficult for you to believe today because many of the commands in His Word admonish you to stop engaging in behaviors you may enjoy. Likewise, the trials God has permitted you to face are difficult—sometimes incredibly so—making you feel as if you're being consumed.

However, to experience the profound life the Lord created you for requires that you allow Jesus to live *His* life in and through you, and that demands a radical transformation. It means you must learn to function in Christ's strength and wisdom rather than your own. In 2 Corinthians 1:8–9, Paul explained, "We were burdened excessively, beyond our strength, so that we despaired even of life; indeed, we had the sentence of death within ourselves so that we would not trust in ourselves, but in God who raises the dead." In other words, the Lord allows the trials so you'll stop being distracted by peripheral issues and focus your attention completely on Him and what He deems important. And in exchange, you live in the extraordinary power of the risen Savior—with His peace, joy, confidence, and assurance.

Friend, the Father hasn't called you to an *adequate* life—He wants your existence to be *extraordinary*. Because of that, everything He sends your way is meant teach you how to truly live for Him. So today, choose His path to the abundant life. Allow Christ to direct you and walk in the power of the living God. Certainly, that is life at its very best.

Father, thank You for readying me for the abundant life.
I die to myself so I can experience the incredible
wisdom, power, peace, and joy of Christ in me.
Amen.

A Feeling for Healing

SCRIPTURE READING: PROVERBS 13; ROMANS 5:8; EPHESIANS 2:8–9

A faithful envoy brings healing.
PROVERBS 13:17

Do you ever feel unworthy of your relationship with God? That no matter how hard you try, you just don't deserve Him? Be comforted today: That's actually a good thing! All of us are undeserving of the salvation Christ has given us. In fact, in order to have a relationship with God at all, the first thing we must do is admit we can't get to Him by our own good works. Ephesians 2:8–9 reminds us, "By grace you have been saved through faith; and that not of yourselves, it is the gift of God; not as a result of works, so that no one may boast."

Thankfully, our heavenly Father had mercy on us. Knowing that we could never help ourselves, God took the initiative to forgive our sins and restore our relationship with Him (Romans 5:8). How did He do so? By coming to earth in the form of a man—as Jesus—to die on the cross as the sacrificial, substitutionary payment for all our sins.

Of course you know that. But every once in a while that feeling of unworthiness reappears. Why? There are four general reasons. *One,* to remind you that your relationship with God is not by your effort and you need to stop trying to earn it. *Two,* because there may be sin in your life that you need to repent of. *Three,* because you have false guilt that you need to release. Or *four,* because there are areas of your life that you refuse to relinquish control of to God. This sense of unworthiness is an envoy meant to give you healing. So ask the Father to identify why you're feeling undeserving, and trust Him to remind you of who you are in Him.

Father, thank You for drawing me back to Yourself. Help me to repent of, release, or relinquish anything that displeases You.
Amen.

APRIL 14

The Father's Provision

SCRIPTURE READING: PROVERBS 14; MATTHEW 6:11; 7:9, 11; JAMES 1:17

In the fear of the Lord there is strong confidence,
and his children will have refuge.
PROVERBS 14:26

Your heavenly Father wants you to be confident in Him. He desires that you face each day with peace and assurance because He is with you. How is that possible?

It comes in understanding God's heart. Jesus tells us, "What man is there among you who, when his son asks for a loaf, will give him a stone? . . . If you then, being evil, know how to give good gifts to your children, how much more will your Father who is in heaven give what is good to those who ask Him!" (Matthew 7:9, 11). What a promise! The Father would never bestow something that would harm you. You may not comprehend what He offers or why He allows it in your life, but you can be certain that His answers to your prayers are always in your best interest.

So Jesus—God's most amazing provision to us—tells us to ask, "Give us this day our daily bread" (Matthew 6:11). Notice that He says *daily.* We are to have a continual, ongoing relationship with the Lord. He wants us to respect Him as the Source of everything we have and receive. As James 1:17 reminds us, "Every good thing given and every perfect gift is from above, coming down from the Father."

Many people won't acknowledge this and will attempt to attain what they want in their own strength. The question is: Where do *you* go for the things you require? Jesus tells you to ask Him for your daily bread so you'll understand that your hope, abilities, and sufficiency are all from Him. So go to Him today and thank Him for perfectly and lovingly providing your needs every day.

Lord, thank You for the good gifts You give me daily.
And thank You for withholding the requests that would
harm me. Truly, You are a wonderful Father.
Amen.

Deep Healing

SCRIPTURE READING: PROVERBS 15; PSALM 16:11

Sheol and Abaddon lie open before the Lord,
how much more the hearts of men!
PROVERBS 15:11

It may seem that the issues of your heart are so deep, dominating, and complicated that no one can search them out and there'll never be a way for you to overcome them. And this makes you feel incredibly lonely and hopeless. However, when Jesus saves you, He sends His Holy Spirit to indwell you. The Holy Spirit searches your heart and mind—repairing your brokenness, counteracting wrong beliefs, and enabling you to overcome your circumstances.

The Spirit sees more deeply into you than you could ever see yourself because He observes areas that are hidden from your sight. Today's Proverb mentions that *Sheol*, the abode of the dead, and *Abbadon*, the place of destruction, are open before Him. God sees into these actual spiritual locations, which indicates how incredibly far His unfathomable understanding reaches. But it also means He perceives the places within you that have died or are destroying you. These are the areas that make you respond and suffer as you do. That's why no matter how many self-help books you read, pills you take, or programs you try, nothing really changes—because they can't reach the true source of the problem. Thankfully, your Savior knows how to free you from them—stopping the devastation and resurrecting the dead places, which is what ultimately frees you. And when you submit to God, wounds begin to heal within you in ways that are beyond understanding.

So what should you do? Your responsibility is simply to walk with God and obey Him as He directs you, and He does the rest. The Father knows exactly how to heal you and is more than willing to make "the path of life" known to you (Psalm 16:11).

Father, thank You for healing my deepest wounds
and transforming me. I will trust and obey You.
Amen.

To Set You Free

SCRIPTURE READING: PROVERBS 16; PSALM 32:1–6; 1 JOHN 1:9

There is a way which seems right to a man,
but its end is the way of death.
PROVERBS 16:25

It's always disheartening to realize that we've sinned or there's something we've been doing wrong. In fact, it can be so demoralizing that we may be tempted to run from God. But understand, the Father makes us aware of our sins out of lovingkindness and compassion because our transgressions are so terribly destructive. They hurt our fellowship with Him, damage our relationships with others, and wound us. When we try to meet our needs in our own way, it always leads to bondage that leaves us broken and without hope. So God will wait to speak with us until we are willing to repent, to turn away from these harmful behaviors, and to seek His life-giving ways.

David affirms, "When I kept silent about my sin, my body wasted away through my groaning all day long. For day and night Your hand was heavy upon me; my vitality was drained away as with the fever heat of summer. I acknowledged my sin to You . . . and You forgave the guilt of my sin" (Psalm 32:3–6). God was pleased to forgive because His goal is always to set us free (1 John 1:9).

Do you feel the same way David did? Is there something bothering you that you cannot identify? Are you bearing some heaviness in your spirit that is depleting your energy and causing everything to go awry? Examine your heart and make sure you are not harboring any sin. And if you are, ask the Father to identify your iniquity and set you free from it. Turn to the cross of Jesus and know that His provision for your sin is more than enough. Then, like David, you can say, "How blessed is he whose transgression is forgiven, whose sin is covered!" (Psalm 32:1).

Father, examine me and purge my life of sin.
Set me free, Lord Jesus, so I may honor You in all things.
Amen.

Barabbas, You're Free

SCRIPTURE READING: PROVERBS 17; MATTHEW
27:15–26; MARK 15:7; JOHN 18:40

He who justifies the wicked and he who condemns the righteous,
both of them alike are an abomination to the Lord.
PROVERBS 17:15

Barabbas deserved the cross. He had violated Roman law and was found guilty of thievery (John 18:40), murder, and insurrection (Mark 15:7). He was sentenced to death because his actions warranted execution (Matthew 27:15–26). So you can imagine the shock he felt when the Roman jailer approached him with the astonishing message: "Barabbas, you are free to go."

If we think about it, the unfairness of the scene is overwhelming. The compassionate, innocent, sinless Son of the living God—who lived to heal and teach others—is crucified instead of the hardened criminal. You can imagine Barabbas looking up at the middle cross and wondering why the innocent Man from Nazareth had taken his place.

Yet this is the ultimate illustration of what the substitutionary death of Jesus does for each of us—*substitution* being the key word. Spiritually, all of us are Barabbas. Each of us has violated the Laws of God and merit eternal separation from the Father because of our sin. But like Barabbas, we've had our death sentence commuted because Jesus has taken our place. He has set us free, though we didn't deserve it.

So today, let's think about that middle cross and consider how—in a spiritual sense—we should have been there too, just as Barabbas should have. Let's not take for granted the grace poured out at Calvary. Rather, let's give praise to the wonderful Savior who mercifully spares us, forgives our sins, and took the judgment for us.

Lord Jesus, I am in awe of how You bore my sin debt
on the cross. You didn't deserve the pain I caused You.
Thank You for loving me so much and saving me.
Amen.

Knowing God

SCRIPTURE READING: PROVERBS 18; EXODUS 33:11;
EPHESIANS 2:8−9; HEBREWS 4:14−16

There is a friend who sticks closer than a brother.
PROVERBS 18:24

In Exodus 33:11 we read, "The Lord used to speak to Moses face to face, just as a man speaks to his friend." Have you ever wondered if this is possible for you? Can you really get as close to God as Moses did? Of course, this is a question many of us struggle to answer. Although we may accept that the Lord is loving, trustworthy, and capable of delivering us from our troubles, we're not certain just how intimate He'll allow us to be with Him.

We know intellectually that the Father's foremost desire is that we would have a close, personal relationship with Him. But as we kneel to pray, our feelings of inadequacy may take over, making us doubt we're worthy of His presence. Yet understand, it's not our worth that hinders the depth of our relationship with God. The Lord accepts us based on Christ's death on the cross, not because of what we've done or have failed to do (Ephesians 2:8–9). Once we trust Christ as our Savior, we're always able to approach the throne of grace with confidence (Hebrews 4:14–16).

Moses was able to enjoy such profound fellowship with the Father because of *how* he spent his time with Him. You see, Moses didn't merely go to God for direction or relief from his troubles. He entered into the Lord's presence in order to *know* Him. Moses listened to God and learned His ways—like a real friend would.

And so today, understand that, yes, you can get that close to God. But you must enter His presence to *know* Him, not just to receive things from Him. That is the key to having the intimacy with Him you desire.

Father, I want to know You as Moses did.
Reveal Yourself to me, my Lord and my Savior!
Amen.

Wrath or Favor?

SCRIPTURE READING: PROVERBS 19; JOHN 3:36;
ROMANS 5:1; 1 THESSALONIANS 5:9

The king's wrath is like the roaring of a lion,
but his favor is like dew on the grass.
PROVERBS 19:12

*A*m I really acceptable to God? Does He really love me? How can I be *sure He isn't angry with me?* These are questions that may rise up unbidden in your mind, especially when fierce trials press in on you. It may feel as if His wrath is being poured out because the pressure is so great.

Yet understand that at the moment you accept Jesus as Savior, you are reconciled to the Father and peace is established between you (Romans 5:1). It's only if you reject Christ that you experience the Lord's wrath. John 3:36 explains, "He who believes in the Son has eternal life; but he who does not obey the Son will not see life, but the wrath of God abides on him." In other words, you receive His fury only if you reject the gift of salvation He has given through Jesus. First Thessalonians 5:9 affirms, "God has not destined us for wrath, but for obtaining salvation through our Lord Jesus Christ."

Therefore, if you're fearful of God's anger today, your anxiety is misplaced. He is not punishing you. So what is really going on? If the Father isn't mad at you, why do bad things continue to occur? For this, you will have to spend time with Him to understand what He is achieving in your life. He may be cleansing you of sin, stretching your faith, or building your character. But whatever His goal, it is out of *love*—not anger. In fact, He most likely sees potential in you He wishes to develop, and that requires discipline. Therefore, what you're experiencing is actually favor, not wrath. So take heart and trust Him to lead you.

Father, I will trust that these trials are evidence of Your love
and favor. Teach me and lead me to better things, Lord.
Amen.

Powerful Enough

SCRIPTURE READING: PROVERBS 20; EXODUS 14:13;
DEUTERONOMY 1:29; 31:6, 8; 2 CHRONICLES 20:15; ISAIAH 41:10;
43:1; MATTHEW 10:28–31; JOHN 8:32; 14:24; PHILIPPIANS 4:6–7

> *Who can say, "I have cleansed my heart,*
> *I am pure from my sin"?*
> PROVERBS 20:9

Do you truly believe that God is powerful, wise, and loving enough to overcome your sins? Perhaps you do from the standpoint of forgiveness. You trust He can pardon your transgressions. However, do you realize He can also deliver you from the bondage your sins cause in your life?

For example, repeatedly in Scripture, God commands, "Do not fear" (see Exodus 14:13; Deuteronomy 1:29; 31:6, 8; 2 Chronicles 20:15; Isaiah 41:10; 43:1; Matthew 10:28–31; John 14:24; Philippians 4:6–7). Yet many people would say, "Yes, I worry, but that's just who I am. I've always been that way and I'm not going to change." In essence, they deny that the Lord can deliver them from the stranglehold of anxiety.

But understand that the Savior who pardons you from the *penalty* of sin likewise wants to deliver you from the *dominion* of it! Jesus wants you to experience His abundant life and works tirelessly to free you from the bondage sin causes you to suffer. As you've probably discovered, you cannot overcome issues such as anxiety by your own willpower. But Jesus can. And when you cooperate with Him—trusting Him in the trials, obeying Him, seeking His face in prayer, and studying His Word—you will find victory in all that currently hinders you.

So today, don't wallow in your sin or close your heart off to real and lasting healing. Rather, trust your Savior to liberate you from the destructive force of sin within you. "You will know the truth, and the truth will make you free" (John 8:32).

> *Lord Jesus, I confess I've accepted my sinfulness as a fixed*
> *part of my life. But I trust You can deliver me from its*
> *dominion and bondage. Thank You for freeing me.*
> *Amen.*

Religion or Relationship

SCRIPTURE READING: PROVERBS 21; HOSEA 6:6; MATTHEW 7:21–23

To do righteousness and justice is
desired by the LORD more than sacrifice.
PROVERBS 21:3

Have you been trying to please God—serving Him the best way you know how—but it just seems to be wearing you out? Often we can get caught up in doing so much *for* the Lord that we actually miss out on experiencing Him. But understand, the key to the Father's heart is not religious activity—it's a loving relationship that results in faithful obedience. This is why He says in Hosea 6:6, "I delight in loyalty rather than sacrifice, and in the knowledge of God rather than burnt offerings." Your personal relationship with Him will always be more important than your grand sacrificial gestures.

Unfortunately, most believers know this but take the truth too lightly because it's easier to submit to a set of religious behaviors. But Jesus said, "Not everyone who says to Me, 'Lord, Lord,' will enter the kingdom of heaven, but he who does the will of My Father who is in heaven will enter. Many will say to Me on that day, 'Lord, Lord, did we not prophesy in Your name, and in Your name cast out demons, and in Your name perform many miracles?' And then I will declare to them, 'I never knew you; depart from Me'" (Matthew 7:21–23).

You can't do God's will without knowing Him. All the religious activity done outside a relationship with Him is in vain. So stop wasting your time and energy! Today, seek to know Him better through His Word and in prayer. Show you love Him by obeying what He tells you. He will certainly energize you with His presence and empower you for all He calls you to do.

Father, I want to experience who You are—my Lord, God,
Savior, Provider, Defender, and King. Show me how to
walk in Your will and exalt You with my life.
Amen.

Let God Handle It

SCRIPTURE READING: PROVERBS 22; ROMANS 12:17–21

The eyes of the LORD preserve knowledge, but
He overthrows the words of the treacherous man.
PROVERBS 22:12

One of the most difficult things to face in life is when someone who hurts you prospers. Despite the fact that the individual acted in an ungodly manner, he or she is still blessed with success. This creates the perfect conditions for unforgiveness to take root in your heart. After all, the offender has gone unpunished, and someone needs to hold him or her accountable. You may feel that if you forgive what has been done, there won't be any justice and the offense will be forgotten. And so you hold on to your bitterness, convinced that somehow you can hold that person responsible.

The problem is that you're not actually punishing the person who wounded you; you're hurting yourself. It's understandable that you're angry and afraid. You don't ever want to be in that situation again, and you don't want anyone else to be either. But what you must understand is that forgiveness doesn't mean you deny that what happened was wrong, and it certainly doesn't mean you allow that person to abuse you again. Rather, you give the situation to God, trusting Him to heal you and to set everything right in His timing. You have faith that He has seen what happened, cares you were hurt, and will bring true justice to the situation (Romans 12:17–21).

Friend, don't let that person continue to wound you. Find freedom through the forgiveness Jesus died to give you and empowered you to give others. Release the offender to the Lord and step out of bondage. Are you willing? Then pray and open your heart to God. Don't hold anything back. Allow the Father to give you the strength to forgive and receive the healing He wants to accomplish in your life.

Father, I trust that You will vindicate me in Your
time and bring justice to this situation. Thank You
for helping me to forgive and find healing.
Amen.

APRIL 23

Conviction

SCRIPTURE READING: PROVERBS 23; DANIEL 1

When you sit down to dine with a ruler,
consider carefully what is before you.
PROVERBS 23:1

When Daniel was a teenager, King Nebuchadnezzar invaded Jerusalem and deported its inhabitants to Babylon. Along with other bright and promising Hebrew captives, Daniel was selected to train for special service to Nebuchadnezzar. This meant undergoing a rigorous process of assimilation into the Babylonian culture, which included eating the delicacies found on Nebuchadnezzar's table.

Unfortunately, the king's cuisine had not been prepared according to Jewish dietary laws and may have been offered to idols, which was strictly forbidden by the Law of Moses. So Daniel and his friends felt strongly that they couldn't eat the king's food. Risking the anger of their captors, they asked the commander for permission to eat only vegetables for ten days. Miraculously, he complied. And at the end of that time, they looked better than the men who were eating from the king's table and were granted permission to continue with their diet of vegetables. Likewise, Daniel 1:20 reports, "As for every matter of wisdom and understanding about which the king consulted them, he found them ten times better than all the magicians and conjurers who were in all his realm."

The story of Daniel provides us with a powerful example of how to stand for our convictions. He was a long way from his home and family, in the midst of a pagan culture that actively sought to strip him of his values. But because Daniel remained true to God, the Lord blessed him. As believers in an increasingly secular culture, we need to learn from his determination. Instead of allowing society to set our values, we should base our convictions on Scripture. Ask the Father to grant you the courage to be a person who stands by your beliefs, no matter what.

Father, I want to be a person of conviction like Daniel.
Help me to honor You with every detail of my life.
Amen.

An Eternal Endeavor

SCRIPTURE READING: PROVERBS 24; JOHN 12:32;
1 CORINTHIANS 2:4; 1 THESSALONIANS 2:19–20

Rescue those being led away to death.
PROVERBS 24:11 NIV

Do you ever wonder about your legacy, about what will continue on after you after you've passed away? Many people seek to gather wealth and build monuments so they won't be forgotten. But there's only one thing that will last in eternity: how you've served Jesus—how you've led others to Christ and taught them to walk with Him.

Certainly, we all agree that rescuing the lost is important. There's even a Crown of Rejoicing for those who do so (1 Thessalonians 2:19–20). However, believers are sometimes averse to sharing their faith because they're fearful of rejection. They're worried they won't know what to say. So they remain quiet—and the person remains lost.

Yet the apostle Paul clearly taught that you don't have to be witty or eloquent to share your faith. He said, "My message and my preaching were very plain. Rather than using clever and persuasive speeches, I relied only on the power of the Holy Spirit" (1 Corinthians 2:4 NLT). This is because we cannot convict people of their sin—only the Lord can. And He wants us to depend upon Him to do so, as we share the Good News of salvation in obedience.

Friend, do you know people who need Christ? God doesn't need you to study fancy formulas or methods. All you have to do is share your heart about what Jesus has done for you; He will do the rest. Jesus said, "If I am lifted up . . . [I] will draw all men to Myself" (John 12:32). So exalt the Savior by sharing the message of the cross. Not only will your efforts endure forever—they may make an eternal difference to someone else as well.

Father, I will trust You to help me share my faith.
Thank You for showing me whom to talk to and what to say.
Amen.

Righteous Rulership

*Take away the wicked before the king, and his
throne will be established in righteousness.*
PROVERBS 25:5

Jesus said, "Your kingdom come. Your will be done, on earth as it is in heaven" (Matthew 6:10). No doubt this statement would have been of interest to those listening. After all, the Jews were awaiting the Messiah, whom they believed to be the mighty Warrior and King who would free them from the Roman Empire and restore the land of their inheritance to them. Roman rule was oppressive—poverty, slavery, and immorality were rampant—and the Jews looked forward to the Redeemer who would free them from all of it, as the prophets had promised He would.

However, Jesus first had to come as the Suffering Servant who would be "pierced through for our transgressions" and by whose "scourging we are healed" (Isaiah 53:6). He would establish His throne in righteousness by first by making us holy. Yes, the Lord will return one day to fulfill all of the other prophecies about Himself, including destroying all wickedness (Revelation 20:10–15). But what He speaks of here is a dominion of God different from what they were most likely expecting.

Likewise, when Jesus tells us to pray, "Your kingdom come," He means the Lord's spiritual and eternal reign in our lives. Jesus affirms, "The Kingdom of God is within you" (Luke 17:21 NKJV). We demonstrate that His kingdom is within us when we allow Him to rule our hearts and when we walk in righteousness in obedience to Him.

The Father wants us to let Him lead. Just like the Jews in Jesus' day, we have ideas when we come before Him about what we want Him to do in and through us. But God expects to be first in our lives, becoming the starting place of our desires, motivations, and every step we take.

*Lord, Your kingdom come, Your will be done on earth
and in my life. Thank You for making me holy.
Amen.*

Work Life

SCRIPTURE READING: PROVERBS 26; PROVERBS 29:5;
1 THESSALONIANS 2:5–8; JAMES 1:15

A flattering mouth works ruin.
PROVERBS 26:28

Do you watch what you say? That is, do you examine the motives you have when you address others? It is always important to ask yourself, "Why I am saying this?" Because, if you are going out of your way to be complimentary and encouraging to your leaders or people with influence, hoping to get their favor in return, then you are actually being deceptive. In fact, Proverbs 29:5 says, "A man who flatters his neighbor is spreading a net for his steps."

Likewise, you may believe you are being kind and understanding when you approve of others' actions, even though the Bible calls what they're doing sin. But the truth is you are condoning the very thing that is destroying them. In their own way, they are trying to fulfill needs that can be fulfilled only by God—and that means a little more is dying inside them every day (James 1:15).

Flattery works ruin. You may think you are doing something good, but you may actually be harming the very people you want to lift up. So how can you ensure that your encouragement to others is sincere and life-giving? When you exalt God and are selfless with what you say (1 Thessalonians 2:5–8). If there is a gift or talent you are grateful for, remind them that it was the Father who endowed them with it. If they are hurting themselves through some sinful behavior, comfort them with the truth that the Savior wants to fulfill all their needs because of His matchless grace. In all things, love and encourage others by leading them to the Lord. Because then you won't be working ruin—you'll be helping them experience true life.

Father, help me to encourage others sincerely in a
manner that builds them up and glorifies You.
Amen.

A Time to Live

SCRIPTURE READING: PROVERBS 27; JOHN 15:5

When the grass disappears, the new growth is seen.
PROVERBS 27:25

At times, you may feel despondent because of the barrenness of your life and circumstances. All your hopes and dreams seem irrevocably gone. Do not despair. This won't last forever. This is merely a season of your life. Just as all nature experiences periods of death and growth, so do we.

Think about it. During the summer, lawns are green and wildflowers cover the countryside. No one thinks about the dreariness of the winter months or how the trees will lose all their leaves. However, it's beneficial to remember that late in the year, as cold winds sweep over the landscape, it's natural for everything to appear completely devoid of life.

But we know that as the days begin to warm, life will miraculously spring forth from the seemingly dead branches, and lovely foliage will thrive where it appeared impossible for it to grow. Life will triumph over death.

The same can be said of the beauty God is bringing forth in you. Of course, the basis of your growth is in a deep relationship with Christ. As Jesus said in John 15:5, "I am the vine, you are the branches; he who abides in Me and I in him, he bears much fruit, for apart from Me you can do nothing." But God brings you through times of pruning and death so that He can cultivate you for the abundant life you were born to live. He promises to do amazing things through you as long as you remain in Him. So do not despair as you face periods of darkness and death. Rather, trust Him who employs resurrection power on your behalf to give you true and lasting life.

Father, it is true that I am mourning some losses today.
But I trust You that this is only a season. Prune me so
that Your abundant life can be found in me.
Amen.

The Spirit-Flesh Battle

SCRIPTURE READING: PROVERBS 28; GALATIANS 5:16–17

He who trusts in his own heart is a fool,
but he who walks wisely will be delivered.
PROVERBS 28:26

There is a constant battle you face every day—to succumb to the drives of your heart or to *choose* to walk in obedience to God. You may not perceive this as a struggle, but it is. And it's not an easy one.

Once you accept Jesus as your Savior, He gives you life so He can *be* your life—living through you so that you can experience true fulfillment, eternal fruit, and ultimate victory. This doesn't mean that you have to constantly engage in "spiritual" activities. Rather, it means that you allow His indwelling Spirit to reign within you—leading you, giving you energy, and enabling you for the tasks He calls you to accomplish. Every day, each circumstance, challenge, and encounter is an opportunity for you either to obey Him or to express your own will. The degree to which you yield to His control is the extent in which you will experience Christ as your life (Galatians 5:16–17).

For example, suppose that at work you overhear a friend speaking critically of your performance. Later in the day you encounter this person in the break room and anger rises up within you. But understanding that forgiveness is the only biblical response, you engage in conversation. Perhaps you even pray for your friend concerning a pressing need. At that point of obedience—as you yield to the Spirit's direction—you're experiencing the supernatural life of Christ.

You're not obeying your heart; you're following Jesus—and that's the road to life at its best. The battle is worth it. Certainly, your Christ-honoring choices will make all the difference today and in eternity as well.

Lord, I want to live by Your Spirit, not my flesh.
Help me to obey You in all things so I can enjoy
the life You created me to experience.
Amen.

The Grip of Sin

SCRIPTURE READING: PROVERBS 29; ROMANS 12:2;
2 CORINTHIANS 10:5; 1 JOHN 1:9

*By transgression an evil man is ensnared,
but the righteous sings and rejoices.*
PROVERBS 29:6

Are you tempted to think about something you know is forbidden in God's Word? If so, remember that sin begins with a thought. You may think such deliberations are harmless, but they aren't—which is why the enemy always begins his onslaughts with your mind. He knows that if he can get you thinking about a behavior, he can ultimately get you hooked to it.

You see, sin is about meeting your needs apart from God's provision. Not only does it enslave us to destructive activities, but it also blinds us from recognizing and receiving God's answers to our deepest needs. We eventually end up in a situation where we feel totally out of control, completely dominated by our raw desires. We give ourselves to people or addictions and then feel helpless to break free from their grasp. That's how sin gets a stranglehold on our lives.

If you ever find yourself in this place, what can you do? *First,* remember that no transgression is too great for God to forgive. The blood of Jesus can cover all our sin. First John 1:9 says, "If we confess our sins, He is faithful and righteous to forgive us our sins and to cleanse us from all unrighteousness." So the first thing you need to do is make the decision to turn away from it and return to the Lord. *Second,* take control of your thoughts (2 Corinthians 10:5) and allow God to transform them (Romans 12:2). Make a commitment to say no to everything that does not line up with His Word.

Sin may seem to have an unbreakable grip on you, but you can overcome it by the power of the Holy Spirit. Because once you have tasted God's freedom and learned His principles, sin will certainly lose its appeal.

*Father, I confess my sins. Thank You for freeing me from
their grasp and teaching me to walk in freedom.*
Amen.

True or False?

SCRIPTURE READING: PROVERBS 30; MATTHEW 7:15–16;
JOHN 14:26; 17:23; ACTS 17:11

Do not add to His words or He will reprove you.
PROVERBS 30:6

At times it can be confusing to know who to listen to—especially when Christian leaders appear to have such different opinions about God. How can you tell who's telling you the truth and who is leading you astray? How can you identify false teachers? Thankfully, Jesus revealed the ultimate litmus test: "Beware of the false prophets, who come to you in sheep's clothing, but inwardly are ravenous wolves. You will know them by their fruits" (Matthew 7:15–16). What kind of fruit was He talking about?

First, is the person increasing your faith in the Word of God, or undermining it? False teachers generally attempt to discredit Scripture, focusing on the passages they like and disavowing the rest. Be very careful of anyone who doesn't preach the whole counsel of God. *Second*, is the person condoning sin? False teachers are often driven by their own lusts and shape their theology to justify their sinful habits. If what the person says doesn't match God's Word, run. *Third*, is the person fostering unity within the church, or dividing it? In John 17:23, Jesus prayed believers would be unified. So someone who goes about attacking others without cause is likely not working for Him. *Fourth*, is the person exalting Jesus, or self? Remember, Jesus said that the Holy Spirit's job is to "teach you all things, and bring to your remembrance all that I said to you" (John 14:26). If a person isn't pointing you to Jesus, then he or she probably isn't submitting to the leadership of the Holy Spirit.

Don't be led astray. Test everything you're taught by comparing it with Scripture (Acts 17:11), and ask the Holy Spirit for discernment to distinguish truth from error.

Lord, help me to be wise. Give me discernment about those
I listen to so I can follow You in truth and obedience.
Amen.

Emotions

It might seem as if wisdom and emotions are incompatible, but that depends entirely on whether you're controlling them or allowing them to drive you. The person ruled by God's incomparable understanding knows how to possess his or her soul and draw victory from seeming defeats.

A Fear of Lacking

SCRIPTURE READING: PROVERBS 1; MATTHEW 6:24; 1 TIMOTHY 6:10

So are the ways of everyone who is greedy for
gain; it takes away the life of its owners.
PROVERBS 1:19 NKJV

Most people would prefer to be wealthy. There's nothing wrong with that as long as we're not basing our security on money and it doesn't become the controlling factor of our lives. As Jesus said, "No one can serve two masters; for either he will hate the one and love the other . . . You cannot serve God and wealth" (Matthew 6:24).

Greed is often based on the emotion of fear—the fear of not having enough or of missing out on something important. For example, if as children we have experienced times when there wasn't sufficient money to buy the necessities or we faced times of deprivation, we may have an ingrained fear of going hungry that drives us. So we attempt to safeguard ourselves by attaining possessions, which we believe will protect us from starvation. But as we grow older, our motivation often moves from fulfilling basic needs to amassing material goods in order to satisfy our desires for significance and achievement—the deeper hungers of our soul. The wealth we acquire becomes our security, identity, and goal in life. Before we know it, our lives are defined by greed and are empty of the meaning God has for us. The fear of going hungry is still there, buried far beneath destructive layers of our defenses, continually driving us in the wrong direction.

This is why 1 Timothy 6:10 tells us, "The love of money is a root of all sorts of evil, and some by longing for it have wandered away from the faith and pierced themselves with many griefs." Only the Savior can fulfill those deepest needs. So look to Him to satisfy you and experience a much better life than money could ever buy.

Father, You are my security and perfect Provider.
Thank You for giving me true life.
Amen.

MAY 2

Your True Worth

SCRIPTURE READING: PROVERBS 2; PSALM 139:13–14; ZEPHANIAH 3:17

Wisdom will enter your heart, and knowledge will fill you with joy.
PROVERBS 2:10 NLT

Often, when we struggle with disappointments or despair, we attribute our failures, painful feelings, and misfortunes to our worth. We believe that we don't deserve acceptance or anything good because something within us is inherently lacking, useless, or broken. Sadly, it may be very difficult to break out of those beliefs because they are so ingrained in our identity.

But friend, if you wrestle with feelings of worthlessness, you must accept the reality that your view of yourself is not right. The only One who truly understands your potential and value is the Father, and He accepts you, promises to love you unconditionally, and enables you to do all He calls you to do. The Lord created you exactly as He wanted you (Psalm 139:13–14). And when the Savior looks at you, He sees someone worth dying for—a person He wants with Him for eternity. So to overcome feelings of hopelessness or insignificance, you must accept His assessment of your value over your own.

Zephaniah 3:17 affirms, "The Lord your God is in your midst, a victorious warrior. He will exult over you with joy, He will be quiet in His love, He will rejoice over you with shouts of joy." Not only does your heavenly Father rejoice over you, but He also is committed to winning the battles for you. Therefore, when disappointments or feelings of despair arise, refuse to entertain any thought of worthlessness or inadequacy. Instead, train your eyes on your Savior and Creator. And accept who He created you to be—a vessel who shines with His glory, regardless of your circumstances.

Father, set me free of feelings of worthlessness and inadequacy.
Thank You for loving me, redeeming me, defending me,
and equipping me to do everything You call me to.
Amen.

Harnessing Our Emotions

SCRIPTURE READING: PROVERBS 3; JEREMIAH 29:11; JOHN 8:32

The LORD will be your confidence
and will keep your foot from being caught.
PROVERBS 3:26

Is there a pervasive agitation that lingers in your spirit? Do your emotions overflow at all the wrong times and without much warning? Do you ever respond with such intensity that it shocks you and those with whom you're interacting?

Our emotions can become a dominating force within us if we do not get hold of them. Of course, most of us like to think that our feelings don't control us. But if we're managing them with anything other than the guidance of the Holy Spirit and the principles of God's Word, we will find it quite difficult to govern how they affect us. Given the right combination of circumstances and stressors, our emotions have the potential to trigger very destructive behavior.

Thankfully, the Father is able to give us the victory over our inner wounds. We are confident of this because we are assured the Lord desires that we experience the fullness of His wonderful plans for our lives (Jeremiah 29:11). Truly, we serve a loving God who will not fail to lead us to freedom if we trust in Him (John 8:32).

Friend, you can harness your emotions. You can choose how you respond to the circumstances of life. You can take control of the powerful force within you. Victory is possible. Genuine healing can occur if you're willing to allow the Father to set you free. Submit to Him one step at a time, obeying even when you don't understand His commands. He will heal your heart, teach you how to rule over your spirit, and lead you to the freedom you long for.

Father, I submit my emotional well-being to You.
Heal what is broken, release me from these wounds,
and teach me to respond in a manner that honors You.
Amen.

What's in Your Heart?

SCRIPTURE READING: PROVERBS 4

*Watch over your heart with all diligence,
for from it flow the springs of life.*
PROVERBS 4:23

Put your head down and imagine God holding you as a loving Father embracing His beloved child. You may be surprised by the emotions you feel. Hopefully, you feel secure in His overwhelming love for you. However, it is possible that you're uncomfortable and wish to push Him away because somewhere in your heart, you don't really trust Him. You may feel a sense of conviction due to some unconfessed sin. Or you may realize that you've been running away from Him all your life, when all you really wanted was to feel safe in your heavenly Father's arms.

Whatever the case, be still and allow God to deal with whatever emotions and issues arise. Do not fear. He will teach you what to do. The Father can remove any encumbrance you have to knowing Him, and He can draw you into a deeper, more intimate relationship than you have ever known.

So consider: Do you truly trust God? Are you confident that He is able to help you? Are you convinced that the Father is willing to listen to you and come to your aid? I hope you are. But if your answer to any of these questions is no, I pray that the Father will do a mighty work in your life and show you beyond a shadow of a doubt that you can place all your hope in Him. Not only is He worthy of your trust; He also loves you unconditionally and wants to show you the extraordinary life He created you for. So spend some time in prayer today and allow Him to reveal to you who He really is.

*Father, You know what's in my heart. Thank You for healing
my wounds, forgiving my sins, and leading me to the awesome
life You have for me. I love You and will trust You, Father.
Amen.*

Waiting for Freedom

An evil man is held captive by his own sins;
they are ropes that catch and hold him.
PROVERBS 5:22 NLT

Today, you may feel tempted to meet your own needs instead of waiting for God to help you. You may be so overcome by your emotions and desires that you're driven to take action, even if it means disobeying the Lord. But don't. Friend, such temptations are meant to lead you to bondage, leaving you trapped within the prison of sin. This is where the enemy would like to keep you—limited by your own resources and unaware of all that is available to you through your relationship with Christ.

You see, after years of self-protection, there are certain areas of your life that the Father must work on to free you. This is why you're facing this time of trial and waiting—because God is surfacing issues in your life He needs to work on. To rid you of the internal prisons you bear, the Lord will allow you to face situations where you have absolutely no choice but to rely upon Him. As you do, He sets you free from those cords of sin and ushers you into the abundant life He created you for.

So don't move forward or succumb to the temptation today. Allow the Father to reveal Himself to you and release you from the bondage that is keeping you wounded. Learn the power of His presence in your pain, the depth of His love in your loss, and His patient wisdom despite your complaints. Because when you do, you will certainly see that you can indeed "stand by and see the salvation of the Lord which He will accomplish for you" (Exodus 14:13).

Father, I don't know how to break free from the bondage
within me, but I am grateful that You do. I will wait on
You, trusting that You lead me to abundant life.
Amen.

MAY 6

Love or Lust?

SCRIPTURE READING: PROVERBS 6; JAMES 1:14–15

Do not lust in your heart.
PROVERBS 6:25 NIV

Are you seeking to alleviate the pain, loneliness, or unworthiness you feel? Then beware the draw of lust—of anything that promises immediate pleasure without penalty. Lust will cause you to become self-centered, focusing inward on your needs and convincing you to quench your desires with methods that will only create more hunger within you. The sinful desires you entertain can only lead you to terrible consequences, including the shame of sinning against God, which means further isolation from the love and acceptance you really need and want. You'll feel even more detachment from the Father, which will tempt you to engage in more addictive behavior because of your desperate need to feel part of something—even if it's only for a moment (James 1:14–15).

Perhaps you've been focused inwardly for a long time. Maybe you've spent a lot of time thinking that no one understands the pressures you face. You feel empty inside and just want something—anything—that will make you feel loved and accepted, even if it's for only a little while. Maybe you've also been so wounded and feel so worthless that you don't think you truly deserve love and happiness—even though you want them so badly.

Friend, it's out of His great love for you that God gave His only Son to free you from the sin that now holds you in bondage. He knows the difficulties of your life and how you feel about yourself. That's why He wants to liberate you from lust and build you up with His edifying and everlasting love. So instead of facing inward, look upward to Him to meet all of your deepest needs and give your life comfort, worth, meaning, and significance.

*Father, forgive me for my sinful desires and the ways
I feed them. I feel so isolated from You. Comfort me
with Your presence and fill me with Your love.
Amen.*

The Healing Word

SCRIPTURE READING: PROVERBS 7; JOHN 8:32

Treasure my commandments within you.
PROVERBS 7:1

We're often told, "Time heals all wounds," but it simply isn't true. Time in itself has no power to heal; it cannot remove the unhealthy thought patterns formed when our wounds are created—it cannot even identify them. Only the Father can pinpoint where we've been injured and what destructive coping mechanisms we've developed to protect ourselves. Only He recognizes what lies we believe about ourselves and which attitudes keep us in bondage.

This is one of the reasons it's so important to study Scripture and treasure His commands. Because as you consume God's Word, you begin detecting the wrong beliefs you have about yourself. This is the work of the Holy Spirit in you: He exposes the false messages that drive your identity, decisions, and interactions with others. God then begins to replace those false ideas with truth that sets you free and makes you whole (John 8:32).

This is not something that happens overnight, of course; it does take time. But the most effective thing you can do is read Scripture and allow the Holy Spirit to teach you through it. Because when you immerse yourself in God's Word, the Father begins to renew you, changing the way you see things and giving you His perspective of the situations you're facing. He reveals the conditions that trigger your damaged emotions and teaches you to respond in a manner that builds you up rather than tears you down. And He shows you how to enjoy the abundant life He created you for.

So don't wait; start today. Get on your knees, open Scripture, and wait before the Father with an attitude of listening. You'll be astounded by how He heals the wounded places within you.

Father, thank You for the healing You bring me through Your Word.
Identify the wrong beliefs I have and help me to walk in Your truth.
Amen.

How to Triumph

SCRIPTURE READING: PROVERBS 8; PSALM 26:2–3; 2 CORINTHIANS 10:5

Joyful are those who listen to me, watching for me daily at my gates.
PROVERBS 8:34 NLT

How did the saints of old triumph over the devastating trials they endured? How did they stay brave despite overwhelming odds and frightening enemies? It was through the principle David wrote about in Psalm 26:2–3: "Examine me, O Lord, and try me; test my mind and my heart. For Your lovingkindness is before my eyes, and I have walked in Your truth." In other words, David overcame his fears by asking God to reveal any wrong way of thinking within him and replace it with the Lord's facts and unfailing principles.

Paul explained it like this in 2 Corinthians 10:5: "We are destroying speculations and every lofty thing raised up against the knowledge of God, and we are taking every thought captive to the obedience of Christ." These men rejected their destructive patterns of thinking, preferring to believe what God said about them.

So what are the most painful experiences you've had? And what emotions assail you as a result of those difficulties? Now consider this carefully: When those feelings rise up within you, what are the thoughts that play repeatedly in your mind? Are there messages you've come to accept as a result of the pain you've experienced? Understand that if your thoughts do not line up with God's Word, they are false and must be supplanted. Identify them so you can find victory over them.

If you will deliberately govern what you think, you will transform your emotions—you will manage them instead of them ruling over you. And as you choose how you feel and bring your beliefs in line with what God says about you, the Lord gives you courage and transforms you into the person He created you to be.

Father, I want to believe Your truth, not stay in bondage.
Please show me when my thoughts fail to align with
Your Word and lead me to freedom.
Amen.

Unconcealed Secrets

SCRIPTURE READING: PROVERBS 9; LUKE 12:2

Bread eaten in secret is pleasant.
PROVERBS 9:17

Isn't it interesting that when we really want to do something we know is wrong, our minds can always rationalize the behavior? We tell ourselves, *No one will ever know. I'm not hurting anyone else, this just involves me.* But do we ever really get away with sin? In our hearts we know that the answer is no. Yet when the consequences of sin seem to differ so greatly, we sometimes choose to take the risk.

However, we must always remember that though the consequences of sin are not always external or immediate, we will eventually reap what we sow, more than we sow, and later than we sow. "Secret sins" such as lying, gluttony, or viewing pornography may go unnoticed for months or even years. However, make no mistake—they destroy the individual from within. And the internal damage done to those engaged in these activities can be life-threatening.

Be assured, God will deal with habitual sin in the lives of believers. He may allow His children to live in sin for a season, but as Luke 12:2 says, "There is nothing covered up that will not be revealed, and hidden that will not be known."

If you are trapped in habitual sin and can no longer hear God's voice, it is time to evaluate your future. Will you continue destroying yourself through disobedience, or will you boldly turn from sin and accept His gift of forgiveness? The choice is yours. Friend, for the sake of your own soul, do not continue down this path. Confess and repent, confident that Your heavenly Father will not just forgive your sin but will also liberate you from its power.

Lord Jesus, I know You can liberate me from the
power this sin has in my life. I confess it to You and repent.
Teach me how to walk in Your ways so I can be free.
Amen.

Your Heart's Desire

SCRIPTURE READING: PROVERBS 10; JOHN 16:23; 1 JOHN 5:14–15

The desire of the righteous will be granted.
PROVERBS 10:24

What is it that you yearn for above everything else in the world? What is the supreme desire of your heart? You probably know what it is because it instantly comes to mind. Perhaps you've asked the Father to provide it for you repeatedly but have yet to see it come to fruition. As the years go by, you wonder if He will ever answer this particular request.

But understand, God cares about your desires. In fact, Jesus said, "I say to you, if you ask the Father for anything in My name, He will give it to you" (John 16:23). That doesn't mean you should expect the Lord to give you whatever you want, whenever you want it. He will not honor your sinful cravings, because He knows they lead to emptiness, suffering, and disappointment. Rather, the key is asking in His name and in line with His will.

First John 5:14–15 confirms, "This is the confidence which we have before Him, that, if we ask anything according to His will, He hears us. And if we know that He hears us in whatever we ask, we know that we have the requests which we have asked from Him." This is why the question you should always ask is: *Do my desires fit God's plan for my life?*

The Father loves to grant your godly longings. Yes, He may wait some time to provide them for you, but that is because He wants to give you His very best. So seek Him wholeheartedly and obey His commands. He will bless you by giving you praiseworthy yearnings, and then will satisfy them in ways beyond your imagination.

Father, thank You for granting the godly desires of my heart.
Root out the longings that don't fit Your will for my life
and help me to seek only those things that honor You.
Amen.

Expressing His Fruit

SCRIPTURE READING: PROVERBS 11; MATTHEW 5:16;
ROMANS 8:29; GALATIANS 5:22–23; JAMES 2:15–16

A gracious woman attains honor.
PROVERBS 11:16

Galatians 5:22–23 tells us, "The fruit of the Spirit is love, joy, peace, patience, kindness, goodness, faithfulness, gentleness, [and] self-control." This means that when the character of Christ is formed in us through the work of the Holy Spirit, these are the qualities that flow out from us (Romans 8:29). The Father does this so we can reflect His graciousness, mercy, and passion to the world. These were never meant to be passive characteristics that merely make us feel better about ourselves. Rather, the Lord gave us these Spirit-born attributes to mobilize us to action.

For example, consider the godly trait of graciousness mentioned in today's proverb. It isn't formed within us so that others will know us as nice people, though that may be a by-product. Rather, the Father gives us His compassion so we'll faithfully express it to others. The apostle James asks, "If a brother or sister is without clothing and in need of daily food, and one of you says to them, 'Go in peace, be warmed and be filled,' and yet you do not give them what is necessary for their body, what use is that?" (2:15–16). In other words, we need to be actively demonstrating kindness. Why? Because as we do so, God works through us to draw others to Himself.

This is in accordance with Jesus' command in Matthew 5:16: "Let your light shine before men in such a way that they may see your good works, and glorify your Father who is in heaven." We reflect His character, graciousness, and love so others can know Him and experience His mercy. And whenever we do that, friend, we're certainly on the path to honor.

Father, I want to be gracious and loving so I can reflect Your
character to the lost. Help me to serve others in Jesus' name.
Amen.

Fighting Anxiety

SCRIPTURE READING: PROVERBS 12; ISAIAH 41:10; 1 PETER 5:7

Anxiety in a man's heart weighs it down,
but a good word makes it glad.
PROVERBS 12:25

Have you ever fallen into bed after a long, hard day only to begin a wrestling match with your thoughts? You close your eyes and immediately you're overwhelmed with problems, burdens, lost opportunities, past mistakes, and injustices. Next come the existential contemplations: What meaning does your life really have? Are you really reaching your full potential? Is this all there is to life? What is the point of going on?

If you continue entertaining these destructive thoughts, they will take you in a downward spiral that is dangerous indeed. The process evolves like this: *First*, a problem, concern, or issue enters your thoughts. *Next*, when no clear solution surfaces in your mind, you begin to experience detrimental emotions such as fear, depression, and guilt. *Finally*, those negative feelings take root and begin to destroy you— stealing your peace, dividing your mind, damaging your relationships, and devastating your health.

Friend, don't allow anxiety to consume you. To effectively combat the downward spiral, you must learn to submit your concerns to God early in the process, even as the first thought surfaces (1 Peter 5:7). Make a conscious effort to turn every difficulty over to Him and replace fearful contemplations with the truth of Scripture. Why should you do so? Because if you believe that you're responsible for solving every problem you encounter, you will inevitably fail. But when you surrender yourself to the Lord, you can sleep peacefully knowing He can handle everything that concerns you. So accept that what He says is absolutely true. And whenever those devastating thoughts arise, remind yourself of His promise: "I will strengthen you and help you. I will hold you up with my victorious right hand" (Isaiah 41:10 NLT).

Father, thank You for helping me with every struggle and
calming my fears. I will trust You with all that concerns me.
Amen.

The Focus of Hope

SCRIPTURE READING: PROVERBS 13; GENESIS 16; ISAIAH 41:10

Hope deferred makes the heart sick,
but desire fulfilled is a tree of life.
PROVERBS 13:12

When you pray for some change or blessing for a long time, the delays can be disheartening, especially when circumstances don't go your way or your burdens get heavier. And in the midst of your waiting times, even greater challenges may arise that make it seem as if hope is gone and lost forever. This has a way on wearing on even the strongest faith—especially when the blessing is so important and the delays are so extensive.

But friend, no matter what you're waiting for today, ultimately you are better prepared and suited for it if you are centered on God. Why? Because when you focus on what you lack, despair takes root in your heart. You obsess over your own limitations, which reinforces the pain and frustration within you. Not only that, but you may become tempted to meet your needs in your own way rather than the Lord's—and that never ends well (Genesis 16).

True hope isn't just based on having a certain outcome; it's absolute confidence in God's unfailing character and ability, regardless of your circumstances. When you single-mindedly set your sights on the Father, you realize the incredible strength, wisdom, and power that are being employed on your behalf. God isn't affected by the obstacles that limit and intimidate you (Isaiah 41:10). Likewise, you can have confidence because the Lord always knows and provides what's absolutely best for you. So today, put your focus back on Him and have faith that what He's planned is what you really need. Then you're assured that your hope won't be deferred but will be fulfilled.

God, You know the heaviness in my heart that I bear from waiting.
But Lord, You are my hope. I will focus on You and not be
afraid, trusting that You lead me in the best way possible.
Amen.

Not Alone

SCRIPTURE READING: PROVERBS 14; PSALM 38:6, 15

Each heart knows its own bitterness,
and no one else can fully share its joy.
PROVERBS 14:10 NLT

One of the most devastating things about our trials is how isolated they make us feel. They can make us think there's something wrong with us—that we're weak, incapable of improving, and that no one will want to be around us. We wonder if we're being punished and may even begin to believe that no one in history has ever felt as low and terrible as we do. But nothing could be farther from the truth.

It's a universal fact: Every person faces hard times, obstacles, disappointments, and some degree of emotional pain throughout his or her life. If you haven't yet faced any difficulties—trust me, you will. Unfortunately, in this fallen world, they cannot be avoided.

The great King David often felt agony, which we can read about in Psalms. He suffered through staggering betrayals, unbearable losses, and heartrending failures. At one point he wrote, "I am bent over and racked with pain. All day long I walk around filled with grief" (Psalm 38:6 NLT). Yet David also wrote, "I hope in You, O Lord; You will answer" (Psalm 38:15). His hymns have often comforted the hurting because he understood firsthand the pain all of us feel—but he still chose to trust God and found victory.

Friend, you are certainly not alone in your feelings. Others throughout history have felt as you do and triumphed over their troubles. Just as it was feasible for them, it is possible for you as well. So take a step in the right direction and choose to respond to God in faith. He delivered David, and He will answer you too. Trust Him.

Father, thank You that I am not alone and that there's
always hope in my trials because of You. Like David,
I will trust in You and know You'll answer.
Amen.

MAY 15

An Uplifting View

SCRIPTURE READING: PROVERBS 15; 2 CORINTHIANS 6:4–10;
12:2–10; PHILIPPIANS 1:12–14; 4:11–13

All the days of the afflicted are bad,
but a cheerful heart has a continual feast.
PROVERBS 15:15

Paul said, "I have learned to be content in whatever circumstances I am. I know how to get along with humble means, and I also know how to live in prosperity; in any and every circumstance I have learned the secret of being filled and going hungry, both of having abundance and suffering need" (Philippians 4:11–12).

Despite the extensive persecution and hardships Paul endured, how did he remain content and joyful? He revealed the secret in verse 13: "I can do all things through Him who strengthens me." Paul looked at every circumstance through the understanding that Christ had allowed it and was in it with him for the greater glory of God.

Each new trial Paul encountered was the stage for the Lord's miraculous intervention and strength (2 Corinthians 12:2–10). Each imprisonment was a chance to deepen the inner freedom the Savior had provided (2 Corinthians 6:4–10). And with each soul that Paul met—even those who stood in opposition to him—came an opportunity for an outpouring of God's grace and salvation (Philippians 1:12–14).

For some people, even the blessings turn negative because of their faulty viewpoint. But for those who see everything as coming from the Father, there is joy even in the trials. Paul was one of those who had a continual feast of joy, and you can be too. Don't remain bitterly bound by a problematic perspective. Turn your eyes to Jesus and trust Him to transform everything you experience for your good and His glory.

Father, thank You that nothing can touch my life without
it first passing through Your hand. Fill my heart with
the joy of knowing You are always my strength.
Amen.

The Basis of Patience

SCRIPTURE READING: PROVERBS 16; LUKE 22:34; JOHN 11:40

He who is slow to anger is better than the mighty,
and he who rules his spirit than he who takes a city.
PROVERBS 16:32

They had unjustly beaten Him, humiliated Him, and stripped Him of His garments, and now they were suffocating Jesus to death by crucifixion. He was the Messiah—the Son of the living God—and He had come to save the world from sin. Although His mission was the most sacred and noble in all history, the people repaid Him by falsely accusing Him and putting Him on a cross to die an excruciatingly painful death.

Yet Christ's response shows us the nature of godly, unconditional love: "Father, forgive them; for they do not know what they are doing" (Luke 22:34). Jesus knew that if the people had realized who He was, they would never have done this to Him. They did so because of their limited understanding of the plans and purposes of the living God. But the Lord worked through their ignorance to bring about the salvation of the world.

The same is true for you. Most people don't comprehend the full impact of their actions. They can see their behaviors only from their point of view, not yours. Realizing this can help you be forgiving to others, as Jesus was. But it's even more helpful to understand that everything you experience is allowed by God for some good purpose. You may not comprehend His reasons, but if you will trust Him in your trials, you will find a redemptive intent in them. Yes, circumstances may seem unreasonably painful and unfair, but the Father has not abandoned or forgotten you. So be patient with others and have faith that God is in control, and you will certainly see His glory (John 11:40).

Father, help me to be slow to anger, and to be forgiving. Show
me Your point of view, Lord, so I can love others as You do.
Amen.

The Joy of the Lord

SCRIPTURE READING: PROVERBS 17; PSALM 32:11; NEHEMIAH 8:10;
ISAIAH 41:16; JOHN 14:26–27; GALATIANS 5:22–23; PHILIPPIANS 3:1; 4:4

A joyful heart is good medicine.
PROVERBS 17:22

Throughout the Bible, we are told to rejoice in the Lord (Psalm 32:11; Isaiah 41:16; Philippians 3:1; 4:4). Of course, that's not always easy, especially with the challenges that arise each day. Or is it? What exactly is joy? And how can joy flow forth from us?

The first thing we need to understand is there is a difference between joy and happiness. Happiness generally has an *external* cause. People are happy when things go their way, when they have what they want and can do as they please. Joy, however, is the result of something that goes on within us; it has an *internal* cause. Joy is an abiding emotion that God gives to His children though the work of the Holy Spirit (Galatians 5:22–23).

Therefore, the source of our joy is actually our personal relationship with Jesus. It's the result of the Holy Spirit conforming us to the likeness of Christ and exhibiting Jesus' characteristics through us. Even when we face difficulties, we can still have joy because the Holy Spirit reminds us of God's presence and promises (John 14:26–27). However, we can lose our joy when we sin against the Lord or refuse to believe His Word, thereby hindering the Holy Spirit's work in our lives.

Friend, God intends for His people to rejoice, which is why He's given you the awesome gift of joy. Therefore, regardless of what you're going through, trust the Father, spend time with Him, and believe His Word. Those are the perfect conditions for the Holy Spirit to express His gladness through you. And the joy of the Lord will be your strength (Nehemiah 8:10).

Father, I confess my sin and believe Your Word. Holy Spirit,
work Your joy in and through me so I may rejoice in Your name.
Amen.

What Did You Say?

SCRIPTURE READING: PROVERBS 18; PROVERBS 23:7;
MATTHEW 12:43; JOHN 8:36; ROMANS 12:2

The words of a man's mouth are deep waters.
PROVERBS 18:4

Today's proverb tells us that the words we speak come from deep within. And it is true. Jesus corroborated this when He said, "The mouth speaks out of that which fills the heart" (Matthew 12:43). However, Proverbs 23:7 tells us that this not only reveals what's in us but also shapes us: As a person "thinks within himself, so he is." In other words, if we continually tell ourselves, "I am worthless. I am inadequate. No one respects me. No one could ever love me," it is no wonder that our emotions are in a devastating mess. This affects everything about us—our health, relationships, and even how our faces look to others.

This is why Paul tells us, "Do not be conformed to this world, but be transformed by the renewing of your mind" (Romans 12:2). He understood that our feelings and behavior could change only when the Holy Spirit's transformational work had begun in our thoughts.

This is the reason it's so exceedingly important to spend time in God's Word and in His powerful presence. We need to take hold of what the Lord—the limitless Creator of heaven and earth, our wise Maker, faithful Savior, omnipotent Defender, loving Father, and sovereign King—has to say about us, rather than believing the lies we've been told by flawed and fallen humanity. So today, listen to what you say and consider whether it lines up with what God has revealed about you. Root out the falsehoods that have gotten stuck in your thought patterns and replace them with His truth. Because "if the Son makes you free, you will be free indeed" (John 8:36). And isn't that what you really long for, after all?

Lord, search my words, my heart, and my thoughts. Reveal the lies and replace them with Your Word so my life may glorify You.
Amen.

Tempted by Fear

SCRIPTURE READING: PROVERBS 19; GENESIS 3:5

He who keeps the commandment keeps his soul,
but he who is careless of conduct will die.
PROVERBS 19:16

Have you ever considered how the serpent used fear to tempt Eve? He did so by planting the seed of doubt in her mind about the Lord's intentions and character. There had to have been questions that arose in her mind after her interaction with him. Perhaps she wondered: *Could it be that God is really keeping something from me? Why wouldn't He want me to be like Him—knowing good and evil? This tree looks fine; it doesn't make sense that I can't have some of this fruit. What is He hiding from me?*

The result was that Eve began to distrust the Father's command and feared missing out on becoming "like God" (Genesis 3:5). So she reached out and took fruit from the only tree in the entire garden that was forbidden to her.

The same happens to us. After all, aren't those some of the questions we ask? *Why did the Lord allow this to happen to me? Why isn't He giving me the desires of my heart? Will I ever get what I want?* We're worried we won't receive what we yearn for, so we rush ahead and take it for ourselves. And like Adam and Eve, we find ourselves worse off— wounded, separated from the true desire of our hearts, and with deeper grief than we could have imagined.

Friend, don't make that mistake. God's commands are for your good; if He forbids you from engaging in some activity, it is to keep you safe. He sees far beyond what you do. So trust that He is not keeping you from anything except disaster. Accept His commands and live.

Father, I confess I fear the unknown—what good things
I may be missing. But Lord, I know You are good and
protect me from evil. Help me to obey You.
Amen.

A Step in the Right Direction

SCRIPTURE READING: PROVERBS 20; MATTHEW 4:4

*Man's steps are ordained by the Lord,
how then can man understand his way?*
PROVERBS 20:24

You may not believe this at the moment, but whenever you express your desires to grow in godliness, find freedom from sin, or ask the Father for healing, you take an enormous step in the right direction. God is always talking to you—continually calling to you about the wonderful plans He has for your life and the liberty you could enjoy if you'd only obey Him. However, you and I do not always hear what the Lord has to say because we're not focused on Him.

But once you turn to God and begin listening to Him, He starts revealing the inner workings of your heart and initiates the maturation process. He does so by sending you circumstances that expose your sins, anxieties, and weaknesses, and helps you work through them—mending the brokenness in you by teaching you His truth.

This is why prayer is so important to the process of growing in your relationship with God and why I am always encouraging you to seek the Father. Friend, you *need* time with God. Whether you realize it or not, your very soul is hungry for His presence—even more than your body needs food and water (Matthew 4:4). He can satisfy you, strengthen your inner person, and calm your fears in a manner none other can. And as you discover His character and His ways—that He is truly sovereign, wise, and caring—you learn to trust Him more and are able to accept what He is teaching you in increasing measure.

So today, listen to Him and allow Him to lead you. And be confident that you have nothing to fear but everything to gain as you walk in obedience to Him.

*Lord, I want to grow. Help me to focus on You
and walk in Your will. I trust You to lead me.
Amen.*

Admission for Healing

SCRIPTURE READING: PROVERBS 21

Every man's way is right in his own eyes,
but the Lord weighs the hearts.
PROVERBS 21:2

Is there an issue in your life that's been plaguing you? A failure or a problem that you've been blaming on someone else? It probably springs to mind immediately. You know exactly what it is because when you're with others, you fight tooth and nail to prove you're right about it and you're unwilling to admit that your actions may have contributed to the issue. Unfortunately, this unwillingness to let it go may indicate that you are harboring pride.

However, when you're before God, it's a different story altogether. The Father knows the whole truth of the matter, including aspects of the situation you can't see from your point of view and the fears buried deep inside you concerning it. No doubt you feel vulnerable when you're in God's presence, which may even hinder you from drawing near to Him in the first place. You're scared of listening to Him because He may tell you you're actually the one in the wrong. Yet understand, you can't experience healing in those areas until you stop holding others responsible for your mistakes and failures and turn your attention to what the Father is telling you.

Friend, stop being afraid of being real before God, and stop shutting out His love because you're terrified about being imperfect. The Father loves you unconditionally—all of you: faults, failures, and all the rest. He will never reject you. Rather, He wants to heal your heart so that you can truly experience what it is to be free. And isn't that what you're really longing for when all is said and done? Let Him into your life and allow Him to restore your heart. You know it's the right thing to do.

Father, please expose my areas of pride. I want to heal, Lord,
and I know it is only You who can free me from this bondage.
Amen.

Train Them Up

SCRIPTURE READING: PROVERBS 21; MATTHEW
7:24–25; 28:19–20; JOHN 14:6

Train up a child in the way he should go,
even when he is old he will not depart from it.
PROVERBS 22:6

A wise person builds others up, especially the members of his or her family. Wise believers encourage their coworkers and are blessings to their employers and customers. They edify other believers and understand that they have a responsibility to be an example in the society, at home, and in church.

This is the challenge Jesus gave believers—to be actively involved in the spiritual development of others (Matthew 28:19–20). And as this proverb suggests, people need training—the continual love, support, and Christ-centered guidance of those who will take an interest in them. We are, as the proverb says, to instruct them in the way they should go. What is that way? It is revealed in the Person of Jesus Christ, who declared, "I am the way, and the truth, and the life" (John 14:6).

God created each person with a personality, gifts, and talents, and when submitted to Jesus in obedience, that person becomes a fruitful member of the Body of Christ. So we admonish others in how to seek God and have an intimate relationship with Him. Likewise, we train them with the difficulties of life in view. We must pass on a faith that sustains the test of time—and that can be done only if we build it on the enduring Word of God (Matthew 7:24–25).

Today, will you stand up to this challenge to help others grow in their relationships with Jesus? Not only are you able—it's Christ's command to you. So look for others to raise up, and pray for God's help in leading them to greater faith and obedience.

Father, I'm willing. Show me whom You want me to mentor
and guide me in teaching them how to honor and serve You.
Amen.

Your Identity Source

SCRIPTURE READING: PROVERBS 23; ROMANS 5:21

Do not let your heart envy sinners,
but live in the fear of the Lord always.
PROVERBS 23:17

Rejection can cause some of the most painful bondage we experience because of how it influences what we believe about ourselves. This is what happens: When a person or group of people—who may have been trying to hurt or control us—has deemed us unlovable, unfit, or worthless, we unconsciously accept that others must hold the same belief. We may not think it bothers us or even remember that we were rejected. But instinctively, we become more self-critical and begin to look for ways others may reinforce the negative thoughts we have about ourselves—at times even provoking people to reject us by acting out.

This is because rejection strikes at the foundation of our identity, distorting what we think is true about who we are and what we're worth. Why? Because of the sinful nature within us. Remember, "Sin ruled over all people and brought them to death" (Romans 5:21 NLT). The goal of sin is devastation, so it's understandable that the injurious messages we hear find fertile soil in our hearts and take root. This is why it is much easier to believe the hurtful things said about us than comments that encourage or edify us.

And the truth of the matter is that if we fail to recognize the presence of rejection in our lives and deal with it, it will continue to cause us pain and corrupt every relationship we have. Therefore, we must root out every false message of being unloved, unwanted, and unworthy that we've internalized and replace it with the truth of Scripture—where we find God's eternal, unconditional love and favor for all who believe in Him.

Father, please root out any way I am acting out of the rejection
I've experienced. Help me to base my identity in who You've made
me to be—holy, loved, accepted, and able through Jesus.
Amen.

Stop Worrying

SCRIPTURE READING: PROVERBS 24; MATTHEW 6:25, 27, 33–34; LUKE 1:37

Do not fret.
PROVERBS 24:19

Many people are intensely worried about their jobs, families, finances, health, world politics, unmet desires, and even how they measure up to others' expectations. Sadly, instead of turning their attention to God's provision, many choose to fret incessantly about their troubles. They remain uneasy about the future and are unable to think about anything other than the difficult challenges before them. Their fears are continuous, affect other areas of their lives, and often feel absolutely insurmountable. Consequently, their incessant focus on their problems makes them feel as if their lives will never improve.

Perhaps you are experiencing something similar today. But let me assure you: The Lord never intended for you to endure a continual onslaught of anxiety. That's not how God wants you or anyone else to live. This is why Jesus instructed: "Do not be worried about your life . . . who of you by being worried can add a single hour to his life? . . . But seek first His kingdom and His righteousness, and all these things will be added to you. So do not worry about tomorrow; for tomorrow will care for itself" (Matthew 6:25, 27, 33–34).

Jesus did not deny that anxiety exists. There are many things in the world that can cause us to become frightened. But He pointed out two significant truths that are important for us to note:

- Our fears do not achieve anything of value.
- Our focus should be on our Father, who faithfully provides.

In other words, we need to look past our problems and center our attention on our all-powerful, wise, and loving Lord, who is ready, willing, and able to handle anything we face. After all, nothing is impossible for Him (Luke 1:37), so there's never really a reason to fear.

Lord, I don't want to fret, but the challenges can get so overwhelming.
Help me to focus on You—the One who always comes to my defense.
Amen.

Worthy

SCRIPTURE READING: PROVERBS 25; PSALM 139:13–16;
HEBREWS 4:12–13; 1 PETER 1:1–2

Like cold water to a weary soul,
so is good news from a distant land.
PROVERBS 25:25

Let this thought refresh your soul: There is a Person who knows your true significance and potential—and that is the One who knit you together in your mother's womb (Psalm 139:13–16). He understands what is in your heart and what is possible for your future. And because of that, only He is worthy of judging your value and can set you free from the false messages that keep you in bondage (Hebrews 4:12–13). That One is the triune God, who loves you without measure—the Father who created you, the Lord Jesus who saves you, and the Holy Spirit who indwells you (1 Peter 1:1–2).

So there is absolutely no need to go through life handicapped by your past experiences. The only accurate, eternal, unassailable gauge of your worth comes from Almighty God. Who has a right to reject you? The answer, of course, is that no one does, because the Lord—the only One with the authority to judge you—has accepted you for all of eternity. On what basis could another person cast you off? Again, any reason for you to be spurned was destroyed at the cross.

Friend, you are worth dying for. Jesus Himself has declared you worthy. You are a coheir with Christ of the kingdom of the living God. You belong to His family permanently and, as such, are an important representative of His presence in the world. So today, don't despair or give in to negative thoughts about your significance. Be patient with yourself. Forgive your failures as He does. And continue embracing His unassailable truth that you are worthy and have great value in His sight.

Father, thank You so much for accepting me, making me worthy,
and reminding me who I am in Christ! You are so good and kind!
Amen.

Shadow Fears

SCRIPTURE READING: PROVERBS 26; ROMANS 12:2; PHILIPPIANS 4:8–9

The lazy person claims, "There's a lion on the road!
Yes, I'm sure there's a lion out there!"
PROVERBS 26:13

The creative mind is an amazing and powerful gift from God. When used for positive purposes such as glorifying the Father and serving others, it can be extremely helpful. Unfortunately, the same imagination can become a prison for us if employed in a negative manner. People can be dominated by *shadow fears*—they fret about problems that aren't real and don't ever occur. Sadly, because of these baseless worries and excuses, they end up missing God's best for their lives.

How can you be sure your life isn't hindered by shadow fears? It's helpful to ask yourself the following questions:

• Do I ever say, "God couldn't bless me because _____"?
• When facing a problem, do I worry that the worst will happen? Does that prevent me from stepping out in faith?
• Are there issues that I fret about constantly—such as a loved one getting sick, people rejecting me, or losing everything I own—that actually have no basis in reality?

If you answered yes to any of those questions, then your imagination may need to be tamed. Ask God to redeem your creativity and help you "be transformed by the renewing of your mind, so that you may prove what the will of God is" (Romans 12:2). Stop contemplating all the negative things that could happen to you and your loved ones. Rather, "Whatever is true, whatever is honorable, whatever is right, whatever is pure, whatever is lovely, whatever is of good repute, if there is any excellence and if anything worthy of praise, dwell on these things . . . and the God of peace will be with you" (Philippians 4:8–9).

Father, You know the shadow fears within me
and when I've used them as an excuse to be disobedient.
Please forgive me and help me always to move forward in faith.
Amen.

MAY 27

Your Inside Voice

Scripture Reading: Proverbs 27;
1 Chronicles 28:9; Psalm 139:23–24

As in water face reflects face,
so the heart of man reflects man.
PROVERBS 27:19

Your heart is always betraying the true condition of your inner person—the unresolved issues, the unforgiveness, the lack of faith, and even the confusion and anxiety you feel. You can cover up all the pain and fear and pretend it's not there, but the wounds of your soul speak constantly. The challenge is to identify your inner pain and then stop it from driving your actions by allowing God to root out its underlying causes.

This is why David prayed, "Search me, O God, and know my heart; try me and know my anxious thoughts; and see if there be any hurtful way in me, and lead me in the everlasting way" (Psalm 139:23–24). David realized that the Lord understood him better than he knew himself. So he invited the Father to release him from his hidden wounds with full confidence in His wisdom, love, and power.

Friend, you'll never be able to become the person God wants you to be until you deal with the things buried deep in your heart. All the religious activities in the world won't make it right. The Father can do without the programs and activities, but He wants all of you. This is why David instructed his son Solomon, "Know the God of your father, and serve Him with a whole heart and a willing mind; for the Lord searches all hearts, and understands every intent of the thoughts. If you seek Him, He will let you find Him" (1 Chronicles 28:9).

So today, listen to what your heart is saying and submit it immediately to the Father. He will show you truth in your inmost parts and set you free from all that's hidden within.

Father, like David, I pray, search me and know my heart. See if
there's any hurtful way in me and lead me in Your everlasting way.
Amen.

Courage

SCRIPTURE READING: PROVERBS 28;
DEUTERONOMY 31:8; 2 TIMOTHY 4:17–18

The righteous are bold as a lion.
PROVERBS 28:1 AMP

Considering the persecution and trials he endured to proclaim the gospel, we can probably all agree that the apostle Paul was brave. He was opposed by religious leaders, beaten by magistrates, and repeatedly driven out of towns by large, riotous crowds. Yet through it all, he stood firm in his allegiance to Christ.

Perhaps such courage seems beyond you on most days, especially when even inconsequential issues throw you off kilter. But remember, Paul was human just like you. He had fears that paralyzed him at times. So what did Paul know that could possibly help you today? How did he stay so bold in the midst of such overwhelming difficulty?

Paul's courage didn't originate from his strength, willpower, or political connections. Paul was confident because of the Father's presence with him. He said, "The Lord stood with me and gave me strength so that I might preach the Good News . . . and the Lord will deliver me from every evil attack and will bring me safely into His heavenly Kingdom. All glory to God forever!" (2 Timothy 4:17–18). With Almighty God standing beside him, Paul was not afraid.

Friend, courage is not the lack of fear; it is the determination that there is One who is greater than anything that could come against you. You can be brave and courageous like Paul. God can use you in mighty ways—filling you with love, joy, and peace you never dreamed possible. But you must accept that what He says is absolutely true: "The Lord is the one who goes ahead of you; He will be with you. He will not fail you or forsake you. Do not fear or be dismayed" (Deuteronomy 31:8). Therefore, today, be bold in Him.

*Father, make me like Paul—a courageous witness for You
in every circumstance. All glory to You forever!
Amen.*

Anger Toward God

SCRIPTURE READING: PROVERBS 29; JOB 1–2; 42

A fool always loses his temper, but a wise man holds it back.
PROVERBS 29:11

When terrible things happen in your life, you may wonder why God allowed you to suffer. Maybe you even store anger in your heart toward the Lord because He didn't stop the situation that wounded you so profoundly. If He's watching over you, why didn't He protect you? This was certainly how Job felt when he lost his children, servants, livestock, land, and even his health. His wife became so overwhelmed that her advice was, "Curse God and die!" (Job 2:9). Maybe you understand her despair.

But the reality is there's evil in the world (Job 1:6–12). Although everything that touches you must be *permitted* by the Father, He does not always *choose* it all for you. However, what He will do is make sure that no tear you shed, no pain you feel, and no tragedy you experience will go without notice and without some kind of redemption, if you'll allow Him to work in your life.

Friend, don't push God away and don't harbor anger in your heart toward Him when bad things happen. That's exactly what the enemy wants because he knows if God's love has its full effect on you, there will be nothing that can stop you from influencing the world for Christ. Instead of allowing the enemy to tempt you into harboring unforgiveness, cling to God more tightly during times of hurt and uncertainty. Like Job, you can say, "The Lord gave and the Lord has taken away. Blessed be the name of the Lord" (Job 1:20). Ask the Father to teach you about His personal love for you and open yourself to receiving it. And wait in confidence for Him to restore you (Job 42).

Father, forgive me for the ways I've been angry at
You. Whether You give or take away, I will bless
Your name. Help me to trust You as Job did.
Amen.

Healing Through Forgiveness

SCRIPTURE READING: PROVERBS 30

The churning of anger produces strife.
PROVERBS 30:33

The Lord wants us to pardon those who have wronged us, to make sure we don't harbor any resentment, bitterness, or grudges against anyone. But that's not always so easy. It is astounding how much pain and devastation one person or a group of people can cause. Perhaps someone is coming to your mind right now. Whether the wound is fresh or has been there for years, it still stings. It may even shape how you live, causing you to avoid situations or people similar to the one who injured you.

At this point you have a choice: You can nurse your anguish and allow bitterness to rule you, or you can turn to the Lord and allow Him to heal you. Just remember, forgiveness does not mean condoning what the person has done. Rather, it means you give up your resentment and animosity so you can be free.

This is complicated and agonizing at times. But please understand: The more difficult it is to forgive an individual, the more important it is to your spiritual, emotional, mental, and physical health that you do so. You see, unforgiveness binds you to the person who harmed you, wounding you more deeply than he or she ever could have alone. At some point, you must deny that individual the power to hurt you.

Friend, there is awesome power in forgiveness—it keeps you from becoming bitter, resentful, and hostile. When you harbor bitterness, your fellowship with the Lord suffers. So when God reminds you of the people you need to pardon, I hope you won't ignore His voice. Bravely decide to deal with those feelings and allow the Father to set you free.

*Lord God, help me break free from the churning of
bitterness. You know whom I need to forgive. Father, help
me to let go and trust You to put everything right.
Amen.*

Unafraid

SCRIPTURE READING: PROVERBS 31; ROMANS 8:28;
HEBREWS 11; 1 JOHN 4:16, 18

She is not afraid.
PROVERBS 31:21

What do you really believe when you face difficulties? Do you question God's character and wonder if He's punishing you? Or do you give Him thanks because you know He has promised to work all things together for your good (Romans 8:28)? In other words, do you express your confidence in Him? Or do you allow your fears and apprehensions to taint what He is accomplishing?

Friend, there should not be any anxiety about your relationship with the Father. The apostle John explains, "We have come to know and have believed the love which God has for us . . . There is no fear in love; but perfect love casts out fear, because fear involves punishment, and the one who fears is not perfected in love" (1 John 4:16, 18). The Father cares for you deeply and unconditionally. He allows challenges in your life so He can teach you to walk more closely with Him. They are never for your harm.

In fact, we know that the great saints of God faced overwhelming difficulties and were commended for their faith—glorifying the Father despite unbelievable odds and staggering adversaries. They "conquered kingdoms, performed acts of righteousness, obtained promises, shut the mouths of lions" (Hebrews 11:33–34) all because they trusted the Father and wanted to honor Him. They didn't focus on the magnitude of the challenges; rather, they "endured, as seeing Him who is unseen" (Hebrews 11:27). And the Lord rewarded their devotion by giving them awesome victories.

The same can be true for you. So choose to believe God above your apprehensions. After all, "Without faith it is impossible to please Him, for he who comes to God must believe that He is and that He is a rewarder of those who seek Him" (Hebrews 11:6).

Father, I want to believe You in all things. Help my unbelief
and fill me with the courage to follow You faithfully.
Amen.

Temptation

Temptations promise pleasure without penalty, but there are always consequences when you stray from God's path. Thankfully, by obeying the Lord, you can avoid the pitfalls and find greater fulfillment in Him than anything this world can offer.

Just Once

SCRIPTURE READING: PROVERBS 1; GENESIS 25:27–34

My child, if sinners entice you, turn your back on them!
PROVERBS 1:10, NLT

We never really imagine that one decision can alter our entire lives. After all, how irrational would it be to sacrifice our future for the pleasure of a moment? But that is how the enemy traps us. If he can get us to fall to temptation once, the rest is a downhill slide. And when it's too late, we look back and wish our decisions had been wiser.

This was certainly true for Esau (Genesis 25:27–34). He sacrificed his birthright—all of his wealth, inheritance, position, and power—for a bowl of stew. No one denies that Esau was truly hungry. But to sell something so valuable for something that would be completely digested in just a few hours? Well, that was plain foolish. But Esau wanted what he wanted, and no one was going to stop him from having it.

Yet this is a decision we face daily: Will we grab what we want at the cost of what is truly valuable? Will we lie or steal and undermine our character? Will we give in to an affair and destroy our family? Will we lash out in rage and forfeit our relationships, our reputation, or maybe even our freedom? Will we engage in addictive behaviors and sacrifice our lives?

There may be something before you that's so tempting, right there for the taking. You keep thinking, *What would it hurt to do it just once? It would feel so good to try it.* But before you proceed, consider carefully what you may lose. It takes just one wrong move to lose everything that's important to you and just one misguided decision to ruin your future. Friend, it's not worth it. Turn your back on that temptation and flee.

Father, deliver me from temptation. Help me to turn
from evil and honor the blessings You've given me.
Amen.

JUNE 2

Stay on the Path

SCRIPTURE READING: PROVERBS 2; 1 SAMUEL 15

Those who leave the paths of uprightness . . .
walk in the ways of darkness.
PROVERBS 2:13

Sometimes you will be tempted to take the easy way out of situations even though you know that's not what God has called you to do. You'll be tempted to take the obvious open door rather than wait for what the Father has planned for you.

I'm sure Saul *wanted* to be a good king who honored God. However, he thought he could do so on *his* terms rather than the Lord's. For example, God told Saul, "I will punish Amalek for what he did to Israel, how he set himself against him on the way while he was coming up from Egypt. Now go and strike Amalek and utterly destroy all that he has and do not spare him" (1 Samuel 15:2–3).

Saul complied with the Lord's command and headed into battle. However, he failed to obey God fully. First Samuel 15:9 reports that Saul and his men spared the Amalekite king "and the best of the sheep, the oxen, the fatlings, the lambs, and all that was good, and were not willing to destroy them utterly." Saul tried to justify his actions by saying he'd saved those spoils as a sacrifice to the Lord. But it was not obedience that motivated Saul; it was pride, and it resulted in being cut off from the kingdom (1 Samuel 15:23–29).

Friend, partial obedience is disobedience, and there is never an excuse for it in the eyes of God. Whatever goal the Lord has placed before you, He has a way for you to achieve it. Don't take the shortcut or wander from His path. Instead, ask Him for wisdom and strength so you can accomplish the goal completely and obediently. Because then you'll certainly receive the rewards He has planned for you.

Father, thank You for warning me against the shortcuts
before me. I will obey You completely.
Amen.

The Choice

SCRIPTURE READING: PROVERBS 3; ROMANS 1:17

Do not be wise in your own eyes; fear the LORD.
PROVERBS 3:7

When you have a relationship with God, He will constantly challenge you to trust Him more and draw closer to Him—relying on Him more with every aspect of your life. He will do so through the things He asks you to give up, the trials of life, the waiting times, and all the ways He asks you to step out in faith. Why does He do so? Because He wants you to experience the fullness of the new life He's given you. Accepting Christ as your Savior is only the first step. There is more freedom, power, joy, and peace awaiting you as you grow in your intimacy with Him.

But understand, these rewards come at a price. You must choose God's wisdom and timing above your own, obeying Him even when nothing makes sense, you cannot see the path ahead, or the road appears too difficult. In every instance, He is saying, "Here is your choice: Do as I instruct and discover all the astounding things I will accomplish through you, or spend the rest of your life wondering what I could have done if you had submitted to My wonderful plans." Everything in you may fight against what God is asking you to do, but this is the process by which your faith grows. You obey Him above your fears, insecurities, and even your natural senses, and He readies you for greater revelations of Himself and more significant fields of service (Romans 1:17).

Will you listen to Him? Will you say yes to the Lord no matter what? I pray you will, because He is leading you to life at its best. Don't spend the rest of your life wondering what could have been. Obey God today.

Lord, I'm scared to do what You ask, but I will step out in faith knowing You always lead me in the best way possible.
Amen.

JUNE 4

Sidetracked

SCRIPTURE READING: PROVERBS 4; JOSHUA 1:7

Don't get sidetracked; keep your feet from following evil.
PROVERBS 4:27 NLT

The enemy will try to get you off the track of God's will for you in any way he can. He does so by focusing your attention on other people, situations, and temptations rather than on what the Lord has called you to do. After you take the bait, of course, comes sin—the trap that holds and destroys you. So whenever you begin to obsess about something, you experience lingering confusion, or there's a conflict that persistently fuels your thoughts and interactions, it is an indication that the enemy may have been successful. You may have gotten sidetracked.

Friend, examine your thoughts and actions. Have you contributed to the inner turmoil you're experiencing by focusing on things other than the Lord? Have you sinned or gotten yourself into a mess because your eyes were on something other than what He's called you to do? It's not too late. You can triumph in this situation, but you must turn your gaze back to the Father and obey His commands (Joshua 1:7).

Remember, the Father's primary goal is to have an intimate relationship with you. But when you get sidetracked, the enemy successfully creates conditions that prevent God from having full access to your heart. Friend, the Lord will not compete to be Master of your life. He wants you to choose Him above every other distraction. So agree with God about your sins and allow Him to teach you. He will show you how to change the way you operate for maximum intimacy with Him, effectiveness in your life, and influence with others. And He will take care of all those peripheral situations in a manner that will astound your imagination.

Father, I don't want to be sidetracked. I confess my
sins and the issues that have taken my attention away
from You. You are my love, my life, and my all.
Amen.

JUNE 5

Tempting

SCRIPTURE READING: PROVERBS 5; AMOS 5:4

The lips of an adulteress drip honey
and smoother than oil is her speech.
PROVERBS 5:3

Some people say that they don't accept Christ as their Savior because they don't want to live by a bunch of rules. They want to be free to do what they wish, whenever they like, with whomever they please, and they don't like the idea that there is a God in heaven who would prevent them from experiencing the pleasure they desire.

As a believer, one may hear this and wonder, *Is there something I'm missing? It seems that the whole world is enjoying things that God forbids in His Word.* Friend, be careful! The enemy may be trying to get you to believe that the Lord is an unappeasable taskmaster who is keeping you from experiencing pleasure. Satan will do whatever he can to convince you to stray from the sanctified life God has called you to by telling you that you aren't going to hurt anyone. The desires of your body are natural—just meaningless fun—and the Lord is being unreasonable.

However, the truth is that the Father gives you His commands to help you avoid ruining your life with something that will never really satisfy the deep needs you're trying to fill. Because whether you know it or not, those sins influence who you become in a negative way, hindering you from being the courageous, powerful witness God created you to be. Don't do that to yourself! Open your heart to the Lord and be willing to put aside what the world has taught you (Amos 5:4). Tell God that you believe His commands are for your good, and ask Him to teach you to live a godly life that honors Him. There's freedom for you if you'll trust Him, so in prayer commit yourself to Him.

Lord, sin is certainly tempting. But I know Your commands
protect me from destruction and are always for my
good. Teach me to walk worthy of Your name.
Amen.

Get Moving

SCRIPTURE READING: PROVERBS 6; PSALM 119:71; JOHN 10:10

A little more slumber, a little folding of the hands to rest—
then poverty will pounce on you like a bandit.
PROVERBS 6:10-11 NLT

We all have times when we feel tired and unmotivated, when we're sick, exhausted, and truly need rest. However, if we make laziness our way of life, expecting someone else—whether it's the government, our families, the church, or others—to bail us out, then we're truly in trouble. Eventually our "I don't feel like it" becomes "I can't." Of course, God understands our limitations and disabilities; however, He will still hold us accountable for the things we can do for ourselves and for others. He expects us to give our best and to live with discipline, purpose, and the motivation of glorifying Him.

Perhaps you have excuses for being unmotivated or disheartened today. However, when you get right down to it, you have a choice of how to respond to your circumstances. You can either allow your troubles to defeat you, or you can use them as an opportunity to grow your faith in God.

David wrote in Psalm 119:71, "It is good for me that I was afflicted, that I may learn Your statutes." Don't let the enemy claim victory over you by disengaging from life. Instead, embrace the amazing hope of Jesus Christ and start seeing yourself the way He does: precious, redeemed, talented, and able. Satan may be telling you that you're a slug, but he's a liar and he has no right to keep you captive. In God's view, you're a caterpillar that's becoming a butterfly—with wings to soar. Therefore, get to work and claim the abundant life God has for you (John 10:10).

Father, give me energy and motivate me for my work today.
I need Your help to keep going forward. I know if I trust You,
You will lead me to the path of life. To You be all the glory.
Amen.

JUNE 7

Keep Listening

SCRIPTURE READING: PROVERBS 7; JEREMIAH 29:11

Listen to me, and pay attention to the words of my mouth.
PROVERBS 7:24

The Lord is speaking to you. The Father is drawing you into a conversation, communicating His plans for your life, revealing Himself to you, and confirming what He would like to do in and through you. Perhaps you are desperate to hear the Father today because some problem, temptation, or conflict is tearing you apart. Don't give up. Even if you have been pursuing His direction for a while, keep seeking Him.

In His love for you, God makes it possible for you to know what His plans for you are in any given situation. Moreover, you can be certain that the Father will move heaven and earth to show you His will. However, what He intends to tell you may be so crucial that He wants to make sure you are fully focused on Him. So any waiting you experience is simply intended to fix your attention on Him and prepare you for His answer.

Why can you be sure of this? Because the Lord says in Jeremiah 29:11, "I know the plans that I have for you . . . plans for welfare and not for calamity to give you a future and a hope." This is His assurance. Think about it: How can God expect you to walk in His will and accomplish His purposes if He doesn't tell you what they are? It would be out of the Father's character to hide what He wants you to be and do. When you look at the promises in Scripture, it becomes clear that the Lord is not merely disposed to showing you what to do but actively seeking to reveal His path of life to you and empower you to walk it. He may unveil the plan only step-by-step, but He will certainly show you the way to go.

Speak Lord, Your servant is listening. I trust You to lead me.
Amen.

JUNE 8

Boundaries

SCRIPTURE READING: PROVERBS 8; DEUTERONOMY 5:32–33

*He set for the sea its boundary so that the water
would not transgress His command.*

PROVERBS 8:29

Stand on any beach, and you can see God's great wisdom in setting the boundaries of the ocean. Watch the footage of tsunamis and hurricanes, and you can see the turmoil that would ensue if His laws were not in place governing the reach of those powerful waters. How could ports—which are vital for commerce and travel—be established? How could islands be settled or coastal cities built if there were no consistency to how the seas behaved?

Yet the Lord shows incredible wisdom in all of the boundaries He appoints for His creation, especially those He establishes for the beloved creatures who bear His image. Generally, when we're tempted, we are enticed to take our God-given desires beyond the limits He sets. For example, hunger is a needed natural impulse. But there are parameters for how much we're to eat and what we are to consume to remain healthy. When we go outside those boundaries, we can do damage to our bodies.

Friend, you may be wondering at the commands the Father has given governing conduct and the manner by which He orders communities and relationships. But He does so because He sees how destructive a massive overflow of boundary-less freedom would be—just as it would be with the oceans. He wants to protect all of the potential within you. So today, don't despise the constraints the Lord gives you even when they feel limiting. Rather, obey Him and thank God for the boundaries He gives you, knowing that so many more possibilities and blessings are available to you because they exist (Deuteronomy 5:32–33).

*Lord, thank You for the boundaries You've set in place to protect
me. I may not see all the ways these parameters help me achieve my
potential, but I trust You to make me all You created me to be.
Amen.*

Better Understanding

SCRIPTURE READING: PROVERBS 9; ROMANS 8:32

"Forsake your folly and live, and
proceed in the way of understanding."
PROVERBS 9:6

Each of us faces the same challenge every day—to look beyond what we can see to what God perceives, to understand our circumstances from His viewpoint, and to faithfully choose His direction. This is one of the reasons it is so important to have a daily quiet time—because we need constant reminders of His truth. We require continual exposure to the Word and its testimony of God's character.

After all, no one is wiser than the Creator of all things when it comes to knowing how you can live a successful life on this earth. No one has deeper understanding about how you can have a healthy and productive life than the God who formed your body. No one has a more profound comprehension of your potential than the Lord who molded your inmost being and caused you to be born in your particular circumstances. No one could possibly have a better plan for you than He does. After all, He created all natural resources and everything of real value on this earth—including the gifts and talents that you possess. No one has a greater stake in seeing you trained and successful than the One who bled on the cross for your redemption. Certainly, if He gave so much for you, He would lead you in the best way possible and never deny anything you truly need (Romans 8:32).

Friend, each day will bring you numerous opportunities to assert God's wisdom over your own. Don't rely on your own limited knowledge. That only leads to trouble. Rather, continuously train your mind, heart, and spirit with His truth. Then you can proceed with confidence on the path of His understanding and live.

Father, You are God! You know and understand all things! I choose
Your wisdom above my own. May I honor You with my life.
Amen.

JUNE 10

Missing Out

SCRIPTURE READING: PROVERBS 10

The LORD will not allow the righteous to hunger.
PROVERBS 10:3

At times we may mistakenly believe that if we obey God, we'll miss out on something good. It is true that when you follow the Lord, you won't always get your way, but the long-term benefits of seeking and serving the Father far outweigh anything you could lose. Here's what you can expect:

- *Contentment.* Beyond the temporary nature of happiness, you experience an abiding sense of joy.
- *Courage.* Because you know that God is with you at all times, in all situations, you can face any situation with confidence knowing He will lead, protect, and defend you.
- *Peace.* Rooted in the knowledge that the Lord is working all things for your eternal benefit, you can have enduring tranquillity in even the worst storms.
- *Growth.* Regardless of how your circumstances may appear, you can know that God is constantly maturing your faith and moving toward His goals for you.
- *Blessings.* As you obey the Father, He will provide for all your needs and bless you in a manner that will most satisfy and edify your soul.

In other words, the person who walks with God experiences His presence, power, and unconditional love. So consider today: Are you tempted to pursue earthly pleasures such as wealth, possessions, addictive substances, or sex—even though they are outside the boundaries the Lord has set for you? Are you afraid of missing out on these temporary—albeit destructive—pleasures? Friend, you'll never lose when you obey God.

Father, I don't want to miss out on anything You have for
me because I know You lead me to life at its best.
Help me to choose wisely in obedience to You every day.
Amen.

What Rules You?

SCRIPTURE READING: PROVERBS 11; DEUTERONOMY 8:18;
MATTHEW 19:21–22

*He who trusts in his riches will fall, but
the righteous will flourish like the green leaf.*
PROVERBS 11:28

When you rely on anything other than God—money, relationships, status, intelligence, ability, beauty, or what have you—you're asking for trouble in that area. The Lord may ask you to give it up or allow you to experience scarcity in it so you will learn to depend on Him. Why? Because He will not compete for lordship of your life.

The rich young ruler is a sad example of this. He asked Jesus how he could have eternal life. The Lord replied, "If you wish to be complete, go and sell your possessions and give to the poor, and you will have treasure in heaven; and come, follow Me" (Matthew 19:21). This was too much for the young man. Verse 22 tells us, "He went away grieving; for he was one who owned much property."

We may think, *I don't really blame him. I would have trouble giving up everything I have too. What would he live on? How could he afford food, clothing, and shelter?* But remember what he was asking about—*eternal* life. He was keeping the temporary and forfeiting what was everlasting—thereby proving he served possessions rather than God. In addition, he forgot who ultimately provided everything for him (Deuteronomy 8:18).

Friend, don't make the same mistake. If the Lord brings you scarcity in an area of your life—thank Him. If He asks you to relinquish something—do it. He is showing you how flimsy your earthly security is so you'll depend on Him. By your words and actions show that you trust in God above all things and serve Him only.

*Lord God, I know that at times I rely on earthly security
more than You. Please forgive me. Thank You for helping
me to have deeper faith and greater trust in You.*
Amen.

Trustworthy

SCRIPTURE READING: PROVERBS 12; HEBREWS 12:13

Truthful lips will be established forever.
PROVERBS 12:19

Do the people who really know you see you as a person of integrity? When they describe you, do they talk about your truthfulness and trustworthiness? Are they inclined to believe and heed what you say when they need counsel?

We live in a culture that tends to obscure the facts and deny reality. People say one thing but really believe another; and it seems that everyone has his or her own version of what is right. It can be difficult to know whom to trust and whom to listen to. But the reality is that the truth does not have versions, and integrity is a major issue in the eyes of God. His desire is that we would be people who represent Him well, with honesty, transparency, dependability, and hearts set on doing what is right. He wants us to be the kind of people who speak the truth in love—not to wound, but so others can be set free and healed (Hebrews 12:13).

Friend, it is so frustrating when others won't listen to us, but often we teach them to do so by lacking integrity in our interactions with them. Is this the case for you? Do others treat you as less that trustworthy? Begin changing that today by being a person of your word, but also by being a person of God's Word. To build and maintain your integrity, submit yourself to the Lord and walk in righteousness. Don't protect yourself with dishonesty; instead, arm yourself with the Sword of the Spirit, which is the Word of God. Surround yourself with honorable people and learn from them. Trust the Lord in everything you do, and confess your failures. In this way, God will establish you as a person people can count on for the truth and good counsel.

Lord, I want to be a person of integrity. Help me to walk in Your truth so others can count on me so I can represent You well.
Amen.

Inward Anger

SCRIPTURE READING: PROVERBS 13; 1 CORINTHIANS 10:13; 1 PETER 1:6–7

*Whoever despises the word and counsel [of God] brings
destruction upon himself, but he who [reverently] fears and
respects the commandment [of God] will be rewarded.*

PROVERBS 13:13 AMP

When we obey God, we know that even when we are tested, He has a good purpose. First Peter 1:6–7 reminds us, "In this you greatly rejoice, even though now for a little while, if necessary, you have been distressed by various trials, so that the proof of your faith, being more precious than gold which is perishable, even though tested by fire, may be found to result in praise and glory and honor at the revelation of Jesus Christ." The adversity that the Lord allows in our lives can be an awesome bridge to stronger faith and a deeper relationship with Him. We also know that if the Father chooses to try our character, He won't give us more than we can handle but will provide the tools necessary so we can persevere (1 Corinthians 10:13).

However, when we realize that our own bad decisions have resulted in painful consequences that we must bear, we can become furious with ourselves—beating ourselves up relentlessly and punishing ourselves more harshly than the Father ever would. If that inward anger goes unresolved, it can eventually turn into deep, paralyzing despair. We condemn ourselves mercilessly and reject God's grace because we feel unworthy.

Friend, the Savior doesn't want you to live that way. If you are often depressed, search you heart for any anger you harbor toward yourself. Confess your feelings to the Father, accept His forgiveness, and learn how to forgive yourself. Then turn back to Him in obedience, knowing that He can turn anything for your good if you'll agree to walk in obedience to Him.

*Father, You know the despair I often feel. Free me from the anger
I have toward myself and help me walk in obedience to You.
Amen.*

The Guardrail of God's Word

SCRIPTURE READING: PROVERBS 14; ROMANS 12:2

The wise are cautious and avoid danger.
PROVERBS 14:16

You are driving down the highway in the middle of the night. How do you ensure that your car remains safely within the lane? You measure your progress by the center line, right? As long as you keep your automobile aligned with the stripe that runs down the middle of the street, you know where you are. You also recognize that if you stay on your side of the road and the other drivers stay on theirs, you'll arrive safely at your destination.

Thankfully, this is what God's Word does for us as believers—it forms the convictions we live by as we grow in our intimate relationships with the Father. Scripture gives us basic principles that will keep us in the center of His will and safeguards us on the path. You see, we exist for a cause much greater and more important than ourselves. After all, we're living for Jesus Christ and for His kingdom, bearing witness to who He is in our lives. If we want to be effective in our homes, churches, and communities, we must first be very clear in our minds as to what we believe and how we live out those beliefs.

The wisdom we find in Scripture is our center line—keeping, directing, and safeguarding us in every situation and circumstance. It is our anchor in times of storm, regardless of the tempest assailing us. This is why it is so important for us to take the Father's commands seriously and seek Him daily. Because there is no place safer than the center of God's will and no better way to know His will than to interact with Him through prayer and His Word (Romans 12:2).

Lord, thank You for guiding and safeguarding me through Your Word.
As I read Scripture today, help me to understand how to respond
in obedience to You and keep me in the center of Your will.
Amen.

JUNE 15

God Sees

SCRIPTURE READING: PROVERBS 15; HEBREWS 3:12–19

The eyes of the Lord are in every place.
PROVERBS 15:3

God sees and knows the struggles you face, and you can trust Him to take care of you. Yet with the pressures you are experiencing today, you may doubt that. Maybe you wonder if the Father truly knows how much you suffer. Let me assure you, your heavenly Father is truly aware of the storms against you. Yet He also sees more deeply than you realize to the unbelief in your heart that must be rooted out.

Scripture regularly warns of the consequences of an unbelieving heart. We see it all through the Old Testament in Israel's repeated faith failures. Even though the Father often delivered them miraculously from their enemies, their unbelief persisted. And because they did not believe Him, they did not experience the joy and victory He'd planned for them, which resulted in even more trials (Hebrews 3:12–19). In other words, unbelief leads only to more suffering.

The same is true for us. We need to realize that unbelief is a poisonous root that infects our hearts, and the Father will stop at nothing to root it out.

So what brings triumph in life? Trusting that the Lord not only sees our struggle but also that He has planned for our victory. So stay focused on Him, reading His Word, fighting your battles in prayer, and having faith that He is leading you in the right way. His eye is on the finish line, where He waits to rejoice with you—so keep your eyes there as well.

Father, thank You for seeing my trials even more deeply than I do.
Truly, You care for my well-being and lead me to victory.
To You be all the honor, glory, power and praise.
Amen.

What's the Motive?

SCRIPTURE READING: PROVERBS 16; PSALM 37:4

All the ways of a man are clean in his own sight,
but the Lord weighs the motives.
PROVERBS 16:2

Today, perhaps you're wondering if your most cherished wish is the Lord's will for you. Maybe you're uncertain whether He inspired the yearning in your heart, or if it's just something you want. And if it's not from Him, will you be forced to give it up? That depends on the nature of your aspirations, of course, and this is where you need to be cautious. If you understand who God is, you know that there are some longings that are inconsistent with His character.

Of course, the Father won't honor the cravings that would ultimately hurt you. Therefore, in order to discern whether your motives fit His purpose for your life, you must seek His guidance. Remember: The Father will move heaven and earth to show you His will, and He always provides His best for you. You can be confident that if something you want doesn't fit His plan for you, He will reveal His opposition to it when you seek Him. Many times you can do this simple test: If what you seek tempts you to sin or hinders your relationship with God, then it doesn't originate with Him.

On the other hand, a righteous longing not only draws you closer to the Father; it's also His gift to you. We know this from His promise in Psalm 37:4: "Delight yourself in the Lord; and He will give you the desires of your heart." Your responsibility is to seek Him wholeheartedly and obey His commands. When you do, He blesses you by giving you a praiseworthy yearning, and then He satisfies it in a manner beyond your imagination.

Father, I want only motives that honor and exalt You.
Purge any longings that don't align with Your will
and fill my heart with those that please You.
Amen.

Be a Peacemaker

SCRIPTURE READING: PROVERBS 17;
1 SAMUEL 18–19; 24; MATTHEW 5:9, 16

Abandon the quarrel before it breaks out.
PROVERBS 17:14

It is both amazing and terribly sad what can stir hatred in someone's heart toward you. King Saul's jealousy wasn't based on anything that David did wrong—it was what he did right. It was because David had God's favor. We're told, "Saul saw and knew that the Lord was with David . . . Thus Saul was David's enemy continually . . . Saul told Jonathan his son and all his servants to put David to death" (1 Samuel 18:28–29, 19:1).

With his incredible popularity, David could have raised an army to challenge Saul, but he didn't. That would have meant an all-out civil war in the nation that represented the Lord—and that would have been incredibly destructive. Instead David fled from Saul and waited for God to take care of the situation. In fact, David had two opportunities to kill Saul and refused to take them, saying, "The Lord forbid that I should do this to my lord the king. I shouldn't attack the Lord's anointed one, for the Lord himself has chosen him" (1 Samuel 24:6 NLT). David avoided any act that could aggravate the situation and demonstrated that he honored God's timing above all else.

Friend, whenever a person attacks you, you'll be tempted to lash back at him or her. But don't. People know what you believe and Whom you trust in to defend you. Is there someone who is unfairly targeting you? Take David's example to heart and behave wisely. Don't allow the quarrel to become greater, but instead remove any fuel and calm the situation. Be the peacemaker Christ called you to be. Because then you'll be known as a child of God to those who are watching how you respond (Matthew 5:9, 16).

Father, You know the unfair attacks I have sustained.
But I will trust You to defend me, Lord.
Make me a peacemaker who glorifies You.
Amen.

Full Surrender

The spirit of a man can endure his sickness,
but as for a broken spirit who can bear it?
PROVERBS 18:14

We all experience devastating times that stretch everything we know and believe. We are in pain—at times physically, at others emotionally, and sometimes both. Frustrations and setbacks bombard us at an alarming rate, undermining our every confidence. We wonder why God would allow all the agony we are experiencing. At the same time, the enemy tempts us to question whether the Father really loves us—bringing up old sins that have already been forgiven and insinuating they disqualify us from the Lord's blessings. What makes it even worse is that joy is just outside our reach, and we have no hope of taking hold of it. The sense of loss, helplessness, futility, and dissatisfaction with ourselves can be absolutely overwhelming.

Is this you today, friend? Then realize that the only remedy for your broken spirit is to fully surrender to the Father. It is in looking to Him that you will ultimately find the greatest hope, joy, peace, and freedom.

The prophet Isaiah testifies, "Although the Lord has given you bread of privation and water of oppression, He, your Teacher, will no longer hide Himself, but your eyes will behold your Teacher. Your ears will hear a word behind you, 'This is the way, walk in it,' whenever you turn to the right or to the left" (Isaiah 30:20–21). This is the actual purpose of the trial—God is teaching you to rely on Him fully. He wants you to recognize that regardless of what circumstances you face, your omnipotent, omniscient, omnipresent, and unconditionally loving God is there to guide you, protect you, and provide for you perfectly. So today, release all the pain you feel into His care and learn to rest in Him.

Lord, heal my broken spirit and increase my faith.
I surrender, Father. Thank You for helping me.
Amen.

Surviving the Storms

SCRIPTURE READING: PROVERBS 19; JOB 23:10; ROMANS 8:37;
2 CORINTHIANS 1:3–4; HEBREWS 5:8; 1 PETER 5:7

The fear of the LORD leads to life, so that
one may sleep satisfied, untouched by evil.
PROVERBS 19:23

The storms of life may hit hard, but they don't have to destroy you, no matter how overwhelming they are. If anyone understood this, it was Job. Many people could stand firm through the loss of all their possessions, but Job also lost his health and children. Certainly, he was devastated in ways few of us will ever know. Yet through it all, he was able to say, "When He has tried me, I shall come forth as gold" (Job 23:10). Job revered the Lord, honored His authority, and was willing to submit to His greater purposes. And because he did, Job came through the challenges victoriously.

This is how we survive the trials as well—by trusting God and realizing that He is achieving good things through them. Yes, there is an aspect of life's storms that is evil, that can wreck us and leave us completely shattered. But when we submit ourselves to the Lord, difficult circumstances can make us stronger, more sensitive, humble, self-sacrificing, and compassionate. They can teach us true obedience to the Father (Hebrews 5:8) and how to minister to others with sympathy and mercy (2 Corinthians 1:3–4). In other words, good can and will come from those storms, if we will allow God to work through them.

Friend, do you want to make sure that the trials you're facing don't destroy you? Then trust the Lord. Surrender yourself to Him and allow Him to sustain you—"casting all your anxiety on Him, because He cares for you" (1 Peter 5:7). And like Job, you will come forth as gold—more than a conqueror through Him who loves you (Romans 8:37).

Father, only You can bring good from the storms I face.
I surrender myself in faith to You.
Amen.

Faith Battle

SCRIPTURE READING: PROVERBS 20; NEHEMIAH 2; 4

Do not say, "I will repay evil"; wait for
the Lord, and He will save you.
PROVERBS 20:22

Although Nehemiah had overwhelming support from the Jewish community when he tried to rebuild the wall in Jerusalem, from the very beginning of his efforts, he faced opposition from enemies who preferred an unfortified and vulnerable Israel (Nehemiah 2:10). These enemies made life miserable for him—criticizing his efforts, threatening the Jews, and even lying to King Artaxerxes about what Nehemiah was attempting to accomplish.

Anyone else would have forgone the work on the wall to wage war against such adversaries. However, Nehemiah understood that those enemies had no real power to thwart the plans of the living God. As he had done previously, Nehemiah turned to the Father in prayer and encouraged the people, "Do not be afraid of them; remember the Lord who is great and awesome . . . Our God will fight for us" (Nehemiah 4:14, 20).

The Lord is fighting for you today too. Perhaps you face a similar battle—people are preventing your progress, you don't have the influence or resources necessary to proceed, and the criticisms of others have wounded you deeply. What you must remember in such circumstances is that the struggles you're facing represent a *faith battle*. Will you listen to the threats of men, or will you trust the promises of God? Will you allow your circumstances to dishearten you, or will you believe in His unfailing character? Either you will believe the Father takes full responsibility for your needs when you obey Him or you won't. Let me be clear: When the Lord calls you to a task, He will help you accomplish it, regardless of what anyone thinks or says. Trust Him.

Father, it seems like there is no way for me to succeed in this
situation. However, I am confident this is nothing for You.
Thank You for fighting for me and leading me to victory.
Amen.

JUNE 21

Impoverished by Desire

SCRIPTURE READING: PROVERBS 21; PSALM 16:11

He who loves pleasure will become a poor man.
PROVERBS 21:17

Does today's verse mean the Lord doesn't want you ever to experience any pleasure? Absolutely not. In fact, Psalm 16:11 promises, "In Your presence is fullness of joy; in Your right hand there are pleasures forever." Rather, Proverbs 21:17 addresses the problem of giving your life over to the pursuit of gratification rather than God. When your desires become your focus, you're going to begin making compromises in order to fulfill them and will eventually act in a way that contradicts your core beliefs. The steps toward disobedience will begin small, but they'll quickly speed up and take you in a very definite direction—which is away from the Lord.

Eventually, you develop an attitude that anything goes, which results in chaos in your life and your relationships. You become increasingly susceptible to peer pressure, and your disobedience to God increases, as does your spiritual weakness and discouragement. Ultimately, you lose sight of the Father altogether, which means you lose your peace, joy, and strength, and you are no longer able to handle the storms that come into your life.

Friend, don't let that happen! Remember who you are in Christ. You're a child of the living God! The Spirit of God has sealed you as His beloved, and He teaches you how to live in the freedom of your salvation. Because of Christ's provision on the cross, you are not only completely victorious, but you're also a coheir with the Savior—which means you have an eternal kingdom waiting for you that is beyond imagination. You have no reason to chase after temporary pleasures and no reason to compromise. So don't! Don't do anything that could trap you on the downward slide. Rather, look up and see all that God's promised you if you'll obey Him.

Lord, I confess the ways my desires have gotten
hold of me. Free me, Father.
Amen.

Your Advocate

SCRIPTURE READING: PROVERBS 21; MATTHEW 11:29–30;
26:47–56; 27:46; LUKE 22:42; HEBREWS 2:17–18; 7:25

The LORD will plead their case.
PROVERBS 22:23

There may be times when it feels as if you just can't say the right thing to God. Perhaps you strain your ears listening, but can't seem to hear His voice. It may be that your dreams seem lost, the path ahead of you appears vague and unpromising, and you don't understand why God has brought you to this painful and difficult place. You try to communicate with the Father, but you feel as if you're doing a terrible job of it.

Thankfully, in all these things, you have an advocate in Jesus, who always lives to make intercession for you (Hebrews 7:25). And even better, your Savior knows exactly what you are experiencing. Hebrews 2:17–18 (TLB) explains, "It was necessary for Jesus to be like us, His brothers, so that He could be our merciful and faithful High Priest before God . . . For since He Himself has now been through suffering and temptation, he knows what it is like when we suffer and are tempted, and he is wonderfully able to help us."

The Lord Jesus knows what you're feeling, comprehends the difficult decisions you must make, and grasps the inner struggles that often accompany doing the right thing (Luke 22:42). He understands the heartache of being rejected and betrayed by others (Matthew 26:47–56). And He recognizes the agony of being forsaken, abandoned in terrible emotional and physical pain (Matthew 27:46). Jesus not only appreciates what you're feeling, He faithfully walks through each challenge with you and offers you rest for your soul (Matthew 11:29–30). And He is praying for you, friend. So keep approaching His throne of grace. Because He ensures that you'll receive mercy and find grace in your time of need.

Lord Jesus, thank You for praying for me and being
my advocate. Lead me in the way I should go.
Amen.

Waiting in Hope

SCRIPTURE READING: PROVERBS 23; ISAIAH 55:11; 64:4

Surely there is a future, and your hope will not be cut off.
PROVERBS 23:18

Once we know that a dream, promise, or goal is from the Father, how do we look forward to it in a way that honors God as time passes? After all, it's easy to keep the faith when we don't have to wait too long, but sometimes that's not the case. Often the Lord asks us to wait patiently for the desires of our heart. And the stronger our longings, the more quickly our patience tends to waver. As the days, weeks, and months go by, we may find it increasingly difficult to trust that He will answer our prayers at all.

In fact, that may be where you find yourself today. If your desire is truly from God, why has He delayed in fulfilling His promises to you? And how do you continue honoring Him until He brings it to fruition?

First, do not be discouraged. As Abraham, David, and Joseph before you have shown, God's delays are not denials of your prayers. Rather, the Lord knows exactly what you need—what graces must be developed in your character, what areas in your faith require growth, and what details should be arranged. And He will wait until you're ready to send you the blessing. But *second*, understand that you can become discouraged and lose hope if your focus isn't on the Father.

Friend, God "acts on behalf of the one who waits for Him" (Isaiah 64:4), and He always keeps His promises (Isaiah 55:11). So give the Lord the time to accomplish His will in your life. Don't give up; just keep watching for Him and obeying Him. Soon enough, He will answer your prayers in ways beyond your expectations.

Lord, the waiting is so difficult, but I will trust in You.
Keep me focused on Your unfailing character
as I cling to Your matchless promises.
Amen.

JUNE 24

Unfaltering

SCRIPTURE READING: PROVERBS 24; ACTS 14:19; 20:17–24;
27:14–44; 2 CORINTHIANS 4:8–9; 11:23–29; 1 PETER 5:10

If you falter in a time of trouble, how small is your strength!
PROVERBS 24:10 NIV

With the lashes, imprisonments, and dangers Paul experienced, one would not have been surprised if he had faltered in his faith (2 Corinthians 11:23–29). The apostle faced terrible difficulties during his missionary journeys, including almost being stoned to death at Lystra (Acts 14:19), leaving his beloved churches in order to suffer in Jerusalem (Acts 20:17–24), and being shipwrecked on his way to Rome (Acts 27:14–44). In constant peril, separated from his loved ones, threatened on every side, and buffeted by innumerable trials, he had good reason to be disheartened.

Yet Paul was able to report, "We are afflicted in every way, but not crushed; perplexed, but not despairing; persecuted, but not forsaken; struck down, but not destroyed" (2 Corinthians 4:8–9). How was he able to endure such heartache and persecution? The apostle had learned to walk by the Spirit and in dependence of His strength. In other words, Paul learned to deal with his troubles in God's way, rather than the ways of the world.

When we experience difficulty, our human nature often tries to express or quench it in ungodly ways: through possessions, addictions, or immorality. However, that only weakens us and speeds our destruction. It is no wonder we falter. Instead, we must trust in the Lord. And when we do, 1 Peter 5:10 promises, "After you have suffered for a little while, the God of all grace, who called you to His eternal glory in Christ, will Himself perfect, confirm, strengthen and establish you." And that, friend, is strength that will carry us to the very end.

Father, I need Your unfaltering strength to sustain me.
Help me to endure, Lord. I trust You to get me through
the trials I am facing and lead me to victory.
Amen.

Increase Love

SCRIPTURE READING: PROVERBS 25; ROMANS 12:20; 1 PETER 4:8

If your enemy is hungry, give him food to eat;
and if he is thirsty, give him water to drink.
PROVERBS 25:21

When someone wrongs you, you will be tempted to rehash all the person has done to you—even as you're in the process of forgiving him or her. The enemy will convince you that the person needs to feel the shame and guilt of the sins he or she has committed. Unfortunately, focusing on this only keeps you trapped in bitterness and unforgiveness because you're taking justice back into your own hands rather than leaving it in God's.

In fact, some people read Romans 12:20, which says, "If your enemy is hungry, feed him, and if he is thirsty, give him a drink; for in so doing you will heap burning coals on his head," and think, *Aha! I'll do something good for him because then the punishment will be worse!* That's not forgiveness—that's a completely wrong attitude. Rather than a chance for vengeance, forgiveness is an opportunity to show the love of Christ and increase our love for one another. Love is both the seed and fruit of forgiveness. When you feed your hungry enemy and give him something to drink, you replace the bitterness in your heart with God's grace.

Friend, are you willing to let God to make you a vessel of His love? Do you want Him to turn your trials into fountains of fruitfulness? Then as 1 Peter 4:8 instructs, "Keep fervent in your love for one another, because love covers a multitude of sins." Be kind to those who have hurt you as Christ has been to you. You'll forgive much, but you'll also learn to love much—and that's always pleasing to God.

Lord God, I know I have to forgive down to the deepest
part of my soul. Show me ways to minister to my foes so
that You will be glorified and I will be healed.
Amen.

JUNE 26

Backward and Forward

SCRIPTURE READING: PROVERBS 26; PHILIPPIANS 3:7–14

A fool repeats his folly.
PROVERBS 26:11 NKJV

If a person is going to succeed, there are two things he or she must prayerfully and conscientiously consider: "Where have I been?" and "Where am I going?" This is because, *first*, a person who doesn't have a clear understanding of his or her history is prone to repeat past mistakes. This is especially true of our sins, which often have consistent triggers. As we're often told, doing the same thing over and over, while expecting different results, is one of the definitions of insanity. So we have to know where our stumbling blocks are in order to avoid them in the future.

Second, it's important to comprehend where God is leading, because when you don't have clear objectives, you are just wandering through life. It is only when you have a goal that is both powerfully motivating and inspiring that you become focused in your use of time, energy, and talents.

But most of all, asking the questions "Where have I been?" and "Where am I going?" invite the Lord into your past and future. Through them, God sensitizes you to the critical decisions that have changed your course—whether for good or ill. He shows you which factors are causing the difficulties you are currently experiencing and equips you to reverse the destructive trends. And He teaches you a new way to live— His way.

Friend, don't be shackled by who you've been in the past, and don't repeat your mistakes. Ask God to reveal where you've been and where you're going, and allow Him to guide you in His truth and teach you to be far more than you've ever dreamed or imagined (Philippians 3:7–14).

Father, only You have a clear view of why I've committed mistakes
and how I can reach Your goals for me in the future.
Lead me, Father, and help me to walk in Your truth.
Amen.

Whom Are You Exalting?

SCRIPTURE READING: PROVERBS 27; LUKE 18:14

Let another praise you, and not your own mouth.
PROVERBS 27:2

There is no more obvious sign of pride than the constant need to talk about yourself. If you constantly feel the need to justify your actions, let people know how well you've done, or replay your past achievements, there may be pride in your life. This comes from the desire to prove your worth—to give evidence to people that you are worthy of love and respect. But friend, there is only One who can truly judge your value or give your life significance, and that is God.

Yet that's why pride is so destructive in the life of a believer—it overemphasizes the self and refuses to admit a need for God. We see ourselves as the source of our success and happiness, and all of our attention is focused on our good rather than on the Father. However, Jesus warned, "Everyone who exalts himself will be humbled, but he who humbles himself will be exalted" (Luke 18:14).

So today, examine what you say. Are you constantly bolstering yourself and your accomplishments? If there is pride within you, you need to deal with it immediately because conceit can lead you only to pain, isolation, and desolation. It cannot protect your reputation or raise you up in others' opinions. It can't make people love or respect you. Rather, it can only warp your understanding and make you an adversary of God— the One who most loves you and best helps you. So root that pride out of your heart by acknowledging your need for the Lord in every area of your life. He is the only One who can empower you to become all you were created to be. And He is the only One who is truly worthy of your praise.

Father, please forgive me for the times I've exalted myself
instead of You. I need You, and I acknowledge that
You are the only One worthy of all my praise.
Amen.

Find Compassion

SCRIPTURE READING: PROVERBS 28; PSALM 23:3; JOHN 14:26; 1 JOHN 1:9

*He who conceals his transgressions will not prosper, but
he who confesses and forsakes them will find compassion.*
PROVERBS 28:13

It may be that you are hesitant to seek and listen to the Lord today because of the guilt and shame you feel. Perhaps you fear that if you open your ears to His voice, all you'll hear is condemnation and wrath, confirming your feelings of worthlessness.

Yet David's testimony about the Lord speaks of His loving grace, which builds up rather than tears down. David writes, "He restores my soul; He guides me in the paths of righteousness for His name's sake" (Psalm 23:3). In other words, when we submit to Him, the Father brings healing, wholeness, and a restored understanding of our purpose.

Friend, it's important for you to understand that the reason God hates sin is that it creates emptiness, guilt, anger, and loneliness within your heart and separates you from Him. Sin hurts you. But God's goal is not to condemn you. Rather, He works to help you become all you were created to be. So He heals you of your transgressions through the death and resurrection of His Son Jesus Christ, and He gives you the Holy Spirit to teach you to walk in His ways (John 14:26).

God understands that you will stray at some point (Isaiah 53:6). But He calls you back to the throne of grace to show you mercy, to restore your soul, and to remind you of your overwhelming worth in His sight— never to make you feel worse. So today, don't run from Him. Go to your loving God and lay your heart open before Him (1 John 1:9). Certainly, you will find compassion from the One who only wants the very best for you.

*Father, I confess and repent of my sin. Thank You for forgiving
me and cleansing me from this unrighteousness that brings
me such shame. Restore me so I can walk in Your ways.
Amen.*

The Better Way

SCRIPTURE READING: PROVERBS 29; JEREMIAH 18:3–4; HEBREWS 12:4–11

The rod and reproof give wisdom.
PROVERBS 29:15

When God addresses something in your life—such as a sin, stronghold, or fear that He desires to root out—it may surprise you to find that your difficulties may actually *increase*, hitting you right where you hurt. This may seem strange to you because you're getting right with the Lord and are willing to change. You may wonder, *Why isn't the Father helping me? Why has this situation gotten worse instead of better?* You cry out to Him and He comforts you, but the trial does not end, and you cannot understand what He is doing.

Believe it or not, what you are experiencing is absolutely normal—and a necessary part of liberating you from the bondage within you. You see, adversity is not only a bridge to a deeper relationship with God, it is also the path to freedom and healing. Like a surgeon expertly cutting out cancer, He must pierce you right where the concentration of pain is, right where the decay lies within you. So He uses trials as His precise scalpel, making meticulous and skillful incisions into your life that are agonizing but absolutely necessary in order for you to be fully free from what is destroying you (Jeremiah 18:3–4).

Is there no easier way? you may wonder. The simple truth is that you learn more in the difficulties of life than in the blessings. And the fact that He is still working on you is evidence that not only does He see your great potential, but He also desires to touch the world through you in an astounding way (Hebrews 12:4–11). So do not despair. Rather, trust your heavenly Father to lead you in the best way possible.

Father, I do not understand Your ways, but I trust Your heart. Thank You for freeing me from this bondage.
Amen.

True Protection

SCRIPTURE READING: PROVERBS 30; JOHN 16:33; EPHESIANS 6:12–17

*Cliff badgers: delicate little animals who
protect themselves by living among the rocks.*
PROVERBS 30:26 TLB

Are you discouraged by the news of wars in various parts of the world? Or worse, are you disheartened as you see the terrible things happening before your eyes in your own community and nation? Do you long for the day when such conflicts cease?

Yet as a believer, it's important that you recognize that the main battle against you and the Body of Christ today "is not against flesh and blood, but against . . . spiritual forces of wickedness in the heavenly places" (Ephesians 6:12). Yes, the conflicts of this world should cause you concern, but the true threat you face is the spiritual warfare that assails you every day.

In Proverbs, cliff badgers are praised for their ability to make effective use of what they have for their protection. Unfortunately, as believers, we often fail to do the same thing. In Ephesians 6:13–17, God reveals the weapons He's given us for fighting this war—the spiritual armor that will enable us to stand firm against the enemy's onslaughts. Yet how often do we consciously put on the helmet of salvation, the breastplate of righteousness, the belt of truth, and all the other armaments we have at our disposal?

Friend, if you've been fighting the battles of life with human plans and methods, it's no wonder you are tired and discouraged. But God has given you mighty weapons so you won't merely survive today's onslaughts; you'll thrive despite them. So put on the armor today and be on the alert. God has given you everything you need for victory (John 16:33); just listen to your Commander in Chief and obey Him.

*Father, I do get discouraged, but I am grateful the victory is
ultimately Yours. Dress me in Your armor and lead me to triumph.
Amen.*

Character

One thing is certain—God builds your character as He leads you on the path of wisdom. This is because His ultimate goal is that you reflect the likeness of His Son, Jesus Christ. And so as your mind is renewed with His understanding, your character is likewise transformed to bear His image in increasing measure.

JULY 1

Your Attention, Please

Scripture Reading: Proverbs 1

*What you learn . . . will crown you with grace
and be a chain of honor around your neck.*
PROVERBS 1:9 NLT

What happens when people who know how to listen to the Father no longer perceive the sound of His voice? Perhaps you're going through such a time right now. For whatever reason, God appears to be giving you the silent treatment. Maybe you've asked for guidance and He does not answer. It could be that He has not provided for a pressing need in your life and you feel as if He is distant and uninterested in your difficult circumstances. Why this lack of communication?

The truth is, our heavenly Father is sometimes quiet, and when we're hurting, His silence can be particularly perplexing. But be assured that God still loves you and has a good purpose for His silence. He will use it to develop your intimacy with Him and mature you spiritually, if you continue to seek Him. However, if the Father is quiet, then most likely there is something especially significant He desires to teach you, and He wants you to listen closely. God will use the silence to get your attention, prepare you to obey Him, reveal your sin, grow your trust in Him, train you to hear His voice, and teach you to persevere.

So if the Father has been silent lately, you can be confident that He is calling you to a new level of intimacy. Therefore, do not be discouraged or afraid. Humble yourself before Almighty God; get on your knees and acknowledge that He is Lord of your life. Wait quietly before Him, willing to hear and obey whatever He says to you. Thank Him for being active on your behalf, and anticipate His awesome answer with confidence and expectancy.

*Lord, I want so badly to hear You. Open my
ears. Lead me powerfully, as only You can.
Speak, Lord, Your servant is listening.
Amen.*

Know God

SCRIPTURE READING: PROVERBS 2; ISAIAH 40:8–26

Understand what it means to fear the LORD,
and you will gain knowledge of God.
PROVERBS 2:5 NLT

Have you ever contemplated what God is like in all of His grandeur and divinity? How immense and unfathomable He is (Isaiah 40:8–26)? Scripture tells us to fear the Lord, but that doesn't mean being terrified to approach Him. On the contrary, it means that we should *respect* Him by acknowledging that He is the highest authority with the greatest wisdom and power. And we should submit to His leadership because He is holy, infinite God—His instructions to us are perfect, He is in control, and He has never broken a promise.

Being close to the One who is sovereign and divine is the highest privilege you and I are ever given. This should motivate us to enjoy and honor our fellowship with Him. Likewise, being in His presence helps us know His character and instill that character in our own lives.

So consider: Are you experiencing a regular, consistent time alone with the Father? Are you really getting to know Him? Take an honest inventory of your attitude toward God and your relationship with Him. If you really see the Lord as your loving and omnipotent Creator, King, and Redeemer—the sovereign God who will lead you to success in every endeavor—you'll want to spend time with Him, and you'll trust the plans He has for you. But if you see Him as a disinterested force or a cruel deity who is looking forward to punishing you, it's no wonder you're not compelled to be near Him. If you don't feel inspired to experience the Lord's presence, examine why that is. Your perception of Him may be inaccurate—formed by negative experiences with other authority figures rather than His truth. You must overcome this because the path to joy begins with a relationship with Him.

Father, open my heart and give me an accurate understanding
of who You are. I want to know You, Lord.
Amen.

Disciplined for Good

My son, do not reject the discipline of the LORD or loathe
His reproof, for whom the LORD loves He reproves,
even as a father corrects the son in whom he delights.
PROVERBS 3:11–12

If you are hurting today, you may be tempted to doubt God's love for you. It is human nature to interpret negative circumstances as His punishment or cruelty. But don't jump to conclusions or suppose that the challenges you're experiencing are because your heavenly Father doesn't care about you. Just the opposite is true—God loves you profoundly and unconditionally. And because He does, He not only blesses you with opportunities to grow in faith and character but also corrects you for your protection.

Hebrews 12:5–6 affirms, "Do not disregard lightly the discipline of the Lord, nor faint when you are reproved by Him; for those whom the Lord loves He disciplines, and He scourges every son whom He receives." With this in mind, it is important that you understand the difference between punishment and discipline. Punishment is God executing His judgment upon the wicked. Discipline is God correcting believers in order to safeguard them from further disobedience and harmful consequences. Of course, it is always important to repent of the sins you have committed. But don't fear losing God's love because of your failures.

So when challenging circumstances arise, the wisest course of action you could ever take is to turn to your heavenly Father and listen. Don't resist Him. Rather, recognize that the Lord wants to use you in a mighty way, and this is His way of preparing you for greater assignments ahead. Trust Him and His undying love as He shapes you into a beautiful vessel that He can use.

Father, thank You for Your discipline. It hurts,
but I understand You do it only out of love to help
me grow. Teach me to walk in Your ways.
Amen.

JULY 4

The Path of Life

SCRIPTURE READING: PROVERBS 4; EPHESIANS 2:10

Watch the path of your feet and all your ways will be established.
PROVERBS 4:26

What is the path of your feet? Which road are you going to take today? The way that most people would phrase the question is, "What do you want to do with your life?" But that is entirely the wrong question. This assumes that you have full understanding of your potential and the road ahead. But you don't. You can't possibly know the future.

But God does, and He has bigger dreams for you than you do for yourself, ones that will lead you to great fulfillment, meaning, and eternal rewards. His plans keep you young, vibrant, happy, and excited to live. Best of all, He takes full responsibility for accomplishing them in your life. He knows the training and character traits you need and how to engineer circumstances to get you to the desired destination.

Wise people of strong character will always ask, "Lord, what would You have me do?" They will allow God Himself to establish the road ahead for them. After all, Ephesians 2:10 teaches, "We are His workmanship, created in Christ Jesus for good works, which God prepared beforehand so that we would walk in them." If God has created us with assignments in mind, surely He will lead us to them!

So learn the awesome things He wants to do in and through your life and get moving. As you give your life freely to Him in faith, you will discover all you were created for. In other words, you obey God, leave the consequences to Him, and He will lead you to life at its very best.

Father, I submit my life to You. What would You have me do?
Thank You for giving me my gifts, planning good works for me to
accomplish, and securing my future. Lead me, Lord. I will follow.
Amen.

JULY 5

The Problem of Envy

SCRIPTURE READING: PROVERBS 5; JOHN 14:27; EPHESIANS 3:20

Drink water from your own cistern
and fresh water from your own well.
PROVERBS 5:15

Do you have a strong yearning in your heart for something someone else has—like a position, possessions, or a particular relationship? Do you think about how much how much better you would take care of it and how much more you deserve it than the person who actually has it? Such envious thoughts can certainly tear you apart. The enemy uses your feelings to draw you into his bondage, enticing you to forget God's purpose for you by focusing your attention on what you don't have or what you can easily lose.

Friend, such jealousy is never worth the price it inflicts on you. Its continuous emphasis on what you lack only serves to discourage you, create strife with your loved ones, and cause conflict between you and God. There's never peace—only enslavement to something that will never truly satisfy. Jesus promises, "My peace I give to you; not as the world gives do I give to you. Do not let your heart be troubled, nor let it be fearful" (John 14:27). Christ's provision is different from the world's because whatever He gives you, no one can take away.

Do you believe that God is sovereign and always does what's best for you? Or have you created an idol out of your heart's desire and an enemy out of anyone who already possesses it? The Father has pledged to meet all your needs exceedingly, abundantly, and above all you could possibly ask or imagine (Ephesians 3:20). Therefore, stop focusing on what you don't have and begin to praise the Lord for all He's blessed you with. Trust that if there's something He hasn't given to you yet, His motivation for withholding it from you is love.

Lord, this envy within me is eating me alive. Please forgive me.
Set me free from this jealousy and renew my faith in Your provision.
Amen.

Strongholds of Pride

SCRIPTURE READING: PROVERBS 6

The Lord hates . . . haughty eyes.
PROVERBS 6:16–17

In what do you excel? What are the qualities in you that others are always praising? It seems counterintuitive, but your strongest characteristics can actually hinder you from following God the way you should. You begin to rely on your strengths because they feel "safe"—there's no faith involved in achieving your goals. You increasingly attribute your triumphs to your own ability and less to His grace. Soon enough, instead of looking to the Lord for wisdom and power, you're avoiding anything that requires the least bit of trust in Him.

Does this sound like you? Have you believed the hype about your own skills and fallen to pride, destroying your relationship with God? Understand, whatever success you can achieve on your own will be mediocre and unsatisfying compared to the awesome things that the Lord can do through you. That's why pride doesn't belong in your life. God despises it not only because it destroys your relationship with Him but also because it drives you away from all you could be.

In your prayer time today, agree with the Lord about any conceit that He reveals in you and repent of it. Be willing to submit yourself to God and attribute everything you have and all that you are to Him. Because when you do, you'll be well on your way to diffusing pride's hold and becoming all the Father created you to be. So don't wait, friend. The Lord hates pride, but He loves you. Invite Him back into your life as your strength and confidence.

Father, forgive me for the ways I've relied on myself rather than on You. I want to live a life of faith that glorifies You. Please purge me of pride and give me a humble heart so I may serve You well.
Amen.

Embracing the Word

SCRIPTURE READING: PROVERBS 7; ISAIAH 55:10–11; LUKE 1:37; 18:27

Bind them on your fingers;
write them on the tablet of your heart.
PROVERBS 7:3

The Father's promises are expressions of His love for you and anchors you can hold on to in times of storm. When everything else seems like it is falling apart, you can stand on what Scripture says because the Lord assures us, "As the rain and the snow come down from heaven, and do not return there without watering the earth and making it bear and sprout, and furnishing seed to the sower and bread to the eater; so will My word be which goes forth from My mouth; it will not return to Me empty, without accomplishing what I desire, and without succeeding in the matter for which I sent it" (Isaiah 55:10–11).

Nothing can impede the fulfillment of God's Word. Nothing. Why are the Lord's promises so unstoppable? Because His character is your guarantee that it will be done just as He says it will. The Lord is perfect, unchanging, truthful, wise, and all-powerful, so He can do exactly as He pleases. Nothing is impossible for Him (Luke 1:37; 18:27). There is no problem that the Lord can't solve and no question He can't answer. This makes every promise in Scripture sure, and if you use His Word as your compass, He'll show you how we should live.

Therefore, it doesn't matter how your situation looks today or how bad things get, because the reality is not in what you can see but in what the Lord has proclaimed. So dig in to His Word today and keep your heart open to what He desires to teach you. Surely, you will receive grace to help you in your time of need and an anchor to hold you steadfast no matter how difficult the storm.

Father, certainly, you are trustworthy, loving, and
true. Lead me to promises I can hold on to.
Amen.

Finding Life

SCRIPTURE READING: PROVERBS 8; PROVERBS
14:12; MATTHEW 16:25; JOHN 10:10

He who finds me finds life and obtains favor from the Lord.
PROVERBS 8:35

We all want life—true, abundant life that fills our soul with fulfill-ment, joy, and peace. However, when we try to pursue such a life in our own wisdom and strength, we often find disappointment. This is because our flesh—and therefore the way we go about things—is fallen and unable to achieve real vivacity (Proverbs 14:12). So how can we experience life? Only through the One who gives it abundantly (John 10:10).

Jesus said, "Whoever wishes to save his life will lose it; but whoever loses his life for My sake will find it" (Matthew 16:25). To have spiri-tual victory, we must submit ourselves to Christ and let go of the right to run our own lives. We don't have the power to be holy people in our own strength. But as we surrender to Jesus and live by faith, we will dis-cover the power to live the bold, confident, and joyful life God created us to enjoy.

So experience the wonderful life Christ has planned for you by yielding control Him. *First*, begin by confessing your inadequacy, ac-knowledging that you have tried to be a godly person but feel spiritually frustrated or defeated. *Second*, recognize that Jesus is God and will give you whatever you need to live the Christian life. *Third*, let go of your own efforts to "be good enough" or "do enough" to please Him by giv-ing Him permission to live His life through you. *Finally*, say out loud, "Jesus, please live through me. I yield myself to Your will." In this way, you will experience the extraordinary life He has for you.

Lord Jesus, I want the abundant life You offer. Live Your life
through me. I yield myself to You and praise Your holy name.
Amen.

A New Perspective

SCRIPTURE READING: PROVERBS 9; MATTHEW 10:38–39; MARK 10:45

Give instruction to a wise man and he will be still wiser,
teach a righteous man and he will increase his learning.
PROVERBS 9:9

Do you realize that accepting Jesus as your Savior has practical implications? It means that you've committed yourself to a new way of living—one of submitting to God, acknowledging His authority, and embracing His values? It means you've died to this world and are alive in Christ (Matthew 10:38–39). Of course, the things of the earth—money, prestige, authority, possessions—will always compete for your loyalty in a compelling manner. But when you belong to Jesus, you realize that those things are temporary and unworthy of your devotion.

It also means that the Lord's plans, not your own, dictate your life. Of course, you dream and have ambitions that He's planted and longs to see fulfilled in you. But you must always be willing to submit *all* your hopes to the will of God, understanding that what He desires for you is better than what you want for yourself. This is why Jesus must have the right to navigate your life according to His wisdom.

Finally, it means that you must always see yourself as a *servant*. Christ, Who is Lord, became a servant of all (Mark 10:45), and you are to reflect that—manifesting His heart of sacrificial and loving service.

Friend, you may be struggling today because you've lost things that were important to you, such as rights, wealth, prestige, dreams, or authority. Such losses hurt because earthly worth is often attached to them. Yet you now belong to Jesus—with eternal value and a new identity. Let go of those things and trust God. He always gives you far more than you can ever lose.

Father, I know what I feel is part of adjusting to the new life
You've given me. I die to these worldly things so I might
have the eternal blessings You've planned for me.
Amen.

The Security of Obedience

SCRIPTURE READING: PROVERBS 10; PHILIPPIANS 2:13

He who walks in integrity walks securely.
PROVERBS 10:9

Are your prayers filled with boldness and confidence? Or are they full of doubt and uncertainty? Often, we can become fearful in our conversations with God when we are unsure about how He sees us. We entertain thoughts or behaviors that we know aren't His will and begin to question whether He hears us. Faced with our qualms and even shame, we eventually fall silent—though He unfailingly continues to call out to us, inviting us into fellowship with Him.

As a believer, you are God's child forever—He will never reject you. His will is for you to have a healthy, vibrant relationship with Him that is secure and continually maturing. He wants you to grow in your intimacy with Him and progressively become more like Jesus in character, word, and deed. But distance and strain in your relationship with Him will occur when you walk away from Him through sin, self-will, and rebellion. Friend, don't do it. Don't allow sinful behaviors, addictions, or shame to mar your understanding of His salvation or stand in the way of your relationship with Him. Turn to your heavenly Father, who is eager and willing to forgive you. Repent of your sin. Then walk with Him in integrity and obedience.

Why? Because there is nothing so wonderful as being absolutely confident in your relationship with the Lord and certain He hears you. When your life is submitted to Him, you can be certain that "it is God who is at work in you, both to will and to work for His good pleasure" (Philippians 2:13). And that is a joy and security that nothing in this world can ever match.

Father, thank You for Your love and grace to me. I confess
and repent of my sins, knowing You are faithful to forgive me.
Thank You for loving me and always drawing me close.
Amen.

Eternal Fruit

SCRIPTURE READING: PROVERBS 11; JOHN 4:34–36; PHILIPPIANS 1:6

The fruit of the righteous is a tree of life,
and he who is wise wins souls.
PROVERBS 11:30

As believers, we serve the eternal God, so our lives can and should have an everlasting impact. We have the privilege of investing the time, talents, and skills the Lord has given us for the sake of His kingdom, knowing that whatever we accomplish in obedience to Him will endure forever.

I have seen an excellent example of this in the many Wycliffe Bible translators I've met throughout the years. Some of them spent decades in remote regions of the world—in dangerous and primitive conditions—translating God's Word for people who often did not even have a written language. By the world's standards, the translators did not achieve wealth, status, or power. But they produced fruit of infinitely greater value—leading souls into a growing relationship with Jesus Christ. There are people who have eternal life because those translators allowed God to work through them. There is no greater reward than that.

As Jesus said, "My food is to do the will of Him who sent Me and to accomplish His work . . . Behold, I say to you, lift up your eyes and look on the fields, that they are white for harvest. Already he who reaps is receiving wages and is gathering fruit for life eternal; so that he who sows and he who reaps may rejoice together" (John 4:34–36).

Friend, if you expend your energies pursuing earthly ambitions, they will pass away. But when you obey God, accomplishing His assignments for you, you are assured that they will continue to produce fruit and joy even when time is no more (Philippians 1:6). So today, don't waste your time. Work for fruit that will last.

Lord, I want my life to count for eternity. Show me how
and where to serve You. Make me a person who makes a
difference for Your kingdom and glorifies Your name.
Amen.

Don't Give Up

SCRIPTURE READING: PROVERBS 12; DEUTERONOMY 31:6;
EPHESIANS 3:20–21; HEBREWS 10:23

The precious possession of a man is diligence.
PROVERBS 12:27

Some days you may feel like the future ahead of you is so dark that there is just no reason to go on. Everything around you is crumbling—except, of course, the real obstacles on your path. Those problems remain before you like a barricade that will never be moved. But the things you counted on for strength—your support, resources, and even you sense of purpose—are dissipating before you and you're left feeling completely defeated.

But no matter what impediments there are to your future and heart's desire, do not give up hope. Remind yourself that no matter what's going on or what goes wrong, Almighty God is with you. He has great and wonderful plans for your life, more awesome than you could ever imagine (Ephesians 3:20–21).

Fulfilling His plans will mean going through times when you cannot see the road ahead and you'll be forced to rely on the only true source of strength and direction—God Himself. So if you choose to give up, you'll be giving up on the One who says, "The Lord your God is the one who goes with you. He will not fail you or forsake you" (Deuteronomy 31:6). And you certainly can't do that.

So don't give up! Depend on Him, make Him your delight, commit your way to Him, and rest in His loving care. And never forget to "hold fast the confession of [y]our hope without wavering, for He who promised is faithful" (Hebrews 10:23). Regardless of how long you must wait, keep trusting and obeying the Lord with diligence, perseverance, and confidence. The awareness of His presence will get you through trials that nothing else will. And if your dreams are from the Father, you can be certain He will bring them to pass.

Father, I won't give up, but diligently cling to You. Help me, Lord.
Amen.

Father Knows Best

SCRIPTURE READING: PROVERBS 13; ROMANS 12:1-2; 1 JOHN 3:2-3

The one who loves their children
is careful to discipline them.
PROVERBS 13:24

At times, we can put enormous pressure on ourselves to make great strides in the Christian life. But 1 John 3:2–3 explains, "Beloved, now we are children of God, and it has not appeared as yet what we will be. We know that when He appears, we will be like Him, because we will see Him just as He is. And everyone who has this hope fixed on Him purifies himself, just as He is pure."

In other words, we're not yet perfect like Jesus is, and we shouldn't expect to be. But as children of God, we don't train ourselves. The Father is the One in charge of our education and makes sure we stay on track. So what we must do is watch and obey the Father, trusting Him to provide what we need, keep us safe in the midst of trials, and lead us in the right way.

Our responsibility is to have our hope and our focus fixed on Christ; His is to purify us. So when we're centered on Jesus, He sanctifies us, instructs us, and empowers us to become everything He created us to be.

This truth takes the pressure off us and puts the responsibility on God, who is the only One who truly knows how to raise us up as His children. We read the Bible and pray not to impress Him or to earn His favor but out of love and gratefulness because we simply want to know Him. We look to the Father, learn from Him, and obey as He instructs, knowing He is faithful to transform us (Romans 12:1–2).

Father, thank You for raising me up as Your child.
I will keep my eyes on You, trusting that You are
faithful to teach me to walk in Your ways.
Amen.

A Godly Example

SCRIPTURE READING: PROVERBS 14; GALATIANS 6:7–8; 1 PETER 4:17

Righteousness exalts a nation.
PROVERBS 14:34

As this Proverb suggests, our choices have consequences that reach farther than we may ever expect. Because of the salvation we enjoy and the knowledge of God we have as Christians, we have a great responsibility—not just to our families but also to our fellow citizens and nation.

The apostle Paul wrote, "Do not be deceived, God is not mocked; for whatever a man sows, this he will also reap. For the one who sows to his own flesh will from the flesh reap corruption, but the one who sows to the Spirit will from the Spirit reap eternal life" (Galatians 6:7–8). This means that when we consider the immorality in our country, we must first look to the church and ask whether we have sown righteousness as we have been commanded. When we complain because of the lack of education in our nation, we must consider whether the Body of Christ has been consistent in teaching biblical truth and leading others into a growing relationship with Jesus Christ. And when we weep because God is no longer honored in our land, we must examine whether we've humbled ourselves before the Father as we should. Have we fallen to our knees in repentance and prayed for the lost souls of our fellow citizens?

Friend, we cannot allow sin to run rampant in our homes and churches and expect the rest of the country to grow in godliness. Life simply does not work that way. As we read in 1 Peter 4:17, "It is time for judgment to begin with the household of God." We must begin with our own hearts and church families. In order to change our country, we must pull up those roots of rebellion in our own backyard. We must be found faithful. The future of our country depends on it.

Lord, lead me in Your righteousness that I may
be Your light to my fellow citizens.
Amen.

Pray to Know Him

SCRIPTURE READING: PROVERBS 15; JAMES 4:8

The prayer of the upright is His delight.
PROVERBS 15:8

Do you realize the joy that you bring your heavenly Father when you approach His throne of grace to know Him? He loves it when you go before Him to fellowship, seek His help and guidance, and worship Him. Perhaps you've never really thought of prayer from His point of view. Maybe your conversations with the Father began as a bedtime routine when you were a child, or it could be you learned the Lord's Prayer in church. Throughout your life, pastors and Christian teachers have probably stressed the importance of praying to God. But did they also tell you how He longs to spend time with you as a good Father yearns to interact with His beloved child?

This is why it is so important to evaluate how you see prayer. Is it something you do hurriedly out of obligation, or do you truly enjoy conversing with the One who loves you unconditionally? Do you merely spit out requests to Him? Or do you experience the eternal presence of the living God, who created the heavens and the earth, who sees what you cannot, and who leads you perfectly?

Friend, "Draw near to God and He will draw near to you" (James 4:8). Seek the face of the loving God you serve and deepen your relationship with Him. Your time in His presence can purify your life, fill it with power, and give you joy unspeakable. So don't just go through the motions. Experience your Redeemer, King, Protector, and Provider fully. He will energize you, equip you to help others, give you peace, and direct you safely through the storms of life. And you, friend, will bring joy to your Savior's heart.

Father, I want to experience Your presence and know
You better. Speak to me, Lord. Reveal Yourself to
me and I will worship You wholeheartedly.
Amen.

Forgive Yourself

SCRIPTURE READING: PROVERBS 16; ROMANS 8:1

By lovingkindness and truth iniquity is atoned for,
and by the fear of the Lord one keeps away from evil.
PROVERBS 16:6

In this world, there is most likely no one who is so critical of you as you are of yourself. In fact, you have the potential to pick yourself apart with greater intensity and cruelty than anyone else ever could. No one else can torment you with negative thoughts every waking minute as you can. Perhaps they are thoughts about the Lord's punishment—you're positive He's just waiting to catch you messing up in order to discipline you. Or maybe they are thoughts that you are inherently damaged and will never experience real love because you've made far too many mistakes. Whatever they are, you cannot forgive yourself for who you are and what you've done. And because of this, you're missing the joy and abundant life God has for you.

Does this sound about right? Do you harbor unforgiveness toward yourself? Do you beat yourself up because of the emptiness you feel, because of unmet expectations, or because of how important relationships have failed? Friend, just as you don't have a right to keep grudges toward others, you certainly shouldn't tear yourself apart or permit yourself to act in a self-destructive manner. Romans 8:1 asserts, "There is now no condemnation for those who are in Christ Jesus." If Jesus is your Lord and Savior, you are forgiven eternally and loved unconditionally. Yes, you've made mistakes—all of us have. But Jesus understands your weaknesses and has mercy for you. He knows the pain, insecurities, and fears you face, and He wants to help you break free from them. Friend, you don't have to live under a terrible cloud of shame that suffocates your soul. Jesus forgives you. So forgive yourself and experience the liberty He died to give you.

Father, this is so difficult. Please help me to
forgive myself and experience Your freedom.
Amen.

Loving Your Friend

SCRIPTURE READING: PROVERBS 17

Whoever would foster love covers over an offense,
but whoever repeats the matter separates close friends.
PROVERBS 17:9 NIV

Whenever a friend wrongs you, it's normal to be consumed with thoughts of his or her faults and failings. It is human to want to vindicate yourself and to turn others against the person who caused you so much pain. That's the *usual* response. But like in everything else, God calls you to a different path as a believer.

You see, that person who harmed you may need your grace and good example. And deep friendships can develop only when both people in the relationship freely forgive. If you cannot look beyond your own emotions and needs to the wounds and feelings of others, you will not be able to build the deep, godly friendships you long for. However, the more you understand others and walk with them through their difficulties, the more profound you'll find your relationships to be.

That doesn't mean you allow people to walk all over you or take advantage of your goodness. Rather, it means you realize that we all make mistakes and hurt others inadvertently in the process. And forgiveness is the only way to bring genuine healing to a damaged relationship so that both people can move forward with freedom and strength.

Even when you're not the one at fault, forgiveness is always the right path and it's wise to say, "Please forgive me for what *I have done* to hurt our friendship. My relationship with you is very important to me, and I don't want anything to come between us. Let's talk about this." It's better to ask for forgiveness than to insist you're right and allow a friendship to be destroyed. Your relationship is worth fighting for. So forgive as Christ forgave you and reach out to your friend as He did for you.

Lord, help me to forgive. Lead me in how to reach
out so this relationship can be restored.
Amen.

Rooting Out Pride

SCRIPTURE READING: PROVERBS 18; 1 JOHN 2:15-17

Before destruction the heart of man is haughty,
but humility goes before honor.
PROVERBS 18:12

Is your life characterized by competition and contention with others? Do you care more about how other people see you than what God thinks about you? Have you grown stagnant in your relationship with Him? Are you tempted by sins that at one point would have disgusted you? Then you may be struggling with pride.

We know that pride:

- hinders our fellowship with God
- leads to broken relationships
- decreases our effectiveness
- sets the stage for conflicts and foolish mistakes
- shuts down the work of the Holy Spirit
- breeds prayerlessness
- causes us to emphasize self more than God

Have you experienced any of the issues listed above? Friend, if you're struggling with sin today, it is likely that pride is at the foundation of your troubles and you need to root it out. Therefore, prayerfully ask God for the strength and wisdom to obey Him even when everything within and around you fights against it (1 John 2:15–17).

Likewise, understand that as a child of God, you're not in a race to see who is the godliest or most influential Christian. When you're obeying Him, you'll work in harmony with other faithful Christians. There's no competition in that, only the outworking of a healthy, vibrant body, where everyone involved receives the prize of being able to worship holy God in heaven for all eternity.

Lord, I repent of the ways I've been competing with others
and causing conflicts. Please forgive me. Root out this pride
and help me to serve You in humility and love.
Amen.

A Character of Forgiveness

SCRIPTURE READING: PROVERBS 19; HEBREWS 12:14–15

A man's discretion makes him slow to anger,
and it is his glory to overlook a transgression.
PROVERBS 19:11

When talking about how Jesus saves us, one must mention His sacrifice on the cross for the *forgiveness* of our sins. Forgiveness is a central theme of the gospel and a core characteristic of our beloved Savior. In His mercy, He doesn't give us what we deserve: eternal punishment. In fact, in His grace, He gives us what we *don't* deserve: an everlasting relationship with Himself.

So if forgiveness is a predominant character trait of Christ, and we are to represent Him faithfully to the lost, then how can we justify being unforgiving? The truth is, our effectiveness for the Kingdom of God is seriously impeded whenever we hold on to hostility toward others. This is why Hebrews 12:14–15 admonishes, "Pursue peace with all men . . . See to it that no one comes short of the grace of God; that no root of bitterness springing up causes trouble, and by it many be defiled." The phrase "see to it" means that we are responsible "that no one comes short of the grace of God." That no one is hindered in his or her salvation by the presence of bitterness in our lives. That means that our standard in every situation is to show the grace and mercy of God—we forgive others when they wrong us just as Christ forgave us.

Therefore, friend, rid yourself of unforgiveness—let go of your feelings of resentment, lay down your "right" to get even, and allow God to deal with anyone who has hurt you. Choose forgiveness so you don't lead anyone away from the Lord or build a wall of regret between you and the Father. And always show His grace and mercy to others so you can truly be His representative in the world.

Lord Jesus, help me to reflect Your character—
always forgiving as You would.
Amen.

Without Compromise

SCRIPTURE READING: PROVERBS 20

*It is by his deeds that a lad distinguishes himself
if his conduct is pure and right.*
PROVERBS 20:11

What are you willing to compromise to feel accepted? Sometimes you may be tempted to yield a little in your beliefs or step over a line you shouldn't cross in order to gain someone's approval. The enemy will tell you, "No one will ever like you if you don't soften your stance. Don't be so narrow or rigid. Go with the flow so you can be successful and people will want to be your friend." He knows that if you capitulate in your convictions, your ability to lead others to Christ will be damaged and even destroyed. Such compromise is always deadly to a believer's testimony.

However, if you stand firm in your beliefs, people will not only respect you more, they'll also look to you when they need love and support. You see, as a believer, you're like an anchor in the storm, and when others are suffering, they'll be drawn to the stability and truth you offer. They don't want to talk to someone who wavers in his or her beliefs in order to be popular or who will tell them what they want to hear even if it's a lie. No, they want someone who knows God's Word and can lead them to the truth. That's why it's so important that you stay strong.

Therefore, stand for your convictions and rely upon God. Your persistent dedication to His Word is a testimony to those around you. When you don't compromise, people you would never expect will come to you for help in the midst of their storms. They'll see you conduct yourself in a godly manner and will know for certain that you have something valuable to offer them.

*Father, I want to remain steadfast in my convictions,
but sometimes the temptation to compromise is so
overwhelming. Help me to stay strong and glorify You.
Amen.*

Release It All

SCRIPTURE READING: PROVERBS 21; 2 KINGS 13:17–18

The righteous gives and does not hold back.
PROVERBS 21:26

When the formidable armies of Aram threatened to attack Israel, King Joash became fearful to the point of weeping. Without other recourse, he went to see the old prophet Elisha, who instructed him in how to proceed against such a mighty onslaught. Elisha told the king to shoot his arrows out of the eastern window, because, he proclaimed, "This is the Lord's arrow, an arrow of victory over Aram, for you will completely conquer the Arameans at Aphek . . . Now pick up the other arrows and strike them against the ground" (2 Kings 13:17–18 NLT). In other words, Joash was to shoot the arrows into the earth as a sign of his trust that God would win the battle for Israel.

Unfortunately, Joash shot only three of the arrows and held the rest back, demonstrating that he didn't really believe God had the situation under control. And because of his lack of faith, he failed to achieve a complete victory over Aram.

The same is often true for us. At times, we hold back the gifts and resources the Lord gives us to serve Him believing He will bless us anyway. We may do so out of laziness, fear, or even greed, but the result is the same—our partial obedience is actually disobedience, and God refuses to honor it.

Friend, everything you are and possess belongs to the Lord, and He expects you to use it exactly as He instructs. So honor Him with all you have and don't hold back regardless of how scary it is to let go. Because He will never ask you to sacrifice without giving you something even better in return.

Father, help me to express full faith in You by giving all You've
instructed me to give and obeying You completely. Thank You
for all that You've done and all that You're going to do.
Amen.

Finding Favor

SCRIPTURE READING: PROVERBS 21; GENESIS 6:9; PSALM 31:19; JAMES 1:17

Favor is better than silver and gold.
PROVERBS 22:1

People often work hard to earn the favor of employers, parents, or friends, believing their respect and approval are crucial to their happiness. But as believers, we are to strive after God's favor, which He freely offers. As David wrote, "How great is Your goodness, which You have stored up for those who fear You" (Psalm 31:19).

Unfortunately, in our cynical culture, we often take the Lord's kindness toward us for granted. Although He provides for needs, puts a limit on our seasons of suffering, listens to and answers our prayers, and bestows the desires of the heart, we still yearn for other people's admiration and applause. And we would willingly violate our relationship with Him in order to please them. Yet we should understand that every good thing that comes our way is from His hand (James 1:17). Nothing on earth can compare to the support, encouragement, and provision that He gives us.

Of course, as you consider this today, perhaps you feel as if God's favor is capricious, that He shows kindness to some and withholds it from others based on a whim. Although it may appear that way from your current perspective, the Lord is holy and just. He loves unconditionally and always acts in your best interest. Likewise, you will experience His favor in greater measure by always responding to Him in faith. For example, consider Noah, who "walked with God" (Genesis 6:9). Noah's willingness to keep a right relationship with the Lord resulted in his entire family being saved from the world-cleansing flood.

So don't rely on the approval of others. Discover God's favor toward you by feasting on His Word, learning His ways, and practicing His principles. You will certainly discover that His kindness is already flowing into every corner of your life.

Lord, thank You for Your favor. I praise You for all
the ways You shower kindness into my life.
Amen.

The Right Course

Keep your heart on the right course.
PROVERBS 23:19 NLT

If anyone understood adversity, it was David. After being anointed the next king of Israel, he was hunted for decades by jealous King Saul, experienced terrible battles and losses, and suffered heartbreak that would send the strongest soul reeling in despair. Yet through it all he wrote, "Preserve me, O God, for I take refuge in Thee" (Psalm 16:1). David's life gives repeated evidence that in the midst of trials and adversity, the best course of action is always to seek God more—not less.

Friend, like David, it is crucial for you to understand that life's circumstances are God's way of drawing you to Himself. Scripture often records David asking the Lord for meaning, encouragement, and the courage to go on. And David often strengthened himself by remembering the great things God had done in the past, calling to mind the goodness and lovingkindness of the Father's character, and repeating the Lord's promises.

Are you going through some dark time in your life right now where you seem to have lost your sense of direction? Does it feel like God is absent from the situation that plagues you? Do you feel like you're facing life's challenges all alone? Then open your Bible to the Psalms and meditate on David's expressions of deep confidence and trust in God, even when all hope seemed lost. The Lord kept every promise to David, and He will do so for you as well. Don't walk in uncertainty about tomorrow. Like David, place your hope and trust in the living God and say with assurance, "Because [You are] at my right hand, I will not be shaken . . . You will make known to me the path of life; in Your presence is fullness of joy" (Psalm 16:8, 11).

Father, I trust You. Preserve, protect, and guide me, for You are
my Savior, Refuge, and Life. I will praise You forevermore.
Amen.

Meaningful Help

SCRIPTURE READING: PROVERBS 24; JAMES 5:16

When I saw, I reflected upon it;
I looked, and received instruction.
PROVERBS 24:32

Have you ever sensed a deep a burden for another person? Perhaps there is someone in your life who desperately needs to accept Christ as Savior. Or maybe there are people you know who are in deep pain and need the Father's loving comfort and instruction. They want to break free from the bondage they're in but either don't realize how to or are afraid to step out in faith. What can you do?

There may even be a young man or woman in your circle of influence who is obviously called into the ministry, set apart to serve the Father. Ahead of that person is life at its best, building the Kingdom of God. But you understand that the future will also hold challenges—trials that will stretch his or her confidence in the Lord and break any self-will. How can you encourage this person?

You may feel powerless to help in a meaningful way, but there is always something very significant you can do—and that's to intercede. James 5:16 instructs, "Pray for one another . . . the effective prayer of a righteous man can accomplish much." Not only do you fight the battle for him or her on your knees, but as you do, the Lord will also show you the best way to offer help and encouragement.

Friend, no Christian has ever been called to "go it alone" in his or her walk of faith. We need one another to grow in our relationships with God. The Lord asks us to intercede for others in order to help us move beyond our own concerns to the spiritual, physical, emotional, and relational needs of others. This is not just for their benefit but so we can grow in His likeness as well.

Father, make me an intercessor. Reveal others who need
my prayer and show me how to encourage them.
Amen.

Brokenness

SCRIPTURE READING: PROVERBS 25; 1 SAMUEL 30

Remove the dross from the silver,
and a silversmith can produce a vessel.
PROVERBS 25:4 NIV

No one would have blamed David for despairing. Everything was going wrong: He'd been unfairly targeted by King Saul and driven from his homeland of Israel. So David settled in Ziklag with the hope of finding some peace. Sadly, while David and his fellow warriors were away, the Amalekites raided Ziklag, burned everything down, and captured their wives and children. The men were so devastated that they sought to kill David. So in the midst of his heartbreak over his family, David had to deal with the pain of betrayal and the fear of losing his life.

David's experience at Ziklag was one of the lowest points in his long ordeal of running from Saul. And perhaps you can relate to the discouragement he felt. After all, losses, defeats, and disappointments are universal—everyone experiences them at one point or another. But why? Why would God allow His chosen servant David and His beloved child—you—to experience such profound heartbreak?

In this we see one of the most vital principles of the Christian life: Whenever God chooses to work through someone, he or she will go through the process of brokenness in order to be molded for His purposes. The Father uses the seemingly disastrous events of life to make you aware of your inadequacy and to help you depend upon Him completely. You see this process borne out in the lives of the great biblical saints and believers throughout history. Through brokenness they learned the secret of relying upon Almighty God. That is what He taught David and what He is demonstrating to you as well. So do not despair. Like David, strengthen yourself in the Lord and trust that what you're experiencing will ultimately work for your good (Romans 8:28).

Father, I trust You to mold me for Your purposes.
Strengthen me that my life may glorify You.
Amen.

What's Really Going On

SCRIPTURE READING: PROVERBS 26; MALACHI 3:18

Pretty words may hide a wicked heart, just as a
pretty glaze covers a common clay pot.
PROVERBS 26:23 TLB

The world says that wisdom is based upon what we can perceive with our natural senses. If a person looks and sounds right, then he or she must be a good person. However, God's wisdom calls for us to walk with discernment through the power of the Holy Spirit, who is not at all limited by our human senses. He gives us the ability to watch the fruit of that person's life and tell whether or not the individual is being directed by the Father or by the unseen wicked desires within his or her heart. As Malachi 3:18 says, "You will . . . distinguish between the righteous and the wicked, between one who serves God and one who does not serve Him."

In other words, the person who functions in godly wisdom is able to discern truth beyond what the average human being can, which flows directly from the Holy Spirit at work in us. He guards and guides us in supernatural ways so we can walk in God's will and avoid evil. What a privilege!

So how can you ensure that you are walking in godly wisdom and operating with spiritual discernment? As with every other blessing in the Christian life, it is by maintaining a close relationship with God. The more time you spend in prayer, study, and meditation, the easier it will be for you to distinguish the message of the Holy Spirit from the chaos of the world around you. So listen to the Lord. He will always show you what's really going on if you're willing to pay attention.

Father, I need Your help because I often end up trusting the
wrong people. Tune my ears to hear You and my heart to obey
You. Give me spiritual discernment so I can serve You well.
Amen.

Passing the Test of Praise

SCRIPTURE READING: PROVERBS 27; MATTHEW 5:16; HEBREWS 3:13

Fire tests the purity of silver and gold,
but a person is tested by being praised.
PROVERBS 27:21 NLT

It is so nice to hear people say good things about us. After all, who doesn't enjoy a complimentary word spoken in love? A kind comment can be uplifting and inspirational. So what, then, could ever be bad about receiving praise?

The problem, of course, comes when we either become too dependent on other people's approval or start believing that we're the source of our success. Because then we begin catering to others or focusing on our own virtues, rather than obeying the One who truly deserves all the honor and praise. We know there's a problem when the "right people" don't say something positive to us and we have a meltdown because of it. Our eyes are off God, who is the only One who makes us truly worthy. So to prevent us from becoming prideful or enslaved to approval, the Bible gives us guidelines for gracefully accepting accolades.

First, avoid self-praise. Proverbs 27:2 says, "Let another praise you, and not your own mouth." In other words, stay humble. Don't look for reasons to exalt yourself. *Second*, give credit to God. Receiving positive compliments can be a wonderful opportunity to recognize what the Father has done in your life. As Jesus taught in Matthew 5:16, "Let your light shine before men in such a way that they may see your good works, and glorify your Father who is in heaven." *Third*, respond from your heart. Tell the person who encouraged you what he or she means to you, and take the occasion to strengthen your bond of friendship (Hebrews 3:13). *Finally*, thank God in prayer. Always remember that what is praiseworthy in you is how He is shining through you.

Father, I want to pass the test and give You the glory.
Help me to honor You regardless of what anyone says.
Amen.

Blessed by God's Wisdom

SCRIPTURE READING: PROVERBS 28; ROMANS 10:11

Blessed is the one who always trembles before God.
PROVERBS 28:14 NIV

What a wonderful thing to have a relationship with the living God. Even at this moment, He knows what you are feeling and thinking, who you are, and how you function. He knows your likes, dislikes, dreams, desires, fears, and hurts. He knows what brings you true joy, peace, and fulfillment. As your Maker, He knows everything about your life and how to make it the very best life possible. Not only that, your heavenly Father also knows every detail about every circumstance you encounter. He sees the beginning and the ending, and every step you take in between.

As you sit and consider the decisions before you today, you may be at odds about which way to turn because your earthly wisdom is limited. You may be thinking, *How have men and women have responded to these stressors before? What works?* You search the Internet, read books, and consult friends, but no answer seems quite right.

Yet you do not have to despair, because God's unlimited, perfect wisdom is available to you. Not only does He have your past in view—and therefore understands how you function—but He also sees your whole future stretched out and realizes how to get you where you were created to go.

Therefore, today, instead of wrangling with your limited wisdom, seek your heavenly Father's perspective. Ask, "Father, what do You want me to do?" and obey Him as the great and wonderful God He is. Respect His wisdom, acknowledge His sovereignty, and be humble before your Lord, your Savior, and your King. He knows what's best for you and will never lead you astray. As Romans 10:11 promises, "Whoever believes in Him will not be disappointed."

Father, I tremble before You in awe and worship.
What do You want me to do? Give me Your wisdom
so I can walk in Your ways. You are my hope. I will obey You.
Amen.

Humbly Hear Him

SCRIPTURE READING: PROVERBS 29; 1 CHRONICLES 28:9

A man's pride will bring him low,
but a humble spirit will obtain honor.
PROVERBS 29:23

If you are reading Scripture and praying but having difficulty hearing God, something in your life may be preventing you from interacting with Him. It's easy to become discouraged, but don't lose heart. Rest assured that your heavenly Father has the power and wisdom to root out whatever is impeding your relationship with Him. Ask God to examine your heart and see if any of the following issues are thwarting you from enjoying meaningful fellowship with Him.

- Am I intentional and expectant when I engage in a conversation with the Father?
- Do I feel unworthy or undeserving of the Lord's guidance or grace? Do I doubt the Father's character or what He has promised?
- Is there any sin in my life that I must confess or person I should forgive?
- Am I afraid of God's will, thinking it may hurt me or those I love?
- Is there anything I am refusing to give up in obedience to the Father?

As you pray, if anything stands out or if you feel convicted about a particular issue, stop right there. In humility, ask God to heal you and show you what to do. He may direct you to talk to a person, to a passage of Scripture, or to repent of a behavior that has impeded your relationship with Him. Regardless of what He shows you, agree with Him and obey immediately. There is no greater reward than unhindered fellowship with the Father.

Lord, I want to hear You. Don't allow any prideful
strongholds to remain. I humbly submit my life to You.
You are my God and deserve my obedience.
Amen.

As the Eagle

SCRIPTURE READING: PROVERBS 30; ISAIAH 40:31

The way of an eagle in the sky.
PROVERBS 30:19

Isaiah 40:31 tells us, "Those who wait for the Lord will gain new strength; they will mount up with wings like eagles, they will run and not get tired, they will walk and not become weary." Isaiah could not have chosen anything more appropriate to express the profound promise of waiting on God. Why? Because eagles rarely bat their wings when they are airborne. If they did so, they would tire quickly and wouldn't be able to travel very far. So instead they wait, find the right air current to support them, and move effortlessly through the sky by the force of the wind stream that carries them.

What a beautiful application of the Christian life. The wind current that can carries us through every trial and time of delay is our trust in God. When we strive, struggle, and impulsively attempt to achieve our goals without Him, we grow tired—weary of life and hopeless to the depths of our soul. Perhaps you've experienced this feeling of utter exhaustion, the intense realization that life cannot continue on as is. It leads to a discouragement and despair that are so difficult to overcome.

But this is the promise our heavenly Father has given us: When we wait upon Him, He will renew our strength by becoming the powerful force beneath our wings—lifting us to new heights, supporting us in the journey, and taking us to our desired haven. So wait on Him. See the wonderful plans God has for you come to fruition by waiting for the mighty wind of His Spirit to support and empower you. Because when you do, He will certainly carry you to the right destination in a way that won't make you weary but instead will give you energy and joy.

Father, I will wait on You. Thank You for renewing
my strength and taking me to new heights
through the mighty power of Your Spirit.
Amen.

Godly Portions

SCRIPTURE READING: PROVERBS 31; JOHN 12:32

She rises also while it is still night and
gives . . . portions to her maidens.
PROVERBS 31:15

Do you realize that you can make an extraordinary difference for the Kingdom of God right where you are? You don't need special training to serve God—you can have a tremendous influence on others just by how you live in obedience to Him. As a faithful believer, you have an awesome opportunity to share the powerful ways the Lord works in your life and answers your requests with those around you. All He wants is that you allow the Holy Spirit to work through you, showing His unconditional love to those you know.

This is what the godly woman of Proverbs 31 did. Verse 15 above says that she gives portions to her servant girls. Some translate the word *portions* to mean food or tasks. But the Hebrew word, *chôq*, can also mean "laws, decrees, or customs." In other words, the woman is providing godly leadership and instruction to those under her care.

The same should be true for you. God calls you to honor Him and submit to His commands so others will be drawn to Him through you (John 12:32). So how do you do this effectively? *First*, be willing to invest time with those in need. *Second*, when you talk to others, listen to them carefully, with an open, compassionate heart. *Third*, love others unconditionally. *Fourth*, help those around you to understand that their most important relationship is the one they have with Jesus. *Finally*, inspire others to be all they can be, helping them to recognize the Lord's plan for their lives. Because when you do these things, people will observe your faithfulness and be motivated to follow the Father in obedience. And that, friend, is the ultimate goal.

Father, help me to be a vessel of Your wisdom, power, and
faithfulness to those around me. Work through me to show Your
unconditional love so others may follow You in obedience.
Amen.

AUGUST

Communication

The greatest evidence of whether or not you have wisdom will always come through the words of your mouth. In fact, what you communicate is a barometer for the true condition of your spirit. That is why it is so important to guard what you say and ensure that what's feeding your spirit is worthy of the God you serve.

AUGUST 1

Earthly or Divine?

SCRIPTURE READING: PROVERBS 1

Wisdom calls aloud outside; she raises her voice in the open squares.
PROVERBS 1:20 NKJV

Each day you are confronted with decisions that will require wisdom. So how can you discern if a choice you're making or what you're communicating is rooted in earthly or divine wisdom? Consider what the outcome would be. Earthly wisdom is limited by our human understanding. It is "doing what comes naturally," which means doing what satisfies our senses and feeds our pride. Earthly wisdom cannot rise above our fallen nature. Therefore, decisions rooted in earthly wisdom will generally result in poor communication, people being at odds with one another, confusion, and all forms of evil behavior.

But divine wisdom is doing what the Holy Spirit compels us to do. It results in what is pleasing to God and, ultimately, what is eternally beneficial to us. When we allow the Lord to lead us, our abilities to communicate, understand, create, and manage life's resources are powerfully enhanced. Therefore, godly wisdom is marked by these attributes:

- *Purity*—producing Christ-centered, holy behavior
- *Peace*—encouraging unity, not estrangement
- *Servanthood*—helping others rather than one's self-interest
- *Justice*—truth without partiality or prejudice
- *Integrity*—consistency, honesty, and transparency
- *Confidence*—because of God's power at work in us

Divine wisdom will always call you rise above your own nature and function according to the indwelling presence and power of the Holy Spirit in order to produce God-sized results. So when you're making decisions, don't be afraid of what He's calling you to do. Submit yourself as a vessel the Father can use to bless others and be confident that He is leading you in the best way possible.

Lord, help me to speak and make decisions with Your godly wisdom.
Amen.

Speak Faith

SCRIPTURE READING: PROVERBS 2; ROMANS 15:4; ROMANS 10:17

Discretion will preserve you; understanding will keep you.
PROVERBS 2:11 NKJV

When circumstances appear to take an unexpected, negative turn, sometimes our faith can waver. We wonder how we will ever endure the tragedy or injustice unfolding before us. However, adversity should never be the end of our faith—it should be the spark that ignites it. No matter how our world is shaken, a strong trust in God will enable us to endure life's toughest hardships.

But what should you do when you discern that your circumstances are indeed rattling your confidence in your Creator? How do you regain your footing? Make the decision to believe that God is trustworthy and speak it out. The Lord always keeps His promises, so quote them often. He desires the best for your life, so give Him thanks for guiding you perfectly. Even when He says no to important requests and leads you down unexpected and difficult paths, praise Him for having wisdom above your own. Undoubtedly, He knows the way to produce the most spiritual fruit, the strongest character, and the greatest faith in you.

In other words, friend, refuse to doubt God—especially in what you say. As Romans 10:17 reminds us, "Faith comes from hearing, and hearing by the word of Christ." Remember that when you look at your circumstances through your limited, worldly eyes, they'll always seem overwhelming. But when you see them from God's perspective, you will always receive His peace and rest. So read His Word aloud and recall how He has blessed believers in similar circumstances throughout the ages (Romans 15:4). Because what you speak in faith will certainly return to you in blessing.

Lord, I confess that I sometimes talk myself out of trusting You.
Help me speak the words of faith that will preserve my soul.
Amen.

Be Kind Anyway

SCRIPTURE READING: PROVERBS 3; LUKE 10:16; 23:34; ROMANS 12:18

*Do not let kindness and truth leave you; bind them around
your neck, write them on the tablet of your heart. So you will
find favor and good repute in the sight of God and man.*
PROVERBS 3:3–4

Have you ever encountered a person who would not allow you to be kind to him or her? Despite your loving comments or gestures, perhaps the person insulted you or accused you of having some ulterior motive. How should Christians respond to those who will not accept another's attempts at friendship?

While the New Testament contains several passages instructing believers to practice kindness, it does so with the understanding that some people will resist you. After all, they rejected Jesus, the most kind-hearted and compassionate Person who ever lived (Luke 10:16). This is why Paul writes, "If possible, so far as it depends on you, be at peace with all men" (Romans 12:18). Did you notice his two qualifications? First he says, "If possible." This indicates that there are times when a relationship with another person simply will not be feasible. Second is "so far as it depends on you." This means that you should go only as far as your God-given principles permit. When someone demands that you transgress the Lord's commands in order to have a relationship with him or her, then you are released from responsibility toward that person.

Even though there may be occasions when a relationship with another person is impossible, we never have the right to be cruel. We still have a duty to be kind and truthful regardless of what is done to us or how we're rejected (Luke 23:34). Why? Because our ultimate responsibility is to honor God, and there are always others judging Him by how we respond.

*Father, I want to represent You well. Help me to be kind even when
I am rejected so that others may see Your compassion and love in action.
Amen.*

Tell Yourself the Truth

Put devious speech far from you.
PROVERBS 4:24

Do you realize that at times you lie to yourself? If you genuinely believe that God desires to bless you, that He approves of you through Christ, and that He loves you unconditionally, then you must ask yourself, "On what is my poor self-image based?" If you're honest with yourself, you'll see that you've believed the deceitful things that the enemy or other people have told you.

Friend, the devil will attempt to deceive you, telling you that God doesn't love you, you're still in bondage to sin, or that you aren't worthy of the Father's blessings. Other people lie to you as well, telling you that you'll never accomplish anything or that no one could ever love or respect you. Likewise, the world will tell you that unless you look and dress a certain way, are wealthy, or achieve certain levels of success and notoriety, you will forever be a second-class citizen. For your own good, do not buy into these destructive lies.

Understand that God's Word is the only accurate witness of your worth—and Christ is the only One who has the right to judge you. So in order to break free of those destructive beliefs, you must acknowledge that what He says about you in Scripture is true and anything beyond that is false. So friend, believe it! You are loved eternally and unconditionally by Almighty God. He approves of you because you've been saved by the blood of Jesus and filled with His Spirit. He has incredible plans for your life, will empower you to achieve them, and will certainly keep all of His promises to you. Therefore, hold on to what He tells you because it is the truth, and the truth will make you free indeed (John 8:32).

Father, please reveal the lies I've believed and replace them
with Your truth so that my life can bring You honor and praise.
Amen.

Active Listening

SCRIPTURE READING: PROVERBS 5; JAMES 1:22

*Turn your ear to my words of insight, that you may
maintain discretion and your lips may preserve knowledge.*
PROVERBS 5:1–2 NIV

Can you identify God's voice? When the Lord speaks to you, do you realize it is Him speaking? Are you motivated to follow when He summons you? Listening to God is essential if you want to walk with Him and understand His specific plans for your life. That is why it is so important for you to learn to hear the Father. Once you do, you can have a truly fulfilling and intimate relationship with Him.

Perhaps the most crucial step in doing so, of course, is becoming an active, attentive, and purposeful listener. If you anticipate that the Father will speak through a preacher or teacher, you will always receive something from their messages, because you're focused on the Lord and paying attention to what He is communicating to you. But what is crucial for you to understand is that God is *constantly* teaching you, patiently demonstrating His love and wisdom to you through every event and detail of your life. Your challenge is to *expect* Him to reveal Himself with an open and willing heart, regardless of what you're facing, and *intentionally apply* what He says (James 1:22).

Friend, if you can make this shift in the way you listen to God, it will radically transform your relationships with Him. The Father speaks to you through *every* situation, but hearing Him is dependent upon your anticipating and paying attention to His instruction. So be of this mind-set: *The Lord has something to say to me, and I'm not going to miss it!* Regardless of the circumstances you experience, you'll know God is teaching you something that will enable you to walk in the wonderful paths He has for your life and experience the best He has to offer.

*Father, open my ears to hear Your voice. Help me to walk in
Your ways and never miss anything You are showing me.
Amen.*

Guard Your Words

SCRIPTURE READING: PROVERBS 6; PSALM 19:14; EPHESIANS 4:29

If you have been snared with the words of your mouth . . .
PROVERBS 6:2

Do you realize how powerful words can be? Have you experienced how profoundly they can affect your life, how you see yourself, and how others view you? Perhaps you've been blessed by a loved one's expressions of care and comfort. His or her words were positive and fruitful in your life, helping you through some of your most difficult days. Or maybe you've seen how extremely destructive people's remarks can be. Their declarations tore at your heart so deeply that you've never fully recovered from them.

This is why it is always so important to guard what you say, making sure that what you're expressing honors God. Words can tear people down in ways that defy imagination. Even those spoken in haste can unintentionally hurt them deeply, injuring them in ways that affect them for years. Because of this, we must realize we cannot carelessly say whatever we wish and expect a quick apology to heal all wounds.

This is why the apostle Paul instructs, "Let no unwholesome word proceed from your mouth, but only such a word as is good for edification according to the need of the moment, so that it will give grace to those who hear" (Ephesians 4:29). This means that we should avoid cursing, yes, but also that what we express should intentionally bless and edify others in a manner that glorifies the Lord. So watch what you say. If you have been cruel—either deliberately or inadvertently—ask for forgiveness. And like the psalmist, always pray, "Let the words of my mouth and the meditation of my heart be acceptable in Your sight, O LORD, my rock and my Redeemer" (Psalm 19:14).

Lord, how difficult it is to control my tongue. Put a
guard on my mouth so that everything I say will be
seasoned with grace and draw others closer to You.
Amen.

Fighting Our Seductive Thoughts

SCRIPTURE READING: PROVERBS 7; 2 CORINTHIANS 10:5

With her flattering lips she seduces him.
PROVERBS 7:21

We're all enticed to sin at some point, no matter how many years we've been walking with God or how committed we are to Him. But it is important for us to realize that the process of temptation starts with what we think about. We fantasize about the object of our desires— how it would feel to possess it and how unhappy we would be without it. As time goes on, the pressure builds. We come to the point where we must make a choice: Will we turn away from the temptation, or will we give in to it and the temporary pleasure it promises and face the consequences? Once we consent, sin takes hold.

Of course, when you are a believer, the Holy Spirit will help you turn away from the enticement during any step in this process. But be warned—it becomes increasingly difficult the farther you go. This is why it is so incredibly important that you take "every thought captive to the obedience of Christ" (2 Corinthians 10:5) as soon as possible. Because where your mind wanders, your feet are sure to follow. You need to respond wisely by guarding your thoughts.

So consider: Is there something in your life today that is tempting you to lose faith in the Father, stray from His will, or go beyond the boundaries He's set for you in His Word? You can overcome the temptation through Jesus Christ. Meditating on God's Word and spending time with Him will empower you to remain steadfast in your struggle against sin. So defend yourself by setting your mind on the things that honor the Father. Honor Him and trust Him to deliver you. You certainly will not be disappointed.

Lord, You know the temptations I face. I can fight
them only in Your strength. Help me to overcome
them by giving me promises in Your Word and by
empowering me through Your Holy Spirit.
Amen.

Speak the Noble Word

SCRIPTURE READING: PROVERBS 8; PSALM 19:7;
ROMANS 12:2; 2 TIMOTHY 4:2; HEBREWS 4:12

I will speak noble things; and the opening of
my lips will reveal right things.
PROVERBS 8:6

Second Timothy 4:2 (NLT) instructs, "Preach the word of God . . . Patiently correct, rebuke, and encourage your people with good teaching." This is because what we have in God's Word are the very thoughts of the Lord Himself. Scripture is the main way we know the Father and the agent the Holy Spirit works through to conform us to His character, transform us into His likeness, and renew our minds, so that we "may prove what the will of God is, that which is good and acceptable and perfect" (Romans 12:2).

Hebrews 4:12 tells us, "The word of God is living and active and sharper than any two-edged sword, and piercing as far as the division of soul and spirit, of both joints and marrow, and able to judge the thoughts and intentions of the heart." In other words, through Scripture, the Holy Spirit speaks to the deepest parts of our soul—healing our wounds, convicting us of sin, encouraging us, and revealing truth to us that we could not know otherwise. This is the inherent power of God's Word. Through it, the Lord moves us to change beyond our own ability to do so. And it doesn't matter who we are, where we come from, or how we grew up, because the Holy Spirit Himself explains it to us in a way we can understand (Psalm 19:7).

There is nothing in this world more noble or worthy of our conversation than the Bible because of Who it reveals to us. So speak out the wonderful Word of God. By doing so you'll spur others to love Him more and follow Him in obedience.

Lord, teach me to lead others to You through
Your Word. Hide Scripture in my heart so I may
always cling to You and walk in Your ways.
Amen.

AUGUST 9

Wisdom and Folly

SCRIPTURE READING: PROVERBS 9; 2 PETER 2:1–2

"Whoever is naive, let him turn in here!"
PROVERBS 9:4

It's interesting that in Proverbs 9, both Wisdom and Folly call out the same thing: "Whoever is naive, let him turn in here!" Wisdom, of course, does so in order to instruct the individual to follow God. Few things have as great an impact on our Christian lives as sitting under the guidance of wise, Spirit-led teachers of Scripture. Through the power of the Holy Spirit, they inspire us to greater heights in our relationship with Jesus and help us break free from our bondage to unhealthy behaviors and beliefs.

However, if we place our confidence in instructors rather than the Word, we can be easily led astray by wrong doctrine. This is when Folly takes hold. Second Peter 2:1–2 warns: "There will be false teachers among you. They will cleverly teach destructive heresies and even deny the Master who bought them . . . Many will follow their evil teaching and shameful immorality. And because of these teachers, the way of truth will be slandered."

So how can you know if a message is wisdom or folly? The only sure way to protect yourself is to measure it against Scripture itself. Does the message come from the Word? Does the teacher's interpretation fit within the greater context of Scripture? If a teaching requires you to disregard any other part of Scripture, you can be sure that the message is not true to the whole, inerrant Word of God.

So be on the alert. Thank God for the many gifted men and women in your life whom you can trust for genuine teaching, and ask His help in identifying any false teachers who compete for your attention.

*Father, thank You for protecting my mind and heart from
false doctrine. Help me to measure all I hear against
Scripture so I can be wise and follow You in obedience.
Amen.*

A Wise Outlet

SCRIPTURE READING: PROVERBS 10

When there are many words, transgression is unavoidable,
but he who restrains his lips is wise.
PROVERBS 10:19

A truly distressing development we've seen in this day of social media is that people often feel free to express everything they feel all of the time with barely any filter. This, of course, is never wise. Individuals vent their emotions without any discipline or discretion—and they do so without realizing how they are impacting their families, jobs, and lives by doing so. Instead of alleviating the suffering they feel, doing so actually serves to deepen and intensify their problems, anger, and anxiety.

This is not to say we don't need an outlet for our feelings. We absolutely do. We all benefit from loving, godly people who will listen to us and give us wise counsel. But even our closest, most devoted friends do not want to know all the complaints we have every time we have them. They could not bear that, and we should not ask them to.

Instead, if you would like a truly safe and restorative place to express your emotions, there is only One who offers that—and that is the Father. He is the only One whom we can safely bring our hearts to 100 percent of the time.

So what should you do when you feel the need to vent? Go to your bedroom, your prayer closet, or wherever you can have some time alone. It is best if no one will interrupt you. Get on your knees, open the Word of God, and tell the Lord whatever you're feeling. Be honest—He will not get mad at you. In fact, He already knows what you are thinking and what's plaguing you. Not only is He always willing to listen, but He'll also gives you the help you actually need.

Father, thank You for listening to me.
My heart and my words are safe with You.
Lead me to communicate in a godly way wherever I am.
Amen.

Encourage Others

SCRIPTURE READING: PROVERBS 11; ISAIAH 35:3–4; HEBREWS 3:13

Whoever refreshes others will be refreshed.
PROVERBS 11:25

What would it mean for someone to encourage you? Can you recall an instance when someone helped you find the courage to go on or lifted your spirits? Sometimes it takes only a kind word or a smile to make a difference in the life of someone who is having a difficult time. It can strengthen a person to feel loved in low moments when he or she cannot see the way ahead clearly or cannot discern the Father's plan. This is why Isaiah 35:3–4 admonishes, "Encourage the exhausted, and strengthen the feeble. Say to those with anxious heart, 'Take courage, fear not. Behold, your God will come . . . He will save you.'"

Encouragement is the wonderful, God-given responsibility of everyone who belongs to Jesus—and it is absolutely indispensable to the Body of Christ. Why? Because when we remind each other of the Father's promises and faithfulness, it safeguards us against sin and unbelief (Hebrews 3:13).

Friend, there is no such thing as a person who doesn't need encouragement. This is why Paul instructed, "Encourage one another and build up one another, just as you also are doing . . . Admonish the unruly, encourage the fainthearted, help the weak, be patient with everyone" (1 Thessalonians 5:11, 14). So today, seek out those who need a kind word or your helping hand. Refresh their spirits with a testimony of the Lord's goodness and provision. Express your confidence of God's plan for their lives. Or simply love them by praying with them. Because by seeking ways to encourage those with whom you interact, you edify your loved ones, strengthen your relationships, and honor the Lord. And that will certainly result in blessings for you in return.

Father, please show me whom it is You wish me to encourage today.
Fill my mouth with words of Your lovingkindness and faithfulness
so that they will be strengthened and You glorified.
Amen.

A Goal of Healing

SCRIPTURE READING: PROVERBS 12; MARK 2:17

The tongue of the wise brings healing.
PROVERBS 12:18

With every person you talk to, you have decisions to make. Will you attempt to win them to your point of view and interests, or will you seek to help them? Will you try to get them to like you, or will you lead them to God?

In Mark 2:17, the Lord Jesus revealed His mission. He said, "It is not those who are healthy who need a physician, but those who are sick; I did not come to call the righteous, but sinners." In other words, He did not come for the purpose of rallying people to Himself so He could establish an earthly kingdom. He came to heal humanity's most devastating infirmity—sin. Likewise, the people Jesus met were in need of much more than a physical touch. They needed a Savior. And once they were set free, Jesus commissioned them to go and share what God had done for them. The woman caught in adultery told of God's forgiveness. The demon-possessed man testified about Christ's deliverance. Mary bore witness of the Savior's unconditional love. Matthew shared how he had been freed from greed. And Peter spoke of God's restoration.

This is how the gospel spread, by the testimony of those Jesus touched and healed. It is also how God equips us for service. Friend, you have been freed from sin and you have an incredible opportunity to share the hope of Jesus Christ with others. Your life is a living testimony of the healing power of the Savior. So ask Him to show you how you can best proclaim His victorious truth, and be sure to share it with someone today.

Lord Jesus, I want to be a person who speaks healing to others.
It is not about drawing them to myself but leading them to You.
Help me to testify about You so others may find freedom.
Amen.

The Significance of Silence

SCRIPTURE READING: PROVERBS 13; 1 KINGS 19

He who regards reproof will be honored.
PROVERBS 13:18

There are times when we get so caught up in our own activities, needs, and relationships that we fail to focus on the Father or spend time with Him. We pursue our goals in our own strength, becoming so busy that we don't even think about Him. At other times, He's not saying what we want to hear, so we shut Him out of our lives. In such instances, God will sometimes use the silence to get our attention.

Although the prophet Elijah was a godly man who loved and served God faithfully, there was a point in his ministry when he took his eyes off the Lord and fixed them on his circumstances. The wicked Queen Jezebel threatened to execute him, which terrified him (1 Kings 19). So Elijah fled far as from her reach as possible. Exhausted and wanting to die, the prophet was obviously focused on Jezebel's threats. So the Father took profound steps to readjust his mind. God sent a destructive wind, earthquake, and fire, but He remained silent through them. The Lord did not speak until Elijah was focused enough to hear Him in the sound of a gently blowing whisper.

God had to remind Elijah that if He could rend the mountains, He could surely take care of that wicked queen. That Elijah had nothing to fear as long as he trusted the Lord. The same is true for you. Whenever you get your focus off the Father, He may send some powerful, earthshaking silences to challenge your perspective. So if the Lord grows quiet, there's probably something He desires to teach you, and He wants your full attention. Don't let your soul get starved for His presence. Be wise—listen to Him.

Father, I want to hear You and obey. Speak to me, Lord, Your servant is listening. I know You can overcome any challenge I face.
Amen.

Revealing Your Hidden Pain

SCRIPTURE READING: PROVERBS 14; PSALM 139:1–3

Even in laughter the heart may be in pain.
PROVERBS 14:13

Some people mask their feelings of pain with jokes. Perhaps you are one of them. It may be that you either don't want to share your emotions with others because of how overwhelming they are or you cannot because you hold a position that requires a certain level of secrecy. It may be that you believe that emotions are your enemies—to reveal what you're feeling is to give power to others. It's even possible that you don't know how to communicate your sentiments in a healthy manner, so you're often tempted to vent your frustrations in covert or detrimental ways.

Whatever the case, you keep your hurts trapped within yourself and experience pain and isolation while doing your best to keep a smile on your face. Friend, this is no way to live. Your loving Father sees beyond your outward facade to the real condition in your heart. You may not be able to communicate what you feel, but He still perceives it. The Lord knows you perfectly, sees your hidden scars, and fully understands the reason you react to situations as you do (Psalm 139:1–3).

So today, don't fake it when it comes to your time alone with God. Entrust the pain of your heart to Him. Be open and honest—after all, He sees everything you are feeling anyway. But as you take the step of faith to trust Him with your struggles and open your heart to His healing, He will reveal the truth that will set you free. He will also give you the profound, enduring joy that you were created to experience. And that, friend, will put a smile on your face that nothing in this world will be able to take away.

Father, Forgive me for trying to hide myself from You.
I open my heart to You and invite Your healing.
Amen.

Bring Peace

SCRIPTURE READING: PROVERBS 15; MATTHEW 5:9; JOHN 10:10

A soothing tongue [speaking words that build up and encourage] is a tree of life, but a perverse tongue [speaking words that overwhelm and depress] crushes the spirit.

PROVERBS 15:4 AMP

As today's proverb suggests, when you speak, you're either building up or tearing down—either serving God or the enemy. In John 10:10, Jesus said, "The thief comes only to steal and kill and destroy." The enemy does so in the church, in people's lives, and in the family by stirring up emotions and aspirations within us that make us imagine that we are at war with one another. But that is why Jesus says, "Blessed are the peacemakers, for they shall be called sons of God" (Matthew 5:9). Bringing calm to a situation with others takes humility, forgiveness, and trust that God will sort everything out in His time. And that is exactly what we need to live this Christian life.

If you're in the midst of a conflict or some painful separation or rejection, you're not alone. We all experience broken relationships and difficult times. The truth of the matter is that when someone you love and trust walks away—even in a subtle way such as slowly cutting off communication—you suffer terribly with the feeling that you've failed. Nothing is more painful or strikes more deeply than that.

But what we often fail to realize is that what may drive people away is not always something within us, but is something within themselves that God is working on. So regardless of how someone hurts us, what we really need to do is forgive and try to bring peace to the situation by how we speak. In this way, we're serving the Savior, and He's working through us to bring healing to those we love.

Father, I want to be a peacemaker. Keep me from crushing other's spirits or creating more conflict. Help me to speak Your wisdom into situations so that You are glorified and others are healed.
Amen.

Acceptable Prayers

SCRIPTURE READING: PROVERBS 16; ROMANS 8:26

Righteous lips are the delight of kings
and he who speaks right is loved.
PROVERBS 16:13

How can we be sure to pray in a manner that pleases God? At times we may not know how to express the full depth of our desires or feelings in an accurate and a reverent manner. Sometimes we are so exhausted, heartbroken, or discouraged that we cannot imagine a way out of our painful circumstances, and we're not really sure how to ask the Father to help us.

Have you ever felt this way? Have you ever been so encumbered by troubles that hopelessness takes over and you just don't know what to say to God? If so, then realize that the Father has given you an awesome gift by sending the Helper to dwell in you. The Holy Spirit is like an ambassador who faithfully conveys the Father's will to you in a way you'll understand, and He represents you before God in a manner worthy of His righteous name. The apostle Paul wrote, "The Spirit . . . helps our weakness; for we do not know how to pray as we should, but the Spirit Himself intercedes for us with groanings too deep for words" (Romans 8:26).

Be assured that the Helper sees the depths of your difficulties. He translates your feelings more accurately than you could articulate them yourself. And He comforts you with the knowledge that He understands what you need. You should never fear whether God will acknowledge the cries of your heart, because His Holy Spirit transforms your petitions into acceptable and pleasing sacrifices. Even when you think you're failing in your prayers, the Holy Spirit ensures that you are heard. He also guarantees that your tribulations are not in vain but will build you up in the faith if you'll respond to Him in obedience.

Holy Spirit, thank You for expressing the deep issues of
my heart better than I ever could. And thank You for
teaching me how to honor God with my life.
Amen.

Now Listen

SCRIPTURE READING: PROVERBS 17; ECCLESIASTES 5:1–2

He who restrains his words has knowledge.
PROVERBS 17:27

Our desire to walk by faith, stepping solely within the will of God for our lives, can begin only when we have a true desire to hear what He is saying. When we have no idea where the Lord is leading us or what He wants to change in our hearts, listening is the first and most crucial component to a greater faith. This is why Ecclesiastes 5:1–2 instructs, "Guard your steps as you go to the house of God and draw near to listen rather than to offer the sacrifice of fools; for they do not know they are doing evil. Do not be hasty in word or impulsive in thought to bring up a matter in the presence of God. For God is in heaven and you are on the earth; therefore let your words be few."

This doesn't mean you will automatically perceive God speaking. The prophet Samuel was a boy when he first heard the Lord speak, and he was unsure of what he was hearing. Yet through gentle guidance from his mentor Eli, Samuel's faith began to blossom. Listening for God's voice became a pattern in his life. And countless times throughout his leadership in Israel he heard—and obeyed—the voice of the Lord.

The same will be true for you. So deepen your faith, strengthen your relationship with the Lord, and improve how you hear His voice:

- Desire to know Him more.
- Meditate upon His Word.
- Establish a consistent daily time to listen to the Father.
- Practice silence.
- Expect Him to speak.

Friend, the Father *wants* to communicate with you. So stop talking long enough to listen. Certainly He will lead you along the path of His will, strengthen your faith, and lead you to life at its very best.

*Speak Lord, Your servant is listening. Increase
my faith and reveal Yourself to me.
Amen.*

Be Salty

SCRIPTURE READING: PROVERBS 18; COLOSSIANS 4:6

Death and life are in the power of the tongue.
PROVERBS 18:21

God's purpose for each one of us is that we will make a lasting impact on those around us. This is why Colossians 4:6 tells us, "Let your speech always be with grace, as though seasoned with salt, so that you will know how you should respond to each person." Salt was an extremely valuable commodity in the ancient world. It was used as an antiseptic, preservative, sign of hospitality, seasoning, and confirmation of a covenant, among other things. In the life of a believer, it is symbolic for many of the ways we can influence others.

For example, salt was used to keep meat from spoiling, because there was no refrigeration. As Christians, we safeguard—or preserve—people in two ways. *First*, God works through our testimonies to encourage others to accept Jesus as their Lord and Savior—preserving them for eternity. *Second*, as we teach others to live a godly life, we help them avoid the destructive consequences of sin—protecting their lives and witness on the earthly level. Likewise, salt changes the taste of food. As believers, we change situations by our presence because the Holy Spirit indwells us, bringing tranquillity and security even in the midst of turmoil.

Finally, it doesn't take much salt for a dish to be affected by its flavor. That's how a godly life is to be: People cannot help but want to emulate it and have it for themselves. Friend, when you've been with Jesus, His love, wisdom, and power will flow through you, drawing people to a relationship with Him. So let your speech be seasoned with the salt of the Lord's presence, and He'll surely work through you to transform every soul you encounter.

Father, help me to be intentional about how I influence
the people I encounter. May my life attract them to You
so they may taste and see how truly wonderful You are.
Amen.

Godward Promptings

Listen to counsel and accept discipline,
that you may be wise the rest of your days.
PROVERBS 19:20

It can begin as a soft tugging in your spirit or a twinge in your heart. Your internal antenna goes up. You are suddenly aware that you should be paying attention to something important. Perhaps you are listening to a sermon and you sense God tell you to follow Him in obedience. Or maybe you walk into a restaurant and are filled with dread, as if you should leave quickly.

If you are a believer, then most likely these feelings are the prompting of the Holy Spirit, who always guides you to understand, accept, and accomplish the Father's will. He is the One speaking to your heart, warning you about danger and encouraging you to submit to His purposes. Why? Because He is the trustworthy Guide who has been given to you by the Father so you can live a godly life. The Holy Spirit empowers you to resist sin, obey God, and understand Scripture. It is through Him that a relationship with the Lord becomes real in your life. You submit to the promptings of the Holy Spirit, and as you do, you recognize His voice more and more. Eventually, you begin to see spiritual realities that only a person who is in constant communion with the Father can perceive (Psalm 25:14).

Because the Holy Spirit lives within you, you have the Lord's constant presence leading you in the way to go. So don't take Him for granted. Yield to the Holy Spirit—submit to His promptings and depend on His ability rather than your own. He will teach you how to live a life that is pleasing to Christ, and will also enable you to experience God in ways you never imagined possible.

Holy Spirit, make me aware of Your promptings.
Open my heart to listen to You faithfully that
I may follow Jesus and glorify Him.
Amen.

Demonstrate Forgiveness

SCRIPTURE READING: PROVERBS 20; MATTHEW 18:21–35

Keeping away from strife is an honor for a man.
PROVERBS 20:3

There may be times you feel justified in your anger toward others. But Jesus taught that we should always be forgiving. In fact, in the Parable of the Ungrateful Servant, He told the disciples about a servant who owed a king ten thousand talents (in modern terms that would be millions of dollars), an amount that the slave would never be able to work off. Such an enormous unpaid debt warranted that the servant and his family be sold into servitude. But when the man begged for mercy, the king forgave his debt completely.

One would think that servant would learn from the incredible generosity and profound compassion of the king. Sadly, Jesus told the disciples, "That slave went out and found one of his fellow slaves who owed him a hundred denarii . . . and threw him in prison until he should pay back what was owed" (Matthew 18:28–30). A denarius was only about a day's wages, so what the servant was owed was a mere pittance compared to what he had been forgiven by the king. Yet the mercy he'd been shown appeared to have no effect. We might wonder at the condition of his heart—refusing to show compassion after being pardoned of so much. But the truth is that we often respond like that ungrateful servant.

Our Savior forgives us of far more than what the king forgave the servant. With His precious blood, Jesus removes all our sins—past, present, and future. His sacrifice destroys any excuse we might have for holding onto bitterness. Though we may think it is wise to have boundaries about the number of times we'll accept apologies or about which offenses we'll pardon, Jesus drew no such lines at the cross. He forgives us fully, just as we should forgive others.

Lord, I am so grateful to You. May I show Your
compassion and mercy to everyone I meet.
Amen.

Eternal Purposes

SCRIPTURE READING: PROVERBS 21; GALATIANS 1; 1 JOHN 2:17

The man who listens to the truth will speak forever.
PROVERBS 21:28

When God speaks to us, He always has something very specific to say, and His message to us generally has eternal purposes. His goal is to transform our human hearts—to free us from sin and equip us for His service.

For example, in Galatians 1, the apostle Paul recounts how God changed his life. He explains how the Lord first revealed the need for salvation to him "through a revelation of Jesus Christ" (v. 12). This was the beginning of Paul's understanding of the truth—his need for the forgiveness of sins. Next, Paul writes that, despite his advancement in the teachings of Judaism, the Lord "called [him] through His grace" (v. 15). This was the beginning of a process that involved Paul being conformed to the image of Christ in order to exalt the Lord Jesus in his character. Finally, we are given Paul's grace-filled account of the Father's plan for his life. "[God] was pleased to reveal His Son in me so that I might preach Him among the Gentiles" (vv. 15–16). Clearly, God called Paul to communicate His truth to others, and Paul did so with joy, dedication, and passion.

Friend, God desires to speak with you in a similar way. He wants to set you free from sin, mold your character, and give your life everlasting significance. The Lord God is fitting your life for eternity in a manner far beyond your imagination. So listen to your heavenly Father. Because everything that worries you today is just a vapor that will pass away, "but the one who does the will of God lives forever" (1 John 2:17).

Lord, thank You for working out Your eternal purposes. Help me to keep eternity in view so I won't be consumed by transient worries, but my life can truly make an everlasting difference.
Amen.

The Vision of Purity

SCRIPTURE READING: PROVERBS 21; MATTHEW
5:8; JAMES 1:17; ROMANS 8:28

He who loves purity of heart and whose speech
is gracious, the king is his friend.
PROVERBS 22:11

J esus said, "Blessed are the pure in heart, for they shall see God"
(Matthew 5:8). The Savior wasn't referring only to our seeing the
Father in His heavenly kingdom someday. Rather, Jesus was comment-
ing on our capacity to perceive the Lord's protection and provision in our
lives right now—in our relationships, work, struggles, and every aspect
of our existence.

People who pursue purity see God—not necessarily in visions or
through illustrious spiritual exploits, but as He works in and through
their lives daily teaching them His ways. Because their hearts are set
on the Savior, their view of Him is not obscured by the confusion and
clutter sin causes. Therefore, they understand in a powerful way how
the Lord is behind every good thing that comes their way (James 1:17)
and that even the trials and difficulties have meaning and purpose
(Romans 8:28). They realize that God is working all things for their ultimate good—changing circumstances, engineering unexpected events
that produce unimagined benefits, and orchestrating relationships so
that God's Word goes forth with greater power and more impact.

Friend, do you want to see more of the Father's work in your life and
experience His presence in a more profound way? Then keep your heart
pure by seeking and obeying Him. Refuse to harbor sin in your heart;
confess and repent of it as quickly as you're aware of it. Invite the Holy
Spirit to cleanse you through the Word of God. And in all things, submit
yourself to the Father. After all, obedience always brings blessing, and
when the reward is seeing God Himself, you are receiving the ultimate
craving of your soul.

Lord, purify my heart—I want to see You. I want to be so aware
of Your wonderful presence that we are in constant fellowship.
Amen.

The Path of Success

SCRIPTURE READING: PROVERBS 23; ROMANS 12:2;
EPHESIANS 2:10; 4:22–32; COLOSSIANS 1:21; 3:2

As he thinks within himself, so he is.
PROVERBS 23:7

God wants you to be a success in the Christian life. He defines success as becoming the person that He created you to be and accomplishing the goals that He has set for your life (Ephesians 2:10). And as you can see from today's proverb, godly achievement starts with your thinking. What you believe about yourself impacts your attitudes and actions, both toward Him and toward others. The more you dedicate your mind and thoughts to the Lord, the godlier you will be. And the godlier you are, they more likely you are to walk in the center of the Father's will for you.

However, Colossians 1:21 tells us that prior to salvation, we were alienated and hostile in mind toward the things of the Lord. In other words, our old ways of thinking are of no value in helping us to become the person God wants each of us to be. That is why Scripture calls for spiritual renewal of our thoughts and instructs us in what to eliminate and what to add to our minds (Ephesians 4:22–32). Our earthly ways of thinking are to be replaced by the truth of the Word.

So "set your mind" on the things that glorify and please Him (Colossians 3:2). Choose to have His viewpoint and reject any thinking that leads to conformity with the ways of the world (Romans 12:2). Because when you fix your attention on who the Lord is, on His plan for you, and on how to please Him, you will be on His track to victory. So seek His understanding. Consider carefully where your focus is. And trust Him. Because this is not just the path to right thinking but the ultimate road to eternally triumphant living.

*Lord, I want success Your way. Help me to think Your thoughts
and see things Your way so I can remain on the path to victory.
Amen.*

A Heart of Obedience

SCRIPTURE READING: PROVERBS 24; JOHN 14:15

Don't excuse yourself by saying, "Look, we didn't know."
For God understands all hearts, and he sees you.
PROVERBS 24:12 NLT

The way we show God our love is by obedience to Him. Jesus taught us this when He said, "If you love Me, you will keep My commandments" (John 14:15). It is not enough that we know what His instructions are, that we agree with them, or even that we teach them to others. Obedience—an act of the will to align our lives with His—is required.

God knows how difficult we find it to obey Him. However, we cannot claim ignorance of His commands or a lack of understanding because He has given His Spirit to help us do all that He requires. The Holy Spirit is our Teacher who reminds us of all Jesus taught and pierces our consciences when we disregard His principles. He also guides us into the truth of Scripture so we cannot claim we have no way to understand it. Furthermore, the Spirit of God enables, strengthens, and comforts us when we encounter difficulties in trying to obey.

People often ask if we are responsible to obey all the laws of both the Old and New Testaments. The answer is no. The ceremonial laws of Israel, including the sacrificial system, were fulfilled in Christ. In addition, God gave certain specific commands to the Hebrew nation that applied only to them. But the moral laws of the Old Testament apply to us, as do the New Testament commands. If we ignore God's Word, we are being disobedient, and that communicates a lack of love and respect for the One who saves our souls. So say, "I love You," to the Lord Jesus by opening Scripture and obeying whatever He tells you to do.

Lord God, I love You and desire to obey You.
Please enable and strengthen me to do all You ask.
Amen.

Be Persistent

SCRIPTURE READING: PROVERBS 25; ISAIAH 55:8–9;
LUKE 18:1–8; HEBREWS 10:35–36

Through patience a ruler can be persuaded.
PROVERBS 25:15 NIV

Has God ever given you the silent treatment? You pray about something so important, but you're not sure if He hears you because there appears to be no answer. Perhaps this is your situation today. If so, understand that the Lord is sometimes quiet because He is teaching you endurance in your relationship with Him. Jesus taught the disciples the Parable of the Persistent Widow for just this purpose (Luke 18:1–8). This woman was in need of protection because of some conflict she was having. So she repeatedly asked the judge to help her until he relented because of her tenacity. Likewise, God will "bring about justice for His elect who cry to Him day and night" (v. 7). He is faithful to answer our pleas.

This is also why Jesus taught them "that at all times they ought to pray and not to lose heart" (v. 1). Perseverance is crucial in our relationships with the Father because His timing is not like ours—nor are His ways comparable to our ways (Isaiah 55:8–9). Sometimes He desires that we wait because He is arranging our circumstances or protecting us from danger. He may be purifying our motives, teaching us to rely on Him, or preparing us to influence others.

The point is: He is working and has not abandoned us. So heed the words of Hebrews 10:35–36: "Do not throw away your confidence, which has a great reward. For you have need of endurance, so that when you have done the will of God, you may receive what was promised." Continue going before the Father for His wisdom, presence, love, and strength. And don't give up. Because you will certainly be blessed when the answer finally comes.

Father, I continue to pray, certain You will answer. Open my
ears so I will not miss whatever You have to say to me.
Amen.

The Godly Response

SCRIPTURE READING: PROVERBS 26; MATTHEW 5:39

Do not answer a fool according to his
folly, or you will also be like him.
PROVERBS 26:4

Suppose you go to work tomorrow morning, and the moment you walk in, one of your colleagues picks a fight with you. He unleashes anger and frustration at you in a way that feels like an assault and leaves you reeling and wounded. From your point of view, there is no cause for this verbal attack—it's nine o'clock in the morning and you haven't even poured yourself a cup of coffee, much less had a chance to converse with this person. How do you respond?

The normal reaction would be retaliation of some kind. It is human to think, *That was uncalled for. I'm going to get back at him for that.* However, the godly response is quite different. Jesus said, "Do not resist an evil person; but whoever slaps you on your right cheek, turn the other to him also" (Matthew 5:39). In other words, a Christ-centered response might be, "Is there anything else you want to tell me? I appreciate your letting me know how you feel. I'll consider what you've said."

The first reaction leads to an argument, division, confusion, unrest, and an escalation of anger, bitterness, frustration, and estrangement. The other way—God's way—leads to peace, understanding, resolution, reconciliation, and potential growth in a relationship. This is why it is so important for us to ponder God's Word—read it, study it, memorize it, think about it, and consider it. The Lord's commandments, statutes, precepts, and principles cover all of life's situations. And by applying Scripture to our lives, we discover the wise way to respond to the difficult situations we face.

Lord, thank You for teaching me how to respond in volatile situations.
Cover my life with Your Word so I can always react with Your
love, wisdom, peace, and assurance regardless of what happens.
Amen.

Restoring the Fallen

SCRIPTURE READING: PROVERBS 27; GALATIANS 6:1

Better is open rebuke than love that is concealed.
PROVERBS 27:5

When a loved one heads down the wrong path, honesty is always the best policy as long as it is proclaimed in a spirit of love. As a godly Christian, you can help restore a fallen saint to fruitful service. However, you must be serious about your walk with the Lord and be committed to helping your struggling brother or sister find his or her way back to Jesus (Galatians 6:1).

The path to healing is often long and painful, requiring many difficult but necessary steps. *First*, the person must recognize his or her failure. We need to help the individual see the nature of the problem, recognize the consequences, and call the failing by its right name: sin. *Second*, he or she must acknowledge responsibility. Although others may have been involved, placing blame will do no good whatsoever. *Third*, the fallen saint must repent. He or she must commit to turning away from the sinful behavior. *Fourth*, the person must make appropriate restitution. *Fifth*, he or she must learn the lesson God wants to teach. Failure is unprofitable only when we refuse to let it instruct us. If we learn and grow, we have taken the opportunity to discover more about ourselves and the Lord. *Finally*, the believer must respond to the Father's chastisement with gratitude. God is the perfect Parent; He disciplines us but will always use what we experience to teach us eternal truth. And for that we can always be thankful.

None of us wants to see a loved one fall. But when that happens, we should gladly participate if the Holy Spirit leads us to restore him or her. After all, what could be more fulfilling than to help a struggling saint back into fellowship with our heavenly Father?

Father, You know my loved ones are hurting. Lead me in
wisdom and love to restore them in a manner
that most glorifies You and helps them to heal.
Amen.

Liberated to Serve

SCRIPTURE READING: PROVERBS 28; MATTHEW 28:19–20; JOHN 8:32

By a man of understanding and knowledge
Right will be prolonged.
PROVERBS 28:2 NKJV

You know how important it is that you know God's Word. Jesus promised, "You will know the truth, and the truth will make you free" (John 8:32). The Holy Spirit works through Scripture to liberate you from the bondage within. However, for you to absorb the truth, you must do more than simply read or even memorize Scripture. It also crucial that you meditate on it. When you do, the Lord teaches you to apply biblical principles to your life.

But God doesn't simply release you from old, negative thought patterns and feelings of inadequacy; He emancipates you to serve Him with your whole being. When you become overly concerned about your security, the opinions of others, or what you are lacking, you have little to give to anyone else and will be motivated to protect yourself. However, the Lord wants your focus to be on obeying Him—pouring your life out like an offering to Him and helping those who are lost and hurting.

Friend, if you believe that God has liberated you only for yourself, then you've missed the point, and you're not truly free. The Lord has saved and equipped you with His love so that you can carry out His primary goal to "make disciples of all the nations, baptizing them in the name of the Father and the Son and the Holy Spirit, teaching them to observe all that [Jesus] commanded" (Matthew 28:19–20). Your freedom grows as you obey God's purpose for your life. That begins with getting in the Word and listening to Him and ends with passing what He tells you on to others. So do it! And as the Father liberates you from the bondage to sin, communicate what you learn to everyone you meet.

Lord, thank You for setting me free. Help me to reach out to others
with the truth You've taught me so they can be delivered as well.
Amen.

AUGUST 29

Your Internal Compass

SCRIPTURE READING: PROVERBS 29

A man who hardens his neck after much reproof
will suddenly be broken beyond remedy.
PROVERBS 29:1

God has given you a conscience so you can distinguish between what is right and what is wrong. It is His gift to help you avoid the consequences of sin. Your conscience serves as a kind of compass or spiritual radar, and how diligently you maintain it and your relationship with the Father will determine how well you can trust it.

The *sacred conscience* is one that is being kept spotless through confession of known sin and reflects a desire to know and follow God's will. Once you are cleansed, you can live without guilt, walking openly and transparently before the Lord. When you do sin, you immediately realize how important it is to get right with the Father. The *struggling conscience* is encumbered by a spirit of legalism that makes us critical. Having created our own radar system of shoulds, ought tos, and musts, we use it to determine right or wrong rather than developing a vibrant relationship with God. In so doing, we fail to understand the Father's love, righteousness, and guidance, which can never be replaced by a set of rules and regulations.

The *soiled conscience* is stained from harboring sin. If we consistently choose our way over God's, we lose sight of what is suitable and true. Even worse, a *seared conscience* is insensitive to sin. When we have continually resisted and ignored its warnings, such a conscience becomes numb to moral alarms and speeds us along on the road to destruction.

Friend, you have an invaluable tool by which to distinguish between right and wrong. So don't harden your heart to the Lord, which only leads to devastation. Ask God to show you how well your internal compass is operating, and then allow the Holy Spirit to restore whatever has gone awry.

Lord, test my conscience and cleanse it from error
that I might love and serve You well always.
Amen.

A Demonstration of God's Power

SCRIPTURE READING: PROVERBS 30; 2 CORINTHIANS 2:1–2, 4

I do not have the understanding.
PROVERBS 30:2

If you've ever heard a gifted speaker deliver a message, you know how convincing inspiring words and a good delivery can be. You find yourself hanging on every sentence, maybe even taking notes as fast as you can write. Somehow, the way he or she communicates makes the difference in how much you listen.

So maybe you feel inadequate talking about your faith in Christ because you are not a dynamic speaker. You hold back, even when a perfect opportunity presents itself, just because you are so self-conscious. But God never intended for you to rely on your own abilities as a witness. You see, the Father doesn't just long for people to listen—He wants them to be transformed. And that means the message needs power that can come only from Him.

This is why the apostle Paul wrote, "When I came to you, brethren, I did not come with superiority of speech or of wisdom, proclaiming to you the testimony of God. For I determined to know nothing among you except Jesus Christ, and Him crucified . . . My preaching [was] not in persuasive words of wisdom, but in demonstration of the Spirit and of power" (2 Corinthians 2:1–2, 4). Although Paul was an excellent public debater, he deliberately approached others with an attitude of humble simplicity, so that God would do the work through him.

Friend, it is good to admit that you don't have the wisdom to lead someone to Jesus, because that opens the door for the Lord to lead and empower you. So don't stop talking about Christ because of your inadequacies. Regardless of your abilities, God will pour His power into your life to enable you to do His work.

Lord, speak to others through me. I rely not on my limited
understanding and persuasiveness but on Your mighty power,
which can completely transform a person's life.
Amen.

What Flows from You

SCRIPTURE READING: PROVERBS 31; LUKE 6:45; COLOSSIANS 3:16

She opens her mouth in skillful and godly Wisdom, and on her
tongue is the law of kindness [giving counsel and instruction].
PROVERBS 31:26 AMP

What does your speech say about you? When you talk, do you reflect the ways of the world, or do your words testify to a deep relationship with Jesus? Do you tear people down or build them up with godly instruction? Do you complain about problems or offer people Christ-centered solutions? If God has transformed you and given you a new nature, hopefully the way you communicate will show it.

This is because what you say reveals the true condition of your heart. Luke 6:45 teaches, "The good man out of the good treasure of his heart brings forth what is good; and the evil man out of the evil treasure brings forth what is evil; for his mouth speaks from that which fills his heart." So what fills you? What flows from your heart? God's will is that you would reflect the character of Christ in both word and deed.

This is why Paul writes, "Let the word of Christ richly dwell within you, with all wisdom teaching and admonishing one another with psalms and hymns and spiritual songs, singing with thankfulness in your hearts to God" (Colossians 3:16). Paul knew that your heart needs constant nourishment from Scripture and time in the Savior's presence in order for it to bring forth the fruit worthy of a child of God.

So fill your heart with the wonderful truth of Scripture. Because when you do, your mouth will produce not only the words that testify to Christ's influence on your life but will also have power to transform the lives of others.

Father, I want to glorify You in both word and deed.
Fill my heart with Your truth and may it flow forth abundantly.
Amen.

SEPTEMBER

Servant Leadership

The words leader *and* servant *have such different connotations in a worldly sense. Most people prefer to be the one giving orders rather than taking them. Yet from God's perspective, servanthood and leadership are two sides of the same coin—with equal value, importance, and responsibility, and each requiring just as much wisdom for success.*

Pass It On

SCRIPTURE READING: PROVERBS 1; ACTS
17:11; 2 TIMOTHY 2:2; 1 PETER 3:15

*Give prudence to the naive,
to the youth knowledge and discretion.*
PROVERBS 1:4

A solid grounding in biblical principles protects us from being mis-
led and prepares us to answer people who are honestly seeking to
know the truth. It is our privilege to help a soul find his or her way to
Christ and show that person to follow Him in obedience. And by having
a strong grasp on God's truth, we can confidently act upon opportunities
to share our faith. The world offers temporary, fleeting "hope" that is
based on fantasy and opinion. But we can offer others hope based on the
reality of Jesus Christ.

Therefore, we must encourage others to saturate their minds with
scriptural truth, knowing that doing so has two important outcomes.
First, a strengthened personal relationship with God. The more individuals study God's Word, the more they will comprehend its deeper truths
and the stronger their faith will become. As we lead others to serve Jesus,
we remind them that their belief system isn't based on our opinions or the
ideas of others. Rather, the Bible—which is the inspired, infallible truth
of God—is to be their primary source of knowledge (Acts 17:11).

Second, the persuasive power of their answers. We must help others
to understand they have a role in passing on their faith in Christ as well
(2 Timothy 2:2). And as they study God's Word, the Holy Spirit works to
show them the opportunities before them and enables them to answer
those who want to know about Jesus (1 Peter 3:15).

Friend, there's nothing more important in our day than meditating
on Scripture to build our faith and leading others to do so as well. Because when we do, we not only experience the presence of God; we also
have the privilege of witnessing others do so.

*Father, thank You for working through me to help others mature in
their faith. May they find people they can help grow up as well.*
Amen.

Surrender to Him

SCRIPTURE READING: PROVERBS 2; ROMANS 12:1–2

You will discern righteousness and justice
and equity and every good course.
PROVERBS 2:9

When you hear the word *surrender*, what do you envision? Many people imagine military conflicts, overpowering forces, and white flags. However, we should never think of the act of submitting our lives to God as traumatic. On the contrary, it is a wonderful experience that can enrich our lives and give us great peace. Why, then, are we so afraid to hand over the reins of our lives to His omnipotent and wise leadership?

The answer lies in our self-centered and fallen nature. We live in a world that encourages us to take pride in what we have accomplished and protect ourselves from anything that could limit our earthly freedom. This is why the concept of surrendering to God is unthinkable for many people.

As a believer, however, the Father has called you to a higher standard of living. He wants to help you reach the goals that He has created you to achieve, and in order to fulfill His plan, you must submit yourself to Him. Until you make this important step toward God, you will find yourself in a state of unrest and uncertainty. However, once you surrender your life to the Lord, He will unleash the storehouse of blessings waiting for you.

In Romans 12:1–2, the Father specifically asks you to present yourself as a living sacrifice to Him and to renew your mind so that you can know His will. God wants to guide, direct, and bless you. So don't be afraid to give your life to Him and experience all the wonderful things He has planned in advance for you to enjoy. Be assured that following His leadership is always the wisest course you can take.

Lord, there is no other leader like You. I surrender myself to You
and Your purposes, confident You always lead me to life at its best.
Amen.

In Humility Serve

SCRIPTURE READING: PROVERBS 3; MATTHEW 20:16; JOHN 13:7−8

Do not withhold good from those to whom it is
due, when it is in your power to act.
PROVERBS 3:27 NIV

It wasn't easy for Peter to restrain himself. He was a natural trailblazer, which meant he was enjoyed and was good at leading others. However, the events of Christ's last week on earth shattered any dreams Peter may have had concerning glory, rulership, and conquest. He watched in frustration as the Savior wrapped a towel around His waist and began washing the disciples' feet—the lowliest task of the most humble servant in a household. So when Jesus approached Peter with the basin of water, the disciple recoiled, "Lord, You shall never bathe my feet!" (John 13:8).

Jesus was firm in His reply, "What I do you do not realize now, but you will understand hereafter . . . If I do not wash you, you have no part with Me" (John 13:7–8). You can imagine the confusion in Peter's heart. Why would a king—God's promised Messiah!—insist on performing such a humiliating task? But the Lord was confronting the motives of Peter's heart.

Peter neither understood the ways of God nor was he ready for service. It takes both humility and grace to serve others, and sometimes we refuse to do so because we imagine the task is beneath us. However, we must follow Christ's example: He served sacrificially to cleanse not only our outer filthiness but also—and more important—the inner uncleanness of our sinful souls. Jesus said, "If you want to be first, you must first learn to be last." (Matthew 20:16). So today, you may encounter some opportunity to bless another person that seems beneath you. Do it anyway, and with joy. That's what the Savior would gladly do and has done for you.

Lord, please forgive me for the times I've been prideful.
I want to serve in humility as You would. May my life
reflect Your compassion and bring You glory.
Amen.

Fruit That Lasts

SCRIPTURE READING: PROVERBS 4; JOHN
15:16; 1 CORINTHIANS 13:12; 15:57

I have directed you in the way of wisdom;
I have led you in upright paths.
PROVERBS 4:11

We see the following principle repeated throughout God's Word: Doing His work in His way results in everlasting victory (1 Corinthians 15:57). Unfortunately, one of the temptations in Christian service is giving up when we don't see immediate results. But the Lord's perspective is eternal—He works to produce fruit that will last, which requires diligence and patience (John 15:16).

The challenge of Christian living can be compared with a large embroidered tapestry draped across the heavens. We see only the underside of the fabric, its many dangling threads revealing very little of a pattern and actually appearing unkempt and disordered. But from the other side, from God's viewpoint, it is beautiful—a well-designed and expertly crafted masterpiece.

This is why serving Jesus requires that we draw strength and sustenance from Him. The only way to do God's work His way is to remain in His Word and in prayer because then we will not be discouraged when things seem to go awry or we see no good result. We hear these admonitions so often that they can almost seem trite, but the truth is we draw God's energy, strength, wisdom, and patience as His Spirit speaks to us through His Word and in prayer.

Paul reminds us that what we see, know, and understand is not complete: "Eye has not seen and ear has not heard . . . all that God has prepared for those who love Him" (1 Corinthians 2:9). So when you face discouragement in serving the Lord, hold fast to your hope in what you cannot see—because the best is certainly yet to come.

Father, I am grateful that You see beyond what I can see and
I can trust You to produce lasting fruit through me.
I trust You. Help me to endure.
Amen.

Who Is Leading You?

SCRIPTURE READING: PROVERBS 5; 2 CORINTHIANS 11:3, 14–15

Do not go near the door of her house,
lest you give your honor to others,
and your years to the cruel one.
PROVERBS 5:8–9

What fruit is flowing from those you are following? Are they building you up or tearing you down? Are they leading you toward God or away from Him? It would have been wise for Eve to ask those questions before she was led astray by the serpent. But Satan is clever. He knew just what to say to get her attention, to cause her to doubt the Lord, and to persuade her to change her understanding of His command. It wasn't long before Eve had given in to blatant disobedience.

Chances are, Satan has never appeared to you as a talking serpent. Nevertheless, it would be wrong to dismiss or ignore his tactics, especially as he works through others to lead you down a destructive path. This is why Paul gives this warning about Satan's influence on the Body of Christ: "I am afraid that, as the serpent deceived Eve by his craftiness, your minds will be led astray from the simplicity and purity of devotion to Christ . . . No wonder, for even Satan disguises himself as an angel of light. Therefore it is not surprising if his servants also disguise themselves as servants of righteousness, whose end will be according to their deeds" (2 Corinthians 11:3, 14–15).

Satan's strategies and instruments change through the years, but his purposes remain the same. If he can weaken and deceive Christians, he can limit the church's effectiveness and power. That is why church leaders are especially vulnerable and need to be on their guard against any falsehood. Of course, it's crucial for all believers to remain on the alert, dedicating themselves to daily time in God's Word, prayer, and watchfulness.

Lord, help me to discern truth from error. Reveal who is
truly Your servant and who is leading people astray. And
Father, please protect the godly leaders who love You.
Amen.

Let Him Fight

SCRIPTURE READING: PROVERBS 6; PSALM 20:6–8; ROMANS 10:11

The Lord hates . . . a person who stirs up conflict in the community.
PROVERBS 6:16, 19 NIV

As leaders, we may be tempted to see the challenges ahead of us as wars to be waged against enemies who would prevent our progress. However, that changes when we become children of God. This is because as people who belong to Him, when we fight our battles we are to do so on our knees in submission to Him. We no longer depend on our own weapons, strategies, abilities, or resources because we realize how much more effective His are for achieving the goals of His kingdom. And God is clear: He doesn't want us to be the originators or perpetuators of conflicts; He wants us to be peacemakers. So we must agree that that battle belongs to the Lord and allow Him to be our Commander in Chief.

David wrote, "I know that the Lord saves His anointed; He will answer him from His holy heaven with the saving strength of His right hand. Some boast in chariots and some in horses, but we will boast in the name of the Lord, our God. They have bowed down and fallen, but we have risen and stood upright" (Psalm 20:6–8).

In order to achieve the victory God has envisioned, you must surrender yourself to Him fully. This may require stepping out in faith when it's uncomfortable or even petrifying to do so. You may need to abandon some of your goals in order to seek the objectives that the Lord has for you. But no matter how much discomfort His commands cause you, obey Him anyway. Trust the Father's direction, knowing wholeheartedly that "whoever believes in Him will not be disappointed" (Romans 10:11). He is a faithful, skilled General who has never lost a battle and will not let you down.

God, I will not stir up conflict.
I will let You fight and trust You for victory.
Amen.

The Slide into Sin

SCRIPTURE READING: PROVERBS 7; 2 SAMUEL
11; 2 TIMOTHY 2:22; 1 PETER 1:13–15

He took the path to her house.
PROVERBS 7:8

It's dangerous to flirt with sin. The young man in this proverb walks by the house of the harlot, perhaps never intending to interact with her. Yet because he was not wise enough to avoid going near her altogether, she lures him in.

The same thing happened to David. We know that during a time when kings usually went to battle, he sent his troops on ahead and stayed in Jerusalem. One night, looking out over the city, David saw a beautiful woman bathing. Instead of looking away immediately, he allowed his gaze to linger. Without his thoughts fixed on God's will for him, David began thinking of the one who caught his eye—Bathsheba. Of course, his imagination took over, wondering what an experience with her would be like. Eventually his desire became uncontrollable, and his feet took him where his mind had already gone—straight into sin (2 Samuel 11).

That's how the process of sin progresses: It begins with a thought, moving quickly through your imagination, to uncontrollable desire, to consent. It all begins in your mind, which is why 1 Peter 1:13–15 warns, "Prepare your minds for action, keep sober in spirit, fix your hope completely on the grace to be brought to you at the revelation of Jesus Christ. As obedient children, do not be conformed to the former lusts which were yours in your ignorance, but like the Holy One who called you, be holy yourselves also in all your behavior."

Friend, don't slide into sin by flirting with temptation. Instead, be wise by avoiding it as much as you can and fleeing from it before it has time to take hold (2 Timothy 2:22).

Lord, I realize the ways I flirt with temptation. Please
forgive me. Show me how to avoid it altogether and
give me the strength and courage to always flee.
Amen.

Forward by God's Wisdom

SCRIPTURE READING: PROVERBS 8; NUMBERS 13–14; JOSHUA 1:5, 7

By me kings reign, and rulers decree justice.
PROVERBS 8:15

Are you feeling discouraged by the choices before you? Are you afraid of something God has told you to do? Perhaps you are facing a decision that seems too difficult to make because of the impact it will have on others. The good news is this: You are not alone. Every person on earth, throughout every generation, has faced or will face the same indecision and hesitancy. But what do you do when you feel inadequate or uncertain because the choices you make will affect others so profoundly?

Joshua knew exactly what it meant to be in such a fearful and daunting situation. His beloved leader, Moses, had just died. And now, Almighty God was asking him not only to take the position Moses once held but also to lead an entire nation to a land where Moses—through whom the Lord had worked many miracles—had not been able to enter. We usually see Joshua as the brave spy who looked to the Promised Land with hope when others saw nothing but challenges (Numbers 13–14). However, Joshua also understood the enormity of his responsibility and was fearful.

Thankfully, it was God's promise that carried him through. The Lord had said, "Just as I have been with Moses, I will be with you; I will not fail you or forsake you . . . Only be strong and very courageous; be careful to do according to all the law . . . so that you may have success wherever you go" (Joshua 1:5, 7). What made Joshua successful is that he heeded the Lord's instruction and led in His wisdom. Joshua went forward by faith and let the Holy Word of God direct his steps—and it made all the difference. As you face your challenge, will you do the same?

Lord, I trust You. Guide me with Your wisdom
so I can lead others successfully.
Amen.

SEPTEMBER 9

Doing One's Part

SCRIPTURE READING: PROVERBS 9; 1 CORINTHIANS 12:7; 1 PETER 4:10

[Wisdom] has sent out her maidens,
she calls from the tops of the heights of the city.
PROVERBS 9:3

Imagine trying to play soccer without someone to guard the goal. Consider a surgical unit with doctors but no anesthesiologists or nurses. Envision an army with no one to coordinate transportation. Sounds foolish, doesn't it? A team, a unit, a squad is not complete and cannot function adequately without the participation of each member. How imprudent, then, for believers to think of themselves independently of the rest of Christ's body. Yet it's all too common to find a believer focusing on his or her spiritual progress without regard for the needs or importance of his or her brothers and sisters in Christ.

But this is why 1 Corinthians 12:7 reminds us, "To each one is given the manifestation of the Spirit for the common good." We desperately need one another. Each member of Christ's body is specially equipped to minister to the burdens of the others. We need encouragement when we are disheartened. We need sound counsel when we are confused. We need help when we are disabled. We need prayers when our own are feeble. We need correction and rebuke when blinded by our sins. And our family in Christ offers that to us.

Friend, you were made to need God and His people and assist them in return. And 1 Peter 4:10 admonishes, "As each one has received a special gift, employ it in serving one another as good stewards of the manifold grace of God." So get involved in a local body of believers who can help you in your time of need and whom you can aid in their struggles. And discover the joy of serving others with your own gifts and talents.

Father, thank You for giving me a loving family to
help me in my time of need and for giving me an
important purpose in the Body of Christ as well.
Amen.

SEPTEMBER 10

Speak Life

SCRIPTURE READING: PROVERBS 10; MATTHEW 5:16; 1 CORINTHIANS 9:16

The mouth of the righteous is a fountain of life.
PROVERBS 10:11

In many instances, evangelism is viewed as a church-sponsored activity that must be directed by the church leadership. Certainly the church is Christ's body of believers and is responsible to proclaim Jesus' gift of salvation to the world. So it is the church leadership's responsibility to lead and teach Christians to effectively share their faith. But instruction on this level is not usually enduring unless there is inner transformation in the life of the believer—unless the he or she understands the urgency and importance of the calling. We are Christ's representatives who proclaim eternal life to those who are spiritually dead and on the path of perdition. There is no more important task than leading others to Jesus.

Paul comprehended it and was "under compulsion" to preach the gospel (1 Corinthians 9:16). True, he was called as an apostle, but it is also true that we are called as disciples of Christ. Our eagerness to share Jesus' life with others should be just as intense as that of the apostles.

Are you compelled to make Christ known to others? Are you motivated by your devotion to Jesus to proclaim Him through your words and deeds? This is the biblical pattern for evangelism—people who love Jesus Christ willingly sharing His Good News of salvation in relevant ways. It may not always be by quoting Scripture or handing out a tract, but by loving others in ways that demonstrate God's tender concern (Matthew 5:16). Friend, don't allow fear or apathy to quench the fire of the gospel within you. Proclaim the Savior's love to others through whatever opportunities the Father gives you. He will show you the way.

Lord, I want to share Your Good News of salvation with others.
Make me aware of open hearts and teach me what to say so that
many may embrace the eternal life You've given.
Amen.

Recompense

SCRIPTURE READING: PROVERBS 11; MATTHEW 25:34–40;
LUKE 23:34; ROMANS 12:9; EPHESIANS 4:32; 1 JOHN 4:20

The merciful, kind, and generous man benefits himself
[for his deeds return to bless him], but he who is cruel and callous
[to the wants of others] brings on himself retribution.
PROVERBS 11:17 AMP

Throughout our lives, we may have seen incredible evil and we may wish to inflict punishment on those who have caused us pain. But the Father says, "Never take your own revenge, beloved, but leave room for the wrath of God, for it is written, 'Vengeance is Mine, I will repay' " (Romans 12:9). Therefore, during difficult seasons when others wrong us, we must remember that each person is loved by God and needs Jesus to be his or her Savior.

I say this because the Lord is clear: "If someone says, 'I love God,' and hates his brother, he is a liar; for the one who does not love his brother whom he has seen, cannot love God whom he has not seen" (1 John 4:20). For this reason, we must make every effort to make sure no anger, bitterness, or unforgiveness takes root in our hearts. Rather, we are called to love others as Christ loved us: with compassion, mercy, grace, and forgiveness (Luke 23:34; Ephesians 4:32). In caring for them, we show our devotion to the Father (Matthew 25:34–40).

Remember, people are not your enemies; sin is. And if you fight your battles on your knees, God will not only help you be victorious, He will also redeem those who oppose you. Therefore, never act in a manner that would disgrace the name of Jesus or hinder others from following Him in obedience. The goal is always to lead whomever we come in contact with back to faith and trust in Christ.

Father, because I love You, I will forgive as You do. Help those who
have hurt me to seek You. I trust You to set everything straight.
Amen.

Spiritual Fruit

SCRIPTURE READING: PROVERBS 12; PHILIPPIANS 1:6

The root of the righteous yields fruit.
PROVERBS 12:12

Discovering your spiritual gift is the first step toward a lifetime of rewarding service in God's kingdom that produces fruit which will endure in eternity (Philippians 1:6). This discovery is not mysterious or difficult to determine. God does not work to confuse you. He wants you to know and exercise your spiritual gift so you can enjoy the fullness of the Christian life and find eternal significance in your daily interactions.

And the truth of the matter is that your spiritual gift is at the root of your personality and works in accord with your unique set of personal inclinations. You were created to express it as the Holy Spirit empowers you. If you enjoy helping others—service may be your motivational gift. If you enjoy study and investigation—teaching is more than likely your gift. If others consistently benefit from your counsel and correction— the gift of exhortation is a good place to start in your search. The second-best indicator of your spiritual gift is verification by others. If you like teaching but no one grows in his or her relationship with Jesus by your instruction, it may be a preference rather than a true spiritual gift. If you enjoy leading others, but no one follows Christ more passionately because of your example, shepherding may not be your calling.

So ask the Lord to reveal your spiritual gifting today. Examine your likes and dislikes, keep watch for roles and activities where you feel the power of God fueling your efforts, and seek the input of others. And above all, remember your gift is determined by the Father, redeemed by the Savior, empowered by the Holy Spirit, and is to be used to bring glory to God. Discover your spiritual gift and experience producing the fruit that will last in eternity.

Lord, thank You for the spiritual gift You have given me. Empower
me to understand it fully and always use it for Your glory.
Amen.

The Path of Eternal Influence

SCRIPTURE READING: PROVERBS 13; EPHESIANS 4:1–3; COLOSSIANS 1:10

A good man leaves an inheritance.
PROVERBS 13:22

Have you ever walked down a path and noticed footprints of some kind stretched out before you? Just as our physical bodies make imprints on the earth, so our spiritual lives mark those around us. Of course, in both cases, where you walk makes all the difference. Just as physical footprints on a rocky cliff side would be impossible to see, spiritual imprints that are not on God's pathway for you are also invisible to the watching world.

How, then, should we tread? Paul instructs, "I, the prisoner of the Lord, implore you to walk in a manner worthy of the calling with which you have been called, with all humility and gentleness, with patience, showing tolerance for one another in love, being diligent to preserve the unity of the Spirit in the bond of peace" (Ephesians 4:1–3). Humility, diligence, gentleness, patience, tolerance, love, unity, peace—these are the qualities that should characterize our path as the people of God. When we stray from this path, our way becomes dark and dangerous, and we lose effectiveness in the world. However, when we proceed in a manner pleasing to God, He works through us to make an indelible, everlasting mark on those around us.

Therefore, today consider: Do you want to have a permanent influence on the world and in eternity? Then, "Walk in a manner worthy of the Lord, to please Him in all respects, bearing fruit in every good work and increasing in the knowledge of God" (Colossians 1:10). Plant your feet on the solid ground of Jesus Christ and accept His challenge to proceed in holiness and obedience to His will. And He will certainly be with you and give you victory every step of the way.

Lord, I do want to leave a lasting influence on all who follow after me. May my life make a difference for Your eternal kingdom.
Amen.

Blessed Through Obedience

SCRIPTURE READING: PROVERBS 14; JEREMIAH 7:23; 29:11

The king's favor is toward a servant who acts wisely.
PROVERBS 14:35

You will never lose when you obey God. Nevertheless, that doesn't mean obedience will always be easy. David practiced this principle and the Lord blessed him greatly for it. For example, even when Saul's jealous rage threatened to end David's life, the future king refused to sin against the Lord by taking revenge against his enemy. Committed to obeying the Father, David would not allow his feelings to shift in a destructive, self-centered direction.

There will be times in your life when God's requests will seem unreasonable. When this happens, you must remember that the Father sees your whole life. He knows the plans He has for you and exactly what it will take to get you to where you need to be in order to fulfill them (Jeremiah 29:11). And He must get you to the place where you declare your dependency on Him, where you're willing to submit your life to Him and trust Him entirely for the future.

Even though you may not understand why you're faced with a trial or when an door of opportunity suddenly closes, your response must always be trust and obedience. Why? Because God says in Jeremiah 7:23, "Obey My voice, and I will be your God, and you will be My people; and you will walk in all the way which I command you, that it may be well with you." In other words, when you submit to Him, He will bless you. So what are you facing today that could tempt you to disobey your loving heavenly Father? Whatever it is, it's not worth missing out on His fellowship and His plans for your life. So choose to obey God, because that is the certain path to hope and blessing.

Father, I will choose to obey You. Thank You for granting
me Your love, provision, and favor. I put my hope in
You and know I will not be disappointed.
Amen.

Confirming Your Testimony

SCRIPTURE READING: PROVERBS 15; MATTHEW 7:17–18; ACTS 7:60

The tongue of the wise makes knowledge acceptable.
PROVERBS 15:2

If you've ever been asked to give your testimony, you've probably responded by telling others what the Lord has done for you. However, while you are commanded to share your faith with others, this action alone does not fully comprise your witness of the Lord's goodness.

Your testimony is threefold. It includes your character (who you are), your conduct (what you do), and your conversation (what you say). All are very important, and when one element of the trio does not match the others, it clouds your testimony. In fact, the most important aspect of your witness is your character. Although it is unseen and unheard, it produces fruit that demonstrates what is really in you. This is because what is truly inside you will directly influence your actions and communication (Matthew 7:17–18).

Stephen was an evangelist who was selected for service among those at the church at Jerusalem. He was chosen because he was "a man full of faith and of the Holy Spirit" (Acts 6:5). This testimony of his godly character became especially clear when some of the religious leaders rose up against him. Although they stoned him until he died, with his last breath he prayed, "Lord, do not hold this sin against them!" (Acts 7:60). Nothing he said or did conflicted with whom he claimed to be; it was his actions and words that confirmed the presence of Christ within him.

Friend, do your character, conduct, and conversation confirm Jesus' ruling presence in your life? People will have an easier time believing your testimony when your life is consistent in all three areas. So ask God to search your heart, cleanse your life, and make your witness as powerful as it can be for His name's sake.

Jesus, I want to be a powerful witness for You. Search me and reveal any ungodly way in me so that my character, conduct, and conversation may all be beautiful reflections of Your grace.
Amen.

Our Source of Success

SCRIPTURE READING: PROVERBS 16; ROMANS 12:3;
PHILIPPIANS 3:4–7; 4:13; JAMES 1:17

Commit your works to the LORD
and your plans will be established.
PROVERBS 16:3

Too often, confidence is thought of strictly as a self-centered belief in one's own abilities. For example, a string of successes may lead a businessman or leader to think very highly of himself. If he learns through experience that he is the best in his career, he could easily slip into a pattern of pride—trusting himself to meet any need that may arise. But is this the confidence that God desires for us?

The apostle Paul would be quick to answer, "No!" Paul certainly experienced life's grandest successes and harshest trials. Through it all, however, he held steadfastly to the conviction that God would empower him to achieve whatever the Lord set before him (Philippians 4:13). Paul realized the futility of placing his confidence in his own abilities. In Philippians 3:4–7, he shows how impressive his accomplishments may have appeared on a human level. But in the end, he testified, "Whatever things were gain to me, those things I have counted as loss for the sake of Christ" (v. 7).

Certainly, God does not want us to place our trust in ourselves. Throughout Scripture, the Lord demonstrates that He alone is capable of meeting every need, every time. We must be careful not to allow our successes to inflate our egos and thereby distract our attention from God (Romans 12:3). After all, we are told quite clearly that "every good thing given and every perfect gift is from above, coming down from the Father" (James 1:17). He gives us our successes. Therefore, today thank Him today for the powerful source of confidence He offers.

Lord God, I commit all my works and plans to You.
Direct my path and keep me faithfully in the center
of Your will. I trust You for my every success.
Amen.

Remember the Reason

SCRIPTURE READING: PROVERBS 17; ROMANS 5:9; HEBREWS 9

Wisdom is in the presence of the one who has understanding.
PROVERBS 17:24 NLT

It is easy to get caught up in our service for the Lord. When we become Christians and begin to grow in our relationship with Him, He ultimately leads us into some form of ministry where we can express His love to others. Maybe it is something formal and organized, such as a children's church teacher or a worship leader. Or perhaps it is something less formal but just as important—such as donating time and money to help needy people or counseling wayward teens.

Regardless of your type of service to the Lord, it is good to continually return to the roots of why you do it. Every so often we can forget the real meaning behind our desire to glorify Him. It is then that we need to remember the great sacrifice Jesus made for us on the cross. It was necessary for Him to shed His blood so that we could know Him, love Him and serve Him. His blood is the only way that we can be cleansed of our sin—past, present, and future—forever (Hebrews 9). Jesus' amazing provision of salvation is the only thing standing between us and an eternity of suffering without God.

Romans 5:9 beckons us to linger in thought about how crucial it was for Jesus to die on our behalf: "Having now been justified by His blood, we shall be saved from the wrath of God through Him." Pause today and think about the sacrifice Jesus made for you on the cross and its significance in your life. Let Him restore the meaning afresh to your heart so you can serve Him with gratefulness and devotion.

Lord Jesus, thank You for the astounding and costly gift of
salvation You have given to me. I serve You out of gratefulness,
my Savior. Help me glorify You to everyone I meet.
Amen.

The Gift of Praise

SCRIPTURE READING: PROVERBS 18; PSALM 22:3;
ISAIAH 43:21; HEBREWS 13:15

*A gift opens the way and ushers
the giver into the presence of the great.*
PROVERBS 18:16

A worship service may look different depending on which church you attend, the country in which you live, the beliefs you have, the gifts God has given you, and sometimes even how you are raised. However, what's most important is not the way you praise the Almighty but that you actually worship Him with awe and reverence in your heart. Whether your church sings, dances, shouts, or a combination of all these, what matters most is that you adore the Lord for who He is.

Worship plays an important, biblical role in our walk with God because it ushers us into His presence. He is enthroned on the praises of His people (Psalm 22:3). Isaiah 43:21 tells us that as believers, we were created to magnify the Lord. And Hebrews 13:15 encourages us to "continually offer to God a sacrifice of praise—the fruit of lips that openly profess his name."

Praise should be a natural expression of our love for our heavenly Father. It should flow like a fountain because of His indwelling presence. We should also offer our thanksgiving to Him in many ways: in public and in private, in words and in song, and even through our deeds. However, our worship is most effective when it comes from a pure heart—one that is free from bitterness and therefore open to honor our heavenly Father in the way He deserves.

When was the last time you truly offered an expression of uninhibited praise to God? Take a moment to consider His goodness, faithfulness, and provision in your life, and express your love and gratitude to Him with all your heart, soul, mind, and strength.

*Father, I truly adore You. How kind, loving, and gracious You are!
I praise Your holy name! Thank You for saving, loving, providing
for, and walking with me through every circumstance of life.
Amen.*

So You May Be Equipped

SCRIPTURE READING: PROVERBS 19;
JEREMIAH 33:3; 2 TIMOTHY 2:15; 3:16–17

Reprove one who has understanding
and he will gain knowledge.
PROVERBS 19:25

In Paul's final letter to Timothy, his son in the faith, he said, "Be diligent to present yourself approved to God as a workman who does not need to be ashamed, accurately handling the word of truth" (2 Timothy 2:15). This meant studying Scripture and learning to flee from the temptations that could keep Timothy from becoming all that the Lord had planned for him to be. Paul would not always be with Timothy to guide Him, but God's Word would never fail to show the young pastor the way he should go.

This is because "all Scripture is inspired by God and profitable for teaching, for reproof, for correction, for training in righteousness; so that the man of God may be adequate, equipped for every good work" (2 Timothy 3:16–17). Immersing yourself in Scripture not only teaches you about Christ's personal love and desire for you but also prepares you for the trials of life and for the blessings that come your way. This is because God's Word is a road map, a framework, and a blueprint to life, and it is crucial that you meditate on it and apply it to your life. Certainly, the Father has many blessings stored up for those who walk in the light of His truth.

Regardless of what you face, as long as Scripture is hidden in your heart and the Holy Spirit is guiding your steps, you can meet all challenges victoriously. Therefore, pick up the Bible and ask God to breathe fresh life into your love for His Word. You'll be surprised at the great things the Father reveals to you through it (Jeremiah 33:3).

Lord God, thank You for Your wonderful Word! Give me a
passion to know You through it. Hide it in my heart so I may
not sin against You but will always follow You faithfully.
Amen.

Opportunities to Teach

SCRIPTURE READING: PROVERBS 20; PROVERBS 11:14;
15:22; 24:6; 2 TIMOTHY 2:2; 1 PETER 5:3

Prepare plans by consultation.
PROVERBS 20:18

As a leader, you may feel as if you need to have all the answers to every question and make every decision. This is an incredible burden for one person, one that the Lord never intended you to bear. This is why you see commands such as today's proverb, "Prepare plans by consultation," repeatedly throughout God's Word (Proverbs 11:14; 15:22; 24:6). You need others to help you make wise decisions. Although there is some comfort in maintaining a sense of control, when you insist on making plans by yourself, you're actually limiting your own effectiveness and unwittingly stunting the growth of those whom God has entrusted to you.

This is what Peter meant when he wrote, "Don't lord it over the people assigned to your care, but lead them by your own good example" (1 Peter 5:3 NLT). Yes, Peter was speaking to elders in the church. But no matter your leadership position or role, your responsibility is to help others grow in their giftedness, developing their ability to make wise plans and godly choices. If you make every choice for others, they will never learn to do so on their own. Of course, you must have spiritual discernment about which counsel you choose to follow, and gently teach others why their ideas are or aren't wise courses of action.

The apostle Paul exhorts, "The things which you have heard from me . . . entrust these to faithful men who will be able to teach others also" (2 Timothy 2:2). So today, whether in your family, at work, or at church, don't keep your plans and choices to yourself. Seek to transform the decisions you make into teachable moments for those around you.

Father, make me aware of how I can teach those
around me through the plans and decisions we're
making and help me to instruct them faithfully.
Amen.

Ungodly Counsel

SCRIPTURE READING: PROVERBS 21; I KINGS 12:1–19

He who shuts his ear to the cry of the poor
will also cry himself and not be answered.
PROVERBS 21:13

We read in Scripture that King Solomon had a very robust building program in Israel—and it came at a great price. In order for him to accomplish his goals, he taxed his people heavily. So when his son Rehoboam took the throne, the people asked for mercy (1 Kings 12:1–19). Sadly, King Rehoboam refused to listen to the godly advice of the elders. He chose instead to do what his young advisers suggested, and the result was a rebellion that swept through the nation of Israel and tore it in two.

What causes a person to listen to ungodly advice? Crucial mistakes often come as a result of selfish ambitions. We weigh our options and choose the ones that appeal to our personal self-interest. It's common for leaders to surround themselves with those who will agree with their plans, even if those plans ultimately lead to destruction. This may sound unbelievable, but it happens—and often. It certainly did for Rehoboam. Before he could be crowned as king, the people rebelled against his misguided power. First Kings 12:19 tell us, "Israel has been in rebellion against the house of David to this day."

Make sure the counsel you receive is from God. Don't be quick to react to the words of others. Instead, spend time in prayer, asking the Lord to confirm, guide, and provide the wisdom you need and act in the loving, compassionate, and merciful manner He directs you to act—no matter how difficult it may seem. Had the king listened to his godly advisers, the nation, at least for the time, would have remained united. Instead, Rehoboam's decision led to a costly mistake from which Israel never recovered.

Lord, I don't want to be foolish like Rehoboam—
I want to be merciful like You. Lead me in the way I should go.
Amen.

Accomplishing the Work

SCRIPTURE READING: PROVERBS 21; EXODUS 3:11–4:17

*Have I not written to you excellent things of counsels and
knowledge to make you know the certainty of the words of
truth that you may correctly answer him who sent you?*
PROVERBS 22:20–21

Has God asked you to do or face something that is far beyond your comfort zone? When He does, it can be daunting. However, the Father will enable you to carry out His plan for your life. When you fall short of accomplishing the goals He has set for you, it's not because He has failed to provide you with what's necessary. Instead, the failure is usually the result of an attitude or belief that short-circuits your faith. As a result, the flow of God's power is hindered in your life.

Moses is a dramatic illustration of the disruptive potential of faith barriers. Called to one of the greatest missions in all of Scripture—the deliverance of Israel from Egyptian enslavement—he responded with excuses for why he should not obey. Of course, reasons for disobedience have not changed much since Moses' experience with the burning bush: poor self-image, ignorance of God's ways, self-doubt, feelings of inadequacy, and fear of failure (Exodus 3:11–4:17). Perhaps some of those are similar to your own.

Thankfully, God's response to faith barriers has not changed since Old Testament days. Each time Moses protested that the Lord had approached the wrong man—a slow-tongued shepherd who had murdered a man—God responded with a firm but gentle rebuttal. The theme of His answers is one we all need to understand as Moses finally did: When we are called to serve, the Lord does the work through us. God does not seek out the best person for a job; He calls men and women who are willing to surrender themselves to Him in faith. And that's what you must do today.

*Lord, I trust You to enable me to accomplish all You
call me to do. I believe. Help my unbelief.
Amen.*

SEPTEMBER 23

How to Overcome

SCRIPTURE READING: PROVERBS 23; JOHN
16:33; ROMANS 8:37; EPHESIANS 5:18

Who has woe? Who has sorrow? Who has contentions?
PROVERBS 23:29

There are people who seem to always have trouble. This proverb talks about how people turn to alcohol to numb their pain but end up only increasing their problems. Thankfully, we know a different way.

To be at peace while the storms of life rage around us, we can be overcomers by maintaining God's perspective on the ups and downs of life and accessing His power—both of which are available to us through the indwelling Person of the Holy Spirit. This is why Ephesians 5:18 admonishes, "Do not get drunk with wine, for that is dissipation, but be filled with the Spirit." Through Him, we can diligently maintain Jesus' perspective on our trials (John 16:33). Likewise, the Holy Spirit enables us to tap in to the divine power of the risen Christ and to become more than conquerors in any situation (Romans 8:37). The key is submitting our will to His. Then, instead of reacting to life based on our own weaknesses and desires—or trying to numb our feelings, which will lead to greater destruction—we respond based on the fact that we belong to Jesus, and that God's strength, wisdom, and will are always available to lead us to triumph.

Friend, the Father's priority for you is transformation into Christ's image, and yielding control of your life to the Holy Spirit allows His will to be done your life. That's when you will experience the inner peace promised to you in a way nothing on earth can replicate (John 14:27). So submit yourself to Him and say, "Lord, whatever You choose to send will be all right with me." And He will be sure you have everything needed to experience the victorious life you were created to enjoy.

Holy Spirit, my inclination is to numb my sorrows, but
instead I turn to You. Help me to overcome these challenges
with wisdom and to glorify God with my life.
Amen.

Submit to Him

SCRIPTURE READING: PROVERBS 24; ROMANS
13:1; 1 TIMOTHY 2:1–3; 1 JOHN 4:20

*Fear the Lord and the king; do not associate
with those who are given to change.*

PROVERBS 24:21

There will always be people who complain about those in leadership. There will always be those who want to shake free from their bosses' rules. But God is clear: Your role as a believer is to honor those in authority and pray for them as long as they are not asking you to do anything that contradicts His Word (1 Timothy 2:1–3). In fact, you can tell a lot about the level of your love and obedience for the Lord by considering the way you deal with those in authority over you. If you can't submit to them, it will be difficult for you to listen to and obey the Father (1 John 4:20).

We see the root of our struggles through the downfall of Satan. He pridefully sought to replace God as the ruler, thinking he knew better than the One who'd created him. Often we wrestle with this same issue. We arrogantly believe we can do a better job of directing the path of our business, organization, or group than those in authority. And so with every decision they make, we feel an unyielding internal urgency to be heard and take control.

However, you must realize that this is not the Lord's way. After all, Romans 13:1 instructs, "Every person is to be in subjection to the governing authorities. For there is no authority except from God, and those which exist are established by God." Therefore, if you have difficulty submitting to your leaders, ask the Father to speak His truth to your heart. Obedience is the only pathway to blessing, and you must be willing to yield even when you disagree with the direction they're going. So submit to them in obedience to Him.

*Father, You know my struggles. Help me to love and
submit to my leaders in a manner that honors You.
Amen.*

SEPTEMBER 25

A Humble Testimony

SCRIPTURE READING: PROVERBS 25; PHILIPPIANS 2:7–8

Do not exalt yourself in the king's presence,
and do not claim a place among his great men.
PROVERBS 25:6 NIV

In our world, humility is not considered a desirable character quality. We're encouraged to promote ourselves and boast of our achievements—asserting our right to be heard. But in the Kingdom of God, meekness is an essential attribute for believers to demonstrate. This is because humility was an integral character quality of Christ.

To become a Man, Jesus relinquished the glory, majesty, and power that were His in heaven. Philippians 2:7–8 tells us that He "emptied Himself, taking the form of a bond-servant, *and* being made in the likeness of men. Being found in appearance as a man, He humbled Himself by becoming obedient to the point of death, even death on a cross." Not only that, but as a Man, Jesus "did not come to be served, but to serve, and to give His life a ransom for many" (Matthew 20:28). He lovingly submitted Himself to His Father's plan and gave up even earthly rights so that He could rescue us from sin. Jesus' life demonstrates the importance of being humble and gives us a clear pattern to follow.

You may think that in order to convince others of their need for Jesus, you must impress them with your Bible knowledge, oratory skills, accomplishments, or wit. However, if you fail to have a humble spirit, then you won't exalt Jesus. He is the One people need to see most through Christians who have been saved by His grace. So don't promote yourself or how great you are. Rather, humbly serve others as Jesus would, in His name. There is no doubt that when you open yourself to being used by Christ for His purposes, you'll be surprised at all the opportunities He brings your way.

Father, please forgive me for promoting myself rather
than glorifying you. In humility I submit myself
to You so others may accept Your salvation.
Amen.

Always Do Your Best

SCRIPTURE READING: PROVERBS 26; MATTHEW 5:16;
2 THESSALONIANS 3:6–13

As the door turns on its hinges,
so does the sluggard on his bed.
PROVERBS 26:14

The Thessalonians had a problem. There were believers who refused to work because they expected the church to take care of them. Many were Greeks who didn't like manual labor, while others thought it was pointless to work because they believed Jesus would return at any minute. However, Paul was clear. They were sinning against God when they failed to provide for their own needs and refused to do what Christ had called them to do, which was preach the gospel (2 Thessalonians 3:6–13).

So today consider: Do you give your very best when you do your work, or do you do as little as possible to get by? Do you look forward to meeting goals with excellence, or do you avoid getting involved with tasks that require too much effort? The Father understands your limitations; however, He will still hold you accountable for the things you can do for yourself and for others. He expects you to give your best and to live with discipline, purpose, and the motivation of glorifying Him.

Jesus said in Matthew 5:16, "Let your light shine before men in such a way that they may see your good works, and glorify your Father who is in heaven." No matter what job you do or assignment you fulfill, you have a unique opportunity to honor God in it. However, you'll never glorify Him and you'll never get ahead if you're being lazy. So do your best, look your best, and be your best at all times. Because when you do, you can be assured that the best the Father has planned for your life is still to come.

Father, please forgive me for the ways I've been lazy. Help
me to be fruitful and do my best so that Your kingdom
will be advanced and You will be glorified.
Amen.

The Counsel of a Godly Friend

SCRIPTURE READING: PROVERBS 27

*The heartfelt counsel of a friend is
as sweet as perfume and incense.*
PROVERBS 27:9 NLT

It is wonderful to have a friend you can go to for counsel, who you know will be wise and discreet in the guidance he or she gives you. But before you take any recommendations from another believer, it's crucial that you look at his or her life and ask, "Is this individual living in God's will?" The last person you want to get counsel from is somebody who is actively disobeying the Father. You want someone who is obviously submitted to the Father—a Christian who clearly understands how to listen to God and has a strong relationship with Him. Someone who is actively walking in the center of His path.

Of course, no matter how godly your friend is, never ask, "Would you please tell me God's will for my life?" or, "What should I do?" Those aren't the right questions. Instead, inquire, "On the basis of your relationship with the Lord and your knowledge of His Word, do you have any insight into what God may be saying to me? What does Scripture say about my situation?"

A good friend will always have your spiritual well-being in mind and will keep your conversations confidential for your protection. Likewise, a godly counselor will be motivated to guide you to the truth—even when it is uncomfortable or it hurts—because he or she will want to see you break free from bondage and follow Christ in obedience. So look for people whose desire is for you to have a strong relationship with the Father so you can experience life at its best. Because that's the kind of friend whose counsel you can always trust.

*Father, thank You for godly friends whose counsel I can
trust. Give me discernment about who to confide in and
lead me to people who will always put You first.
Amen.*

Discerning Motives

SCRIPTURE READING: PROVERBS 28; MATTHEW 7:23;
LUKE 18:14; GALATIANS 6:7

*He who leads the upright astray in an evil way will himself
fall into his own pit, but the blameless will inherit good.*
PROVERBS 28:10

People with misplaced motives are often easy to identify. Athletes who love money more than the game they play usually stand out. Workers who are consumed by their personal ambitions and professional success are often blinded to the good of the company, their coworkers, or their families. Likewise, those who appear to serve God in order to attain fame or favor are always revealed by the fruit they bear. Such individual often see no problem with manipulating others in order to get their way and exalt themselves.

But Galatians 6:7 warns, "Do not be deceived, God is not mocked; for whatever a man sows, this he will also reap." The Lord knows if the desires of our hearts are pure or not. In our service to Him, we are called to do everything in a manner that honors Him and glorifies His name. To proceed with any other reason in view would be to betray Him. Therefore, we should never imagine that it is okay use the Savior's name for our personal gain, because those who do so will be told by Christ, "I never knew you; depart from Me, you who practice lawlessness" (Matthew 7:23).

Therefore, friend, it would be wise for you to examine your heart today. Are you serving God out of love for Him or because of some other purpose? The Father will honor you when you're pure in heart, when you serve Him with the desire of seeing His name lifted up and His kingdom advanced. Therefore, do not seek recognition or glory for yourself. Because as Jesus promises, "Everyone who exalts himself will be humbled, but he who humbles himself will be exalted" (Luke 18:14).

*Lord, search my heart and reveal if there be any selfish motive in
me. May I serve You with a pure heart for Your glory alone.
Amen.*

Keep Your Eyes on God

SCRIPTURE READING: PROVERBS 29; PSALM 111:10

Where there is no vision, the people are unrestrained,
but happy is he who keeps the law.
PROVERBS 29:18

The *Living Bible* phrases today's verse as, "Where there is ignorance of God, the people run wild." In other words, without a palpable reminder of the Lord's presence and authority, people forget that they are accountable to Him—that their actions have both immediate and eternal consequences.

This is why Psalm 111:10 says, "The fear of the Lord is the beginning of wisdom; a good understanding have all those who do His commandments." Of course, you may wonder, *But what is there to be gained if people are afraid of God?* When Scripture refers to "the fear of the Lord," it does not mean that people should be scared of the Father or live in constant terror of what He will do. Rather, it indicates the attitude we should exhibit before Him, which is extreme awe at His holiness, majesty, and splendor. We bow down in humility before the Creator and King of all creation—the One who is omnipotent (all-powerful), omnipresent (always with us wherever we are, during every moment), omniscient (all-knowing and wise), and omnibenevolent (unconditional and perfect in His love for us).

Having a fear of the Lord at its core means having a heart of worship and reverence for God and His Word. So respect what the Father says, honoring Him by obeying His leadership. Acknowledge that He is the highest authority with the greatest wisdom and power. Keep your eyes on Him and submit to what He says because He is holy God. His instructions to us are good, He is in control, and He has never broken a promise. Certainly it will lead you to the stability, success, and well-being you long for.

Lord, You are God! I worship and obey You, knowing that You
are the best Leader, the Wonderful Counselor, my Almighty
King who always leads me in the best way possible.
Amen.

Diligent Obedience

SCRIPTURE READING: PROVERBS 30; MATTHEW 19:26

The ants are not a strong people, but they
prepare their food in the summer.
PROVERBS 30:25

If you've ever watched ants, you've probably noticed that they don't worry much about obstructions in their path or big challenges. It's not unusual to see an ant carrying a crumb of food several times its size up the trunk of a tree. They're committed to their task, whether they have to go up, down, over, or through the obstacle to accomplish it. They're an incredible example of diligence.

Unfortunately, one of the reasons that people sometimes give up is that they're overwhelmed by their circumstances and past failures. They think, *What's the use? Why even try? I'm just going to fail again.* But that attitude does not fit a child of God, and it never will. As people indwelt by His Spirit, we are to be steadfast—diligent about everything we do in obedience to God. We are to have faith that with His help nothing will be impossible for us (Matthew 19:26). By faith we trust that the Lord's plan will be accomplished, whether He has to take us up, down, over, or through the obstacle to do it.

Friend, is there some task that God has called you to that you've avoided? Don't concentrate on the difficulty of your circumstances. Rather, spend time in worship and praise, focusing on God's love, power, wisdom, and provision. Express your thanks for how He will help you in this situation and state your confidence that He will lead you to victory. Then obey and trust that God will empower you to conquer whatever challenge may come along, no matter how big or overwhelming it seems.

Lord, I confess I have procrastinated in certain areas out of
fear of failure. But I will obey You even when everything seems
overwhelming because I trust You to lead me to victory.
Amen.

October

Stewardship

Every day of your life is an investment—either for what is temporary or for what is eternal. And as you walk with God as steward of all He has blessed you with, you have the daily privilege and confidence that you're leaving a legacy with everlasting significance.

The Trap of Debt

SCRIPTURE READING: PROVERBS 1; ROMANS 13:8

If a bird sees a trap being set, it knows to stay away.
But these people set an ambush for themselves.
PROVERBS 1:17–18 NLT

There are several definitions of the word "debt." Some would say, "Anything you owe anybody, at any time." Others would refer to it as being overdue in one's payments or being overextended, having contracted beyond one's ability to repay. Yet Romans 13:8 is a verse that has some insight for us: "Owe nothing to anyone except to love one another." Does that mean that you should never owe anybody anything?

Most of the time when the Bible refers to debt, it's in a negative light. God gave very strict instructions about borrowing money in the Old Testament. The problem today is not that the Bible says you should never, under any condition, owe anybody anything—but whatever you owe, as a believer, you're to pay it off on time. You're not to be overdue, overextended, or unable to pay your debts because that leads us to further bondage, which can become impossible to overcome.

It is wonderful to live in a country where you can get a loan if you need it, such as for a house or a car. But you must do so rarely, with wisdom and caution. There's nothing wrong with a proper amount of debt if it is in the will of Father, if it something that He has told you to do, and if you can fulfill your obligations. But some people buy far more than they could ever afford with no idea about how to pay it back. They indulge themselves with purchases that are far beyond their means, unwilling to wait for God's permission or provision. That is the point at which a debt becomes a sin and a trap that will be difficult to escape from.

Lord, lead me away from temptation
and teach me to be wise in my finances.
Amen.

Faith and Finances

SCRIPTURE READING: PROVERBS 2; MATTHEW 6:24;
2 CORINTHIANS 5:1–10

Seek skillful and godly wisdom as you would silver
and search for her as you would hidden treasures.
PROVERBS 2:4 AMP

There are more verses about money and stewardship in the Bible than there are about heaven. Heaven is assured for us at the moment of salvation, but until we get there, we will have to deal with money in some form or another every day. And for many people, it becomes the driving force of their lives.

But the truth is that you cannot separate your faith and your finances. You will either obey God and submit your wealth to Him or you will be faithless and allow money matters to rule you. Jesus is clear: "No one can serve two masters; for either he will hate the one and love the other, or he will be devoted to one and despise the other. You cannot serve God and wealth" (Matthew 6:24). One reason why you cannot divide your relationship with the Father from your resources is that He will hold you accountable for what you do with what He allows you to make or to possess—whether it is the fruit of your labor or something someone gives you (2 Corinthians 5:1–10).

Realize, friend, that it is through the finances of faithful believers like yourself that God has chosen to supply His work throughout the world. And it is through your resources that the Lord will teach you some of the most priceless principles in His Word. So serve the Father with your money and express love toward others through it as well (1 John 3:16–18). Don't allow money or the need for it dominate you. Scripture is clear, seek wisdom—respect for God—as passionately as you would great treasure. Because when you have Him, you have all you truly need, and He will take care of the rest.

Father, You are the Lord of all of me—including my
finances. Guide me in the way I should go.
Amen.

A Tithe of Blessing

*Honor the LORD with your wealth, with the first fruits of all
your crops; then your barns will be filled to overflowing.*
PROVERBS 3:9–10 NIV

God has set forth specific directives in His Word about what He expects us to give back to Him. Malachi 3:8–12 clearly teaches we are to give Him a tithe, which is 10 percent of what we produce or earn. It is our acknowledgment that all we have and all we're able to achieve comes directly from His hand. It is also the way we open the door to receive His blessing.

But the Lord is specific about the ways we are to present our tithes and offerings. *First*, we are to bring them into His storehouse. We are to give our tithes wherever we regularly worship the Lord—not only to care for the church building and those who work there but also to support the expansion of His kingdom (2 Corinthians 9:7–14). *Second*, we are to make our gifts on a regular basis. In this way, we make our obedience to God a consistent practice and have a constant reminder of His Lordship and provision in our lives. *Third*, we are to make our gifts joyfully. We need to give with a willing heart, knowing that He has blessed us with more than we could ever give back to Him. And the joy that fills our hearts as we give is a direct result of our trust in God to meet our needs (Philippians 4:19).

Friend, when you give the first tenth of your earnings back to the Lord, you're simply returning to Him what was His in the first place. But by doing so, you ensure that He remains your priority. And that, friend, is the path to blessing—you'll never be disappointed as long you keep Him first.

*Father, I acknowledge that all I have and all I am comes
from Your omnipotent hand. Thank You, Lord!
Amen.*

Straight Ahead

SCRIPTURE READING: PROVERBS 4; LUKE 9:62; PHILIPPIANS 3:13–14

Let your eyes look directly ahead and let your
gaze be fixed straight in front of you.
PROVERBS 4:25

How often do you find yourself thinking of the past? How frequently do you reminisce about events from days gone by instead of being expectant for the future? Whether your past was good or bad, God doesn't want you to get stuck in it. He wants you to move forward.

In fact, Jesus said, "Anyone who puts a hand to the plow and then looks back is not fit for the Kingdom of God" (Luke 9:62 NLT). Any farmer knows that when plowing, you have to keep focused straight ahead, because if you look away from the goal, your rows will be crooked. That means less effective use of the field, more difficulty spotting the weeds, and uneven exposure to sun, pollen, and water.

You can probably see the parallels to your own life. When you focus on the past instead of Jesus, your life is less fruitful, it is harder to root out the sin, and you don't receive what you need for growth. This is why Paul declares, "Forgetting what lies behind and reaching forward to what lies ahead, I press on toward the goal for the prize of the upward call of God in Christ Jesus" (Philippians 3:13–14). The past may influence who you are, but it should not hinder who you become.

Therefore consider: Are you focused on the past or on what is ahead of you? Where you're focused will shape where you end up. So today, fix your eyes on Jesus, and you'll find Him taking you to heights beyond your imagination.

Jesus, You are the Author and Perfecter of my faith.
Forgetting what is behind and reaching forward to what is ahead,
I will fix my eyes on You, rejoicing in the future You have planned.
Amen.

The Road of Debt

SCRIPTURE READING: PROVERBS 5; PSALM 37:21; PHILIPPIANS 4:19

*Do not go near the door of her house . . . lest strangers feast
on your wealth and your toil enrich the house of another.*
PROVERBS 5:8, 10 NIV

Looking back, sometimes our first step down a troubled path is obvious to us. Other times, we consider our circumstances and wonder, "How did I get here? Where did it start?" More than likely, it began with something that appeared to be insignificant at the time. But even a "minor" unwise choice can have major, lasting consequences.

Take excessive debt, for example. It begins like other sins, with the *desire* for things we do not need and often are not in the will of God for us. Next is *deception*—we allow ourselves to be deceived that not only do we need something, but we need it *immediately*, which may lead to hasty and unwise decisions. Then comes *doubt* that the Lord could provide for our needs. We want things on our terms rather than His, so we ignore the fact that "My God shall supply all your needs according to His riches in glory by Christ Jesus" (Philippians 4:19). The next step is *decision*—we purchase something that we know we're going to struggle to repay. The natural consequence is *delay*. Because we have made irresponsible purchases and decisions, we begin to experience financial strain, which results in a delay or default on our payments. The result is *disobedience*. When we fail to pay our debts, we disobey God (Psalm 37:21). The last stage in the debt process is *damage*. When a believer does not repay his or her bills on time, that damages his or her Christian testimony.

Friend, do not take even the first step down the road to debt. A little self-denial now will save you a great deal of heartache later. Be wary of the minor choices and always proceed with wisdom.

*Father, help me to be wise with my resources
and pursue only those things You desire for me.
Amen.*

Wise Stewardship

SCRIPTURE READING: PROVERBS 6; MATTHEW 25:14–30

They labor hard all summer, gathering food for the winter.
PROVERBS 6:8

Today's proverb talks about the wisdom of ants, who honor the Lord by diligently storing away what they will need during months when food will be scarce. Jesus taught that those who likewise handle God's resources wisely, will be rewarded, while those who disregard the Lord's principles will lose out. Matthew 25:14–30 gives us five principles to help us:

1. Investing what we have and wisely putting it to work for the Kingdom of God is the Lord's will for every believer. However, saving (with interest added) is always better than squandering.
2. Mismanaging even a little money indicates that we will also misuse it if we have a lot.
3. Failing to be faithful with God's money will deprive us of even greater riches. The Father offers true wealth—increased opportunities and comprehension of deep spiritual truths—only to those who rightly employ what He's given them.
4. Mishandling that which belongs to another will deprive us of possessing our own resources. If we borrow something and do not take care of it, we cannot expect the Lord to reward us with a similar gifts.
5. Allowing a love for money to rule us will cause us to dismiss scriptural teachings about money and justify ungodly behavior. Our reaction to financial appeals or biblical teaching on stewardship reveals whether money has taken control of us.

Friend, by heeding God's warnings, you can become a faithful steward of all He's given you. So return control of all your resources to your heavenly Father and enjoy the blessings He has for you.

Lord, I want to honor You. With every decision and purchase, remind me of the principles that should guide my life and help me to obey.
Amen.

Ritual or Relationship?

Today I have paid my vows.
PROVERBS 7:14

As we can see in today's proverb, even the adulteress gave offerings to God. This shows that we can do so as a ritual pointing to our own righteousness rather than out of a sincere and obedient love of the Father. This was the problem with the religious leaders in Jesus' day and why they made such a mess of things. In their pursuit of prominence through acts of piety, they had become prideful, trusting in their own works rather than in an ongoing relationship with the Lord.

In a sense, it's a trap we are all in danger of falling into. Many of those Pharisees probably had a sincere desire to know and serve God, so they practiced the disciplines that were supposed to bring them closer to Him. Eventually, the deeds themselves became more important than the Lord. Sadly, the scribes and Pharisees were destroying people's lives by their example—teaching them that keeping the Law was the only way to God. Not only were the people discouraged, they were also prevented from experiencing the loving relationship with the Lord that they longed to have.

That's not what the Savior wanted for them, and He doesn't desire it for you, either. True, it is much easier and more comfortable to abide by a set of rules and regulations than to truly know and obey the Father (Matthew 7:21–23). However, it is nowhere near as fulfilling, and it will eventually put you in terrible bondage. Instead, the Savior asks you to come to Him unguarded and without fear because He loves and accepts you just as you are. So don't try to impress God with your offerings—He already loves you and knows what you need. Just love Him and do as He asks.

Lord, may everything I do to reflect my devotion to You.
I honor Your commands and faithfully obey because
of how profoundly I love and respect You.
Amen.

True Wealth

SCRIPTURE READING: PROVERBS 8; 1 CHRONICLES 29:12;
PHILIPPIANS 4:19; JAMES 1:17

*Wisdom is better than jewels and all desirable
things cannot compare with her.*
PROVERBS 8:11

Today, perhaps you're wondering why the Lord has chosen to place you in the financial situation you're in, with the burdens and bills you bear. Wealth is a desirable blessing, of course, but understand that from God's viewpoint, it is not limited to currency. Monetarily rich people are often miserable: Although their bank accounts are overflowing, their souls are impoverished because material blessings cannot fill the soul's deepest needs. This is why biblical wealth is defined as *the ability to experience and enjoy the Lord's blessings.* The poor individual who knows Jesus as Savior has indescribable resources compared to the rich person who rejects Him.

This is why it's so important that we realize that God is the Source of all we have. As David proclaimed in 1 Chronicles 29:12, "Riches and honor come from You, and You rule over all." Without the Father's love, we would have nothing. He is the Fountainhead of our life, health, and every necessary element for living. And He always gives us exactly what we need. As James 1:17 reminds us, "Every good thing given and every perfect gift is from above, coming down from the Father."

So don't be discouraged by the financial situation you find yourself in today. It is for a purpose—to teach you the importance of your relationship with God. The Lord owns it all and He promises that He will "supply all your needs according to His riches in glory in Christ Jesus" (Philippians 4:19). So cling to Him, rely on Him, and trust Him. And thank Him that because He's in your life, you are wealthy in every way that's eternally important.

*Father, thank You for being my true wealth and providing
for my needs. You are worthy of all my praise.
Amen.*

OCTOBER 9

The Wisdom of Preparation

SCRIPTURE READING: PROVERBS 9; MATTHEW 5:45: JAMES 1:5

She has prepared.
PROVERBS 9:2

Whether you are new in your Christian faith or have been a believer for many years, you can be certain of one thing—you will face times of trial and difficulty. This is because you live in a sinful, fallen world, and the "rain [falls] on the righteous and the unrighteous" (Matthew 5:45). Tough times are more than likely to arise. Thankfully, once you become a child of God, your loving heavenly Father strengthens and prepares you to face the problems you will encounter.

Yes, the Father helps you get ready. But is there anything you can do to prepare for the challenges ahead, especially since you don't know what the future may hold? In fact, there is. You can effectively ready yourself for the trials to come by seeking the Lord when your life is problem-free. When you become accustomed to seeking God during the good times, your first response to a problem will be to call on Him for wisdom and guidance.

Many people make the mistake of deciding on a course of action before praying to discover the mind of God. But disastrous choices can be easily avoided by going to our heavenly Father first and asking Him for guidance. We should never let anyone push us into moving forward until we've heard from the Lord. And we can be sure that when we call upon Him, He will be faithful to answer and to give us wisdom (James 1:5).

Therefore, take the best course of action and prepare yourself for the troubles ahead by seeking the Father in prayer and through His Word today. And trust in faith that regardless of what challenge arises, He will faithfully help you overcome it.

Father, lead me today. Prepare me for what's ahead
through Your Word, as I kneel before You in prayer.
I trust You to strengthen me and give me wisdom.
Amen.

Your Father's Gifts

SCRIPTURE READING: PROVERBS 10;
LEVITICUS 11:1, 9–12; MATTHEW 7:9–11

*It is the blessing of the LORD that makes
rich, and He adds no sorrow to it.*
PROVERBS 10:22

Friend, today you can pray with confidence in the trustworthiness of your heavenly Father. Why? Because Jesus said, "What man is there among you who, when his son asks for a loaf, will give him a stone? Or if he asks for a fish, he will not give him a snake, will he? If you then, being evil, know how to give good gifts to your children, how much more will your Father who is in heaven give what is good to those who ask Him!" (Matthew 7:9–11).

Pay attention to what Jesus is saying. The stones around the Sea of Galilee were round, the same color and shape of the daily bread. But no parent would knowingly give stones to his or her child. Likewise, the snakes probably looked like fish that could be caught there. However, they were not only poisonous; finless fish such as eels were prohibited by Levitical law (Leviticus 11:1, 9–12). No good parent would allow his or her child to eat such a creature.

With this in mind, how much more will your loving Father give when you ask Him to lead you? In other words, there are things in life that seem to be what you may want. Perhaps there is a certain person you want to marry or a job you wish the Lord would give you. But God knows when what you desire is not what will satisfy you. And you can rest assured that He will divert you from danger as long as you are listening to Him. Therefore, seek Him confidently, knowing He will never steer you wrong or fail to keep His promises to you.

*Father, thank You for giving me good gifts without sorrow.
I trust You to lead me and provide what I need.
Amen.*

Enduring Contentment

SCRIPTURE READING: PROVERBS 11; PHILIPPIANS 4:11–13

He who is steadfast in righteousness will attain to life.
PROVERBS 11:19

Do you have a vision of how your life would have to change in order for you to say with confidence, "I am content"? Many people associate contentment with money, recognition, and successful relationships—only to be disappointed with the void that remains when their goals are accomplished or when adversity arises. However, as believers, God offers us a different, more enduring kind of contentment.

In fact, the apostle Paul claimed to have it, saying, "I have learned to be content in whatever circumstances I am" (Philippians 4:11). What was the source of his peace? He revealed the key component: "I can do all things through Him who strengthens me" (v. 13). In other words, Paul learned to trust God completely regardless of his circumstances, knowing the Lord could help him overcome whatever he faced.

Such confidence is available to you as well. So how can you embrace and experience this abiding contentment? The answer is simple: Put your total trust in God's ability to help you by relinquishing control to Him. When you do so, you will have the contentment you seek. Because when you carry your burdens—rather than allowing Him to handle them for you—it's like carrying a hundred-pound weight on your back, which becomes more cumbersome with every step you take. But envision His mighty hand reaching down and lifting that burden from your back. Wouldn't that give you peace?

Friend, the Father wants to relieve you of the worries you're carrying. They're too much for you, but nothing for Him. So trust Him. Release your anxiety and open your heart to the peace that He offers. When you're ready, God is waiting—and so is the contentment He longs for you to have.

Lord, I want to let go. Help me to release my burdens to You.
Thank You that I can face anything as long as You're with me.
Amen.

OCTOBER 12

You Reap What You Sow

Scripture Reading: Proverbs 12;
Malachi 3:10; 2 Corinthians 9:6–7

The deeds of a man's hands will return to him.
PROVERBS 12:14

God knew how important the issue of money would be to us, so He placed special emphasis on how to handle it in His Word. Do you realize that there are more verses in Scripture on the subject of money—some 2,350 of them—than on any other topic? Knowing where our greatest temptations and pitfalls would lie, God, in His grace, gave us wise principles to help us. This is because our Father is personally interested in the details of our life and wants to help us succeed.

So how do we honor the Lord with what we have? *First,* we are to give confidently, knowing that God honors His promises. Malachi 3:10 instructs, "Bring the whole tithe into the storehouse . . . and test Me now in this . . . if I will not open for you the windows of heaven and pour out for you a blessing until it overflows." The tithe is 10 percent of your income, and if you'll trust God with it, He will bless your life in unimaginable ways.

Second, we are to give generously. Second Corinthians 9:6 warns, "He who sows sparingly will also reap sparingly, and he who sows bountifully will also reap bountifully." In other words, those who invest in God's kingdom generously because of their reverence for Him and trust in His provision will reap the fruit of their faith. Therefore, always sow abundantly so you can experience the Lord's amazing bounty.

Third, we are to give cheerfully. Second Corinthians 9:7 reports, "God loves a cheerful giver." Why? Because it means you're giving out of love for Him rather than obligation. So make your giving into an act of worship to the Father. Not only will it bring Him pleasure, but it will bring you joy as well.

Father, I will give confidently, generously, and cheerfully,
in gratefulness to You. Lead me in my finances.
Amen.

A Look at God's Provision

SCRIPTURE READING: PROVERBS 13; PHILIPPIANS 4:19

The righteous has enough.
PROVERBS 13:25

In Philippians 4:19 the apostle Paul writes, "My God will supply all your needs according to His riches in glory in Christ Jesus." Perhaps you've lacked many things in your life and have a hard time believing this promise. But the Lord wants you to have what is best, so He will always give you what you truly need.

So let us examine this assurance in order to have a clearer understanding of it. The Lord will supply all our what? *Needs.* So the first assessment a person must make in considering whether or not this promise applies to his or her situation is, "Is what I'm asking for *really* a need?" A need is something that you require for living or that is essential to your existence.

The second consideration is whether this promise is *limited* or *general.* Does it relate only to a specific person in history, or is it relevant to us today? Thankfully, Philippians 4:19 is intended for all believers. However, as we examine this verse, we find there is a requirement for its fulfillment. We must be "in Christ Jesus," which means that Christ has to be the priority of our lives. And as we look to Jesus to be our Provider, we must be willing to do whatever He calls us to do—walking in the center of God's plan for our lives.

Philippians 4:19 is not a blank check for whatever you may desire, but because of your relationship with Jesus, He *will* meet your every need—not only what you require for your physical health and well-being but also for your emotional and spiritual needs. He will satisfy your soul with love, acceptance, companionship, and worth as no one else can.

Father, thank You for Your perfect provision. Help me
to walk in the center of Your will so that I'll always be
aware of the miraculous ways You supply all I need.
Amen.

Messy, but Worth It

SCRIPTURE READING: PROVERBS 14; HOSEA 8:7; GALATIANS 6:7–8

*Where no oxen are, the manger is clean, but much
revenue comes by the strength of the ox.*
PROVERBS 14:4

You've heard me say that you reap what you sow, more than you sow, and later than you sow. This principle comes from Galatians 6:7–8, which admonishes, "Whatever a man sows, this he will also reap. For the one who sows to his own flesh will from the flesh reap corruption, but the one who sows to the Spirit will from the Spirit reap eternal life." If you obey the Lord, you open yourself up to all the promises and blessings He has for you. But if you don't, it's going to cause all kinds of problems in your life because you won't be in the center of God's will and under His protection.

So consider: Are you trying to evade stress by avoiding life? Do you refuse to sow the seed of the gospel because you don't want to go through the trouble of dealing with the harvest? Or maybe you're avoiding obeying God because of how complicated it could get. Understand that by refusing to engage, you're making a terrible choice.

Hosea 8:7 warns, "They sow the wind and they reap the whirlwind." What you're really doing is inviting more problems and stressors into your life. You're turning down God-given opportunities because they involve emotional and physical commitment. Yet you're actually setting yourself up for even more emotional and physical pain that won't bring you peace, prosperity, or success. Rather you'll reap sorrow, poverty, and penalties beyond what you can imagine. Don't allow that to happen! Obeying God may be messy, but it's worth it. So submit yourself to Him regardless of how complicated it may make your life. You'll be grateful for all He produces through your obedience.

*Lord, I confess that at times I haven't obeyed You because
I didn't want to complicate my life. Please forgive me
and help me to submit to You with faith and devotion.
Amen.*

OCTOBER 15

The Basis of True Worth

SCRIPTURE READING: PROVERBS 15; PSALM 62:10–
12; PROVERBS 11:28; HEBREWS 13:5

Better is a little with the fear of the LORD
than great treasure and turmoil with it.
PROVERBS 15:16

Part of what plagues us today as a society is our focus on material wealth. Because of our prosperity, we've grown somewhat comfortable and self-serving, thereby losing much of our understanding as to what is really important. In most cases, we have more than sufficient resources for ourselves and our families. Sadly, many have come to believe that if we wish to be significant in this world, there are critical items we should own, essential levels of wealth and notoriety we should attain to.

Understand that much of this is fear-driven. We are afraid of missing out, of not being good enough, of being judged, of not having the same opportunities as others. As a result, we rely on money as our source of worth and security, rather than on our Savior, Jesus. We fail to save for the future, choosing instead to pursue possessions, even to the point of putting ourselves and the nation into truly serious jeopardy.

Yet God's Word is clear: "He who trusts in his riches will fall, but the righteous will flourish like the green leaf" (Proverbs 11:28). In fact, Psalm 62:10–12 teaches us, "If riches increase, do not set your heart upon them. Once God has spoken; twice I have heard this: that power belongs to God; and lovingkindness is Yours, O Lord, for You recompense a man according to his work."

Friend, your value comes from our relationship with the Savior, not your portfolio of investments, your bank accounts, your salary, or what you own. Those things will fade away and fail you. Only intimacy with the Father will give you true worth or security (Hebrews 13:5).

Lord, thank You for being the true, unfailing source of my worth
and security. Whenever I'm tempted to feel inadequate because of
what I don't have, help me to remember all You given me in Jesus.
Amen.

The True Measure of Success

SCRIPTURE READING: PROVERBS 16;
2 CORINTHIANS 12:7; PHILIPPIANS 4:13

A just balance and scales belong to the Lord;
all the weights of the bag are His concern.
PROVERBS 16:11

What is your definition of success? Humanly, we often describe it as the financial gain of a businessperson, the fame of a celebrity, or the exceptional ability of an athlete. Regardless of the field, we generally equate success with fame, money, accomplishment, and power. However, if these were truly the way to measure, then we could never call the apostle Paul successful.

Was Paul famous? In his lifetime, he was actually despised. The Jews and strict Roman rulers deemed Paul a notorious troublemaker. Was he wealthy? As a Pharisee and leader among the Jews, he most likely was. However, when Jesus called him to spread the gospel to the world, his financial status changed quickly. He lived the rest of his life as an itinerant preacher, supporting himself on his three missionary journeys by making tents. Was Paul popular? In the eyes of the world, he was simply a strange, brash preacher of a strange new religion. He was in and out of prison, often unimpressive in appearance, and the victim of an unspecified ailment (2 Corinthians 12:7).

But was Paul powerful? In his own strength, Paul was just as weak as any other man. However, Paul had access to the most amazing power the world has ever known: Jesus Christ. In the face of weakness, he exclaimed, "I can do all things through Him who strengthens me" (Philippians 4:13).

Friend, that same power is available to you today. You may not be much in this world, but what matters is who you are in the Father's eyes. Praise God for making you a success through Jesus Christ our Lord.

Lord, thank You that the true measure of my worth and success
comes through You. Help me to obey You so that in all things
I will be more than a conqueror like the apostle Paul.
Amen.

The Real Issue

SCRIPTURE READING: PROVERBS 17; MATTHEW 19:16–26

*Why is there a price in the hand of a fool
to buy wisdom, when he has no sense?*
PROVERBS 17:18

The rich young ruler had it all: wealth, fame, and power. Yet something was missing, especially when it came to the question of eternal life. Therefore, he asked Jesus, "Teacher, what good thing shall I do that I may obtain eternal life?" (Matthew 19:16). Of course, faith in Christ was the answer. But this young man remained determined that there must be a good deed that he could do in order to receive an eternal reward.

Like this young man, many people spend their lives doing good in order to earn salvation. Whenever they sin, they immediately try to balance their blunder with an act of kindness. They hope that in the end the good they do will outweigh the bad. This man was no different. So Jesus said to him, "If you wish to be complete, go and sell your possessions and give to the poor, and you will have treasure in heaven; and come, follow Me" (Matthew 19:21).

You see, Jesus knew that how much good the man had done wasn't really the problem. The issue at hand was what ruled his heart—the fact that he had more faith in his wealth than in God. The riches of this world had a hold on him; therefore, he could not give himself fully to the Lord even though he'd been convicted by the message of the gospel.

Friend, money, good deeds, and acts of kindness will never give you access to God's kingdom—and the notion that they can is the greatest mistake you can make. Thankfully, Jesus Christ sacrificially gave you all you need on the cross. So believe in Him and thank Him for paying your sin debt in full and providing all you need for salvation.

*Lord Jesus, please forgive me for allowing anything to have hold of me
other than You. You are my Savior and worthy of my whole heart.
Amen.*

OCTOBER 18

Investing Eternally

SCRIPTURE READING: PROVERBS 18; LUKE 12:34; 2 PETER 3:9

He who is slothful in his work is a
brother to him who is a great destroyer.
PROVERBS 18:9

Time is precious—we never seem to have enough of it. Therefore, how we invest our lives demonstrates where our heart is and reveals what is most important to us. Throughout the New Testament, we find men and women who devoted themselves to the advancement of God's kingdom, no matter what the cost. They lived lives that reflected Christ. They told stories of Jesus' love. They invited others to join them in their quest to find a deep, intimate relationship with the Savior. And they did so because they shared God's heart, "not wishing for any to perish but for all to come to repentance" (2 Peter 3:9).

And that relationship is what Jesus Himself wants us to have. He invested His life in others. He loved His disciples, the individuals who came to hear Him teach, and the people He healed. But He also cared for the Pharisees, those who were hostile to Him, and the people who crucified Him (Luke 12:34). Jesus actively gave us His best regardless of the difficulty because He wanted us to be saved—blessed with eternal life—not destroyed.

This is why it's so important that you're not slothful in sharing your faith and obeying God. As you invest your life in others, you may find resistance, but you'll also find amazing satisfaction and joy because you are reflecting His character and fulfilling His purpose in creating you. Therefore, keep watching patiently for God to turn others' hearts toward Himself as you diligently lift Him up. When others see the Lord working through you, they will desire to have that same intimacy with the Father that you do. And the fruit from such investment is not of the fleeting variety—it is eternal, and has a permanent impact on the world.

Lord Jesus, I want my life to count for eternity. Keep me focused
on what is important and lead others to You through me.
Amen.

OCTOBER 19

Rewarding Service

SCRIPTURE READING: PROVERBS 19

One who is gracious to a poor man lends to the Lord,
and He will repay him for his good deed.
PROVERBS 19:17

Do you long to do something that makes a difference and provides you with a sense of fulfillment? Then understand that when your work is motivated by love and performed in Jesus' name in order to exalt God, you will find yourself enthusiastic and energized by it. The Lord sends opportunities every day to positively impact the lives of people around you, and He loves seeing your faith shine as you help others.

Your service may simply be an encouraging word, a listening ear, or a cup of cold water given in His name. Or the Father may ask you to sacrifice your time or give generously of your resources to those in need. Whatever the case, the love God gives you for others will motivate you. And as you pour yourself into ministering to them, you'll discover a deep sense of fulfillment and joy. However, make sure your service is always done "in Jesus' name." This means that whatever you do should be in accordance with God's revealed will and in a manner consistent with Scripture. Serving in Jesus' name also means that you are acting in submission to His authority—that is, doing things in His way and time and dependent upon His Holy Spirit's power. Only by yielding to His control—and exalting God rather than yourself—can your work yield real spiritual fruit and an eternal reward.

As an ambassador of Christ, your true fulfillment will come from serving with excellence so that the Savior can receive the glory He deserves. So watch for opportunities to exalt Him among those in need and be ready to live out your faith with joy and enthusiasm.

Lord, I want to serve You. Whether to those in need in an
earthly sense or spiritually—fill me with love for others
and help me reach out to them in Jesus' name.
Amen.

Faithful and True

SCRIPTURE READING: PROVERBS 20;
DEUTERONOMY 31:8; JOB 42:2; PSALM 139:7–12; LUKE 12:2–3;
2 CORINTHIANS 1:20; TITUS 1:2; HEBREWS 13:8

Differing weights and differing measures,
both of them are abominable to the Lord.
PROVERBS 20:10

In our troubled world, injustice, crime, and dishonesty appear to run rampant and the only thing constant seems to be change. Thankfully, we serve the Lord God, whose actions are perfect, whose character is flawless, and who keeps every promise (Hebrews 13:8). We can have complete confidence in Him because He is:

- *Omniscient.* Our Father's knowledge is complete—no circumstance is hidden from Him (Luke 12:2–3). There is no motive or thought process that He does not discern.
- *Omnipotent.* God has total power over all things; nothing is outside His control. No authority in heaven or on earth can thwart His purposes (Job 42:2).
- *Omnipresent.* There is no person or place in all of creation that is outside of the Lord's presence (Psalm 139:7–12). All of space and time are within His sight, and He never misses anyone or anything that can impact your life.
- *Truthful.* God cannot lie (Titus 1:2). He always speaks the truth, and His words are flawless. So you can trust His answers to your prayers and the reliability of His Word.

Friend, the Father's character is not affected by time, place, people, or circumstances. He makes no mistakes in what He says or does because His knowledge is perfect, His sovereignty is complete, and all is within His sight. Every promise is guaranteed in Jesus Christ (2 Corinthians 1:20). He will never fail, forsake, or deceive you (Deuteronomy 31:8).

Lord, I praise You for bringing truth and stability to a world that is ever deceiving and shifting. To You be all the honor, glory, power, and praise. Amen.

Be Diligent

SCRIPTURE READING: PROVERBS 21; DEUTERONOMY 4:9;
JOHN 9:4; 2 TIMOTHY 2:15; 2 PETER 1:5

The plans of the diligent lead surely to advantage.
PROVERBS 21:5

Have you ever considered the fact that diligence is a crucial character trait that is vital to the successful Christian life? Paul instructed Timothy, "Be diligent to present yourself approved to God as a workman who does not need to be ashamed, accurately handling the word of truth" (2 Timothy 2:15). Likewise, before the apostle Peter listed the character traits of faith, virtue, knowledge, and self-control, he exhorted his readers to apply "all diligence" in acquiring them (2 Peter 1:5). This is because such qualities are not found in superficial Christians. They take root in one's character only through steadfast application and pursuit.

However, the overriding motivation for our diligence cannot be our material gain; because that will not endure. Rather, our persistent efforts must be applied to seeking God and proclaiming the Good News of salvation through our Savior, Jesus Christ. In fact, Jesus said, "We must work the works of Him who sent Me as long as it is day; night is coming when no one can work" (John 9:4).

And so to walk in wisdom, we must actively and conscientiously obey and apply God's Word to our lives and proclaim it to others without fainting or failing. As Deuteronomy 4:9 instructs, "Keep your soul diligently, so that you do not forget the things which your eyes have seen and they do not depart from your heart all the days of your life; but make them known to your sons and your grandsons." Our time here on earth is brief, and as believers, we must be alert to every opportunity to share Christ while we can. So don't give up—even when the road is difficult. Instead, diligently honor Him in all you say and do. Because certainly, that is the unquestioned path to blessing.

Lord, I confess that sometimes I want to give up.
Help me to be diligent—to endure with faith in You.
Amen.

Enslaved

SCRIPTURE READING: PROVERBS 21

The borrower becomes the lender's slave.
PROVERBS 22:7

There are many verses throughout the book of Proverbs that deal with money, debt, loans, and repayment, but today's verse is especially powerful. Of course, you may wonder, *How does debt enslave people?* One way is that they no longer have the freedom to use their resources as they should. They must use their resources to meet their obligations.

Another way we are enslaved by debt is that we can't do what God asks us to do with our resources if we already owe all that we have. One reason people do not honor the Lord with a tithe is that they say, "I don't have any left over." Likewise, debt is harmful to a believer's witness and testimony. Think of the impression it makes when you say to a creditor, "I'm sorry. I cannot pay this." You forfeit the opportunity to tell that person about Christ. Then there is the emotional stress a family endures as a result of indebtedness. It can cause division in the home, which will affect the entire family. It can even result in divorce. Furthermore, debt causes the loss of opportunity. One has no discretionary funds to use for special purchases or investments.

Can you fully obey the Lord when you've already obligated yourself to creditors beyond what you are able to pay? Are you obeying Him when you give Him only what's left over—if you give anything at all? You cannot be in the will of God and operate your finances in that manner. So don't give in to debt. Instead, seek His best regarding your finances. He will show you the path to get you out of debt so that you can be the person He wants you to be, free to do whatever He calls you to do.

Father, I don't want to be indebted—unable to
accomplish what You call me to do. Lead me in wisdom
so that even in my finances You are glorified.
Amen.

Better Priorities

SCRIPTURE READING: PROVERBS 23; ACTS 4:12

Do not weary yourself to gain wealth,
cease from your consideration of it.
PROVERBS 23:4

People long to feel safe, and in order to do so they often pursue affluence at the cost of everything else—their communities, friendships, families, and even their own health and well-being. Some do so by becoming workaholics, while others do so by illicit means. And what do they buy? More things that do not satisfy the longings within them. They may purchase items that outwardly indicate worth—such as cars, homes, jewelry, beauty treatments, or what have you. Or they may acquire things that attempt to dull their inner pain—such as alcohol and drugs. Sadly, this only drives them farther from what they really need.

What a waste of life and resources. Can you imagine what awesome things might be done if people were to redirect all of that effort and energy into pursuing the Kingdom of God? Think about the change that could occur in our nation if the money that was spent on things that harm us physically, psychologically, relationally, and spiritually were instead spent in a godly way, teaching people how to have a fulfilling relationship with the Lord. Undoubtedly, we would be absolutely amazed. We could reach those who have never heard the gospel, comforting those who are hurting and giving hope to those who have none. Those who are hungry could be fed, those who are cold could be clothed and sheltered. The uneducated could learn to read and write, and those who are unskilled could become proficient in the abilities they need to earn a living and improve their quality of life. And it would all be done in the name of the One who saves our souls from the grave—the only One who truly gives us safety and security (Acts 4:12).

Lord, what a different world this would be if we redirected our
resources to serving Your kingdom rather than trying to satisfy
spiritual needs only You can fulfill! May You always be my priority.
Amen.

Ten Words for Freedom

SCRIPTURE READING: PROVERBS 24; PSALM 32:8; PROVERBS 3:9–10

By knowledge the rooms are filled
with all precious and pleasant riches.
PROVERBS 24:4

Financial freedom is what every child of God should desire for themselves, and it is certainly what God desires for us as well. Here are ten words that will point you in the right direction.

1. *Conviction.* You must be convicted that you are in debt and that it's not the will of God.
2. *Confession.* Beyond conviction, you must confess: "Lord, I have let my desires control my expenditures and I have not been a good steward."
3. *Commitment.* A commitment is a decision to do something, backed up with the courage to make it happen.
4. *Confidence.* You can be confident that God will guide you and enable you to get out of debt (Psalm 32:8).
5. *Cooperation.* Every member of the family must cooperate.
6. *Construct.* Construct a realistic budget that involves repayment of debt. It won't happen without a plan.
7. *Change.* You must change your spending habits.
8. *Counsel.* Find someone who will hold you accountable.
9. *Contributions.* Honor God with the first fruits of what you have (Proverbs 3:9–10).
10. *Consistency.* Stick with it, whatever it takes.

You can do one of two things with these words. You can ignore them and keep getting deeper in debt, or you can be wise enough to apply them to your life. God wants you to experience financial freedom. Trust Him to lead and enable you, and He will take you there.

Lord, I want to be free in my finances. Help me to
apply each of these ten words so I can experience the
abundant blessings You've planned for my life.
Amen.

The Problem of Excess

SCRIPTURE READING: PROVERBS 25; 23:20–21

Do you like honey? Don't eat too much, or it will make you sick!
PROVERBS 25:16 NLT

Having anything in excess is dangerous. People who are self-indulgent are not in control of their own desires. Self-indulgence may be manifested as gluttony (consistent overindulgence in food or drink), immoral behavior (an uncontrolled drive to satisfy sexual desires), or greed (an insatiable desire for more possessions). Self-indulgent individuals may be power hungry or manipulative because they are always seeking what they want, when they want it, without regard to the needs and concerns of others. But regardless of the area of excess, it assuredly leads to devastation.

Such people generally have no trouble consuming others' time, resources, and energy, or dragging others down with them. This is why Proverbs 23:20–21 warns, "Do not be with heavy drinkers of wine, or with gluttonous eaters of meat; for the heavy drinker and the glutton will come to poverty." Have you ever gone to lunch with a plan that you're not going to have dessert or overindulge in carbohydrates, only to find yourself with a person who wants to try everything on the menu? In the end, you walk away from that lunch having blown your intention of having a light, nutritious meal.

The fact is, self-indulgent people can influence us greatly. They may appear to embrace life fully—they're eager to try new things and are a lot of fun to be around. But beware! In the end, they can cause you to throw away your own disciplines and get off track with God's best plan for your life—all in the name of experiencing more of life or having a good time. Don't give in. Allow the Lord to guide and limit your appetites.

Lord, I realize that too much of anything is unhealthy. Teach me wise habits and moderation so that I may experience all You have for me.
Amen.

The Enemy's False Philosophies

SCRIPTURE READING: PROVERBS 26; JOHN 8:32

Enemies disguise themselves with their lips,
but in their hearts they harbor deceit.
PROVERBS 26:24 NIV

The enemy knows exactly what to do to get you to fall. His goal is to turn you away from the Father by tempting you through his provocative promises of pleasure without penalty. This is why countless people have become spiritual prisoners through the enslaving philosophies of the world system. The enemy deceitfully crafts appealing schools of thought that promise freedom but in reality bring only frustrating bondage and servitude. Some of the worldly ways of thinking include:

- *Materialism*—which promises a fulfilling life through the accumulation of wealth and possessions.
- *Humanism*—which teaches that man is the center of the universe and that the Lord is irrelevant. In fact, humanism claims that in essence, man is the god of his own world, the arbiter of his own truth and able to do anything he desires.
- *Hedonism*—which is the pursuit of personal pleasure and happiness through alcohol, drugs, sex, recreation, or what have you. Its motto is, "If it feels good, do it."

Regardless of which belief an individual falls prey to, the outcome is the same: spiritual bondage and destruction because each belief lacks the capacity to impart genuine spiritual life and fulfillment.

Friend, you don't have to be one of the walking wounded. Defeat the enemy by declaring your trust in your loving heavenly Father. Reject the enemy's lies no matter how good they sound and embrace the truth God teaches you in and through His Word. Commit yourself to the Lord wholeheartedly and let Him show you how to truly walk in freedom (John 8:32).

Father, free me from whatever way I have fallen prey to the world's
empty philosophies, so I may walk in Your wisdom and truth.
Amen.

The God of Tomorrow

SCRIPTURE READING: PROVERBS 27; MATTHEW 6:33-34

*Do not boast about tomorrow, for you do not
know what a day may bring forth.*
PROVERBS 27:1

Have you ever found yourself focused on the future? You look at what's ahead and make your human calculations about whether the future appears bright or foreboding. When everything seems to be going as you've planned and your dreams begin to come true, perhaps you are hopeful, confident, and content. On the other hand, if challenges arise and you don't see much hope, you grow disheartened and disillusioned.

But notice that whether you boast about tomorrow or are bothered by it, the same thing is true—you're focusing on what *you* can see or accomplish in your own strength. However, bragging about tomorrow and worrying about it are two sides of the same coin—you're centered on what you can achieve for yourself.

This is why Jesus said, "Do not worry about tomorrow; for tomorrow will care for itself. Each day has enough trouble of its own" (Matthew 6:34). Instead, Christ admonished, "Seek first His kingdom and His righteousness, and all these things will be added to you" (v. 33). Do you see the Savior's focus? It is not on ability, circumstances, or even time. It's on God.

It is good to plan for the future, but not to be consumed by it or believe you are in control. So if you find yourself overly absorbed by what may or may not happen tomorrow, it's time to remember that there is only One who really knows what is in store for you—and He has promised to care for you. So seek His face and His presence, because that's the only way to ensure that you will have hope and joy regardless of what happens.

*Father, I am so grateful that the future is in Your hands. Because
of this, I can always have hope. Praise Your wonderful name!
Amen.*

Where Are You Running?

SCRIPTURE READING: PROVERBS 28; LUKE 15:11–32; ROMANS 8:32

They who long for and seek the Lord understand.
PROVERBS 28:5 AMP

Do you wonder why your life has turned out the way it has? Are there times you wish you could escape your troubles—run away from life and not look back? Most of us are quite familiar with the Parable of the Prodigal Son (Luke 15:11–32). He struggled with the same desire but came up with a plan to carry it out. We can probably picture him packing his belongings and walking out the door.

Where did the prodigal go? Apparently, he got as far away from his home life as possible. That makes sense, doesn't it? After all, if you really want to get away from it all, then you would most likely get as much distance between yourself and your old life as is feasible. This is almost always true in our physical lives, but what about our spiritual lives?

The truth is, it's entirely possible to move farther away from God without even leaving the safety of your favorite chair. And if you are having thoughts of escape, it is possible that He is the main One you're trying to avoid. So consider: Is your heart running away from the Lord? Have you approached your heavenly Father, demanded the blessings that you believe He owes you, and then turned your back on Him?

Stop for a moment today and examine your spiritual location. Are you surviving in pig troughs, or are you feasting at the Father's table? Friend, you don't need to escape. What you really need is to spend time with the One who freely gives you all things (Romans 8:32). So wherever you are, turn around and seek Him. You'll find God running toward you with open arms.

God, in many ways my soul has become distant from You,
and it weighs on me heavily. Father, let these moments with
You bring us closer together in a real and powerful way.
Amen.

Financial Wisdom

SCRIPTURE READING: PROVERBS 29; 22:7

The poor man and the oppressor have this in common:
the LORD gives light to the eyes of both.
PROVERBS 29:13

Nothing in our lives is ever truly separate from the Lord; in fact, everything that concerns us is in His sight and benefits from His commands. The day we give our lives to Him, we acknowledge that He is in charge of it all and wise enough to lead us. This includes the area of our finances. However, too often we make financial decisions of our own accord without asking the Father what to do. And when we violate this biblical principle of asking God about every aspect of life—including stewardship of the money He gives us—we're inviting all sorts of calamity.

There are two simple ways we violate His principles on wise stewardship. *First*, we are wasteful. Either by carelessness or indifference, we do not govern what God has given us wisely. And *second*, we choose debt. We spend more than we earn or we borrow money from others. Either way, it causes us to be indebted to—or to owe—others. This is not the way God intended us to live (Proverbs 22:7).

The point of looking at finances through the window of Scripture is to see where you stand in your relationship with God. If you are under pressure and stress about finances, or if you owe more than you can pay, then you may be out of step somewhere in your walk with the Lord. The good news is that it's never too late to turn to God. Tell Him your troubles, ask His forgiveness, and let Him be Lord over your entire life. He wants to bless you so that you can bless others with what you receive. Will you let Him?

Lord, give light to my eyes regarding my finances. Reveal where
I am wasteful or indebted so I can repent and walk in Your
will. I know that Yours is the only path to true blessing.
Amen.

The Right Provision

SCRIPTURE READING: PROVERBS 30; 1 KINGS 17:1–16;
PSALM 84:11; MATTHEW 6; PHILIPPIANS 4:19

*Give me neither poverty nor riches, but give me only
my daily bread. Otherwise, I may have too much and
disown you and say, "Who is the LORD?"*

PROVERBS 30:8-9 NIV

Jesus instructs you to ask, "Give us this day our daily bread" (Matthew 6:11). When He does so, He's not referring to a mere loaf of whole wheat or pumpernickel but to the sum of all your needs—physical, financial, spiritual, emotional, and relational. You are assured that your heavenly Father will take care of you.

In fact, in Matthew 6:25–26, Jesus tells you, "Do not be worried about your life . . . Is not life more than food, and the body more than clothing? Look at the birds of the air, that they do not sow, nor reap nor gather into barns, and yet your heavenly Father feeds them. Are you not worth much more than they?"

As a believer, you can always count on God to provide for you and assume full responsibility for your needs as you obediently follow Him (Philippians 4:19). When your resources run dry and you feel as if you cannot go on any longer, the Father continues to provide for you in ways you never could have dreamed or imagined (1 Kings 17:1–16).

You may be thinking, *Are you sure about this? There are many things I've asked God for that He has not yet provided. Will He really come through for me?* Absolutely He will (Psalm 84:11). Though He may not answer you in the way you expect, I can assure you that what He gives is always far better than anything you could provide for yourself.

Father, thank You for providing for me.
I say this in faith today because I am waiting on You.
But I trust You to give me what in Your wisdom is the very best.
Amen.

Setting Goals by Faith

SCRIPTURE READING: PROVERBS 31

She watches over the affairs of her household
and does not eat the bread of idleness.
PROVERBS 31:27 NIV

The godly woman of Proverbs 31 certainly ran an effective household. But much of that is because she was proactive about the goals she wanted to accomplish. Of course, the world is full of advice on how to set and achieve objectives. The process usually starts with us—identifying who we want to become and what we should do to be successful. But Christian goal setting—as we see with this woman—is to start with a God-centered focus. The attitude is, *I want to be who the Lord wants me to be—who He created me to become. So I will look to the Father for direction in all areas of my life and obey.*

Seems easy enough. So why do we often fall short? Sometimes we *lack knowledge* of how to identify the Lord's plan. The solution is to give attention to the Word of God. We meditate on Jesus' life and words, learning His pattern for living and identifying specific steps to take. *Lack of faith* can be another hindrance. Why should we set goals when we are convinced we cannot do what God is asking? The answer is to build our faith through studying the Bible and applying it to our lives. Finally, *fear of failure* can prevent us from establishing goals. We can overcome this obstacle by remembering that in Christ, there is no condemnation, and He will enable us to accomplish all He calls us to do.

Do you desire to move ahead in your Christian life, growing more like Jesus and acting less like your old self? Goal setting with the right attitude and focus will help. So ask the Father to lead you become all you were created to be.

Father, only You know what You want to accomplish through my life.
I want to be who You want me to be. Lead me, Lord. I will obey.
Amen.

November

Blessings of Wisdom

If you think that obeying God means only trouble and difficulty, you've forgotten Whom you are serving. The Lord has planned incredible blessings for those who walk on the path of wisdom with Him—expressing His goodness and love in every area of your life.

A Faith-Building Focus

SCRIPTURE READING: PROVERBS 1; LUKE 6:21–23; ROMANS 8:28–29

He who listens to me shall live securely
and will be at ease from the dread of evil.

PROVERBS 1:33

When you can come to the place where you know God is interested in your problems, that He is greater than anything you could ever face, and that He knows exactly what to do, your troubles will feel less intimidating. Why? Because you're focused on the Lord: your all-powerful, all-knowing, ever-present, and completely loving Father.

This is one of the greatest blessings of wisdom: You realize that not only does God have the best plan for overcoming your struggles but He's also using your difficulties to build you up. As Romans 8:28 reminds us, "We know that God causes all things to work together for good to those who love God, to those who are called according to His purpose." He understands your emotional and spiritual makeup—exactly what you need to grow closer to Him, mature in your faith, and be "conformed to the image of His Son" (Romans 8:29). Therefore, even if His solution is slow in coming, or His answer requires you to take a step of faith, you can be certain that it will result in deeper peace, joy, and contentment than you've ever known. You're also assured that your trust in the Father's plans and purposes will result in eternal blessings. When you stand before Him on judgment day, you will be rewarded for your obedience to Him in ways beyond imagination (Luke 6:21–23).

Therefore, today, focus on the Father's awesome power and trust Him to resolve your situation in His timing. In His hands, problems aren't roadblocks—they are awesome opportunities for you to develop a more intimate and dynamic relationship with Him and grow in your faith.

Father, I praise Your wonderful name. Thank You for helping
me be more than a conqueror in every difficulty on my path
and for turning whatever touches my life for my good.
Amen.

The Throne of Grace

SCRIPTURE READING: PROVERBS 2; HEBREWS 4:15–16; 7:25 REVELATION 4

He stores up sound wisdom for the upright;
He is a shield to those who walk in integrity.
PROVERBS 2:7

Hebrews 4:16 instructs, "Let us draw near with confidence to the throne of grace, so that we may receive mercy and find grace to help in time of need." The reason we can be confident as we approach God's throne is that it is described as a place of kindness and mercy for us. Our loving heavenly Father continually extends His unmerited favor to us even when we don't deserve it.

This should fill us with praise today. Think about it: The Lord's throne of grace is described in Revelation 4 as a place of authority, power, and majesty. Most important, it's the place where God the Father rules over the universe with wisdom, strength, and justice. At His right hand is His Son, our Savior Jesus Christ, who "always lives to make intercession for" us (Hebrews 7:25). In fact, it is Jesus who enables us to be confident as we approach the Father's throne, because, "We do not have a high priest who cannot sympathize with our weaknesses, but One who has been tempted in all things as we are, yet without sin" (Hebrews 4:15). Jesus understands everything we face and also how to overcome all our challenges in a manner that is pleasing to the Father.

Friend, there's nothing hidden from the Lord. He knows every fiber of your heart and every struggle you endure. And Jesus lovingly serves as your great High Priest. The blessing of wisdom is that you know for certain that He defends you, answering the accuser's every indictment with words of forgiveness and restoration. So go daily to the throne of grace with everything that burdens your heart—and go with confidence. You'll always find it to be a place of overflowing love, mercy, and goodness for you, where you'll find grace and wisdom for whatever you face.

Lord, thank You for always receiving me with mercy and
giving me help. You are worthy of all my praise!
Amen.

Wisdom for Life

SCRIPTURE READING: PROVERBS 3; GALATIANS 5:22–23; PHILIPPIANS 4:7

Let your heart keep my commands; For length of days
and long life and peace they will add to you.
PROVERBS 3:1–2 NKJV

When you choose God's wisdom over the world's, you begin to develop a depth to your life that would never have been possible before you came to know Christ as your Lord and Savior (Galatians 5:22–23). This is because the Father's wisdom is given not only so you can make wise decisions but also so you can live the life He created you to enjoy as a believer.

Living wisely includes many things, one of which is abiding peace. When you exercise true wisdom—seeking the Lord for direction and walking in the center of His will—you will have "the peace of God, which surpasses all comprehension" guarding your heart and mind (Philippians 4:7). This is because when problems come, you can rest in the fact that the Father's omniscient wisdom is guiding you, which alleviates feelings of anxiety and stress. Likewise, a wise believer trusts in the abilities of other members of the Body of Christ—other Christians who are serving God faithfully. In other words, you are not in this life alone; you have others you can depend on with confidence. Another benefit is that you discover the things that truly give meaning and fulfillment to your life—the values, activities, relationships, and disciplines that can only be spiritually discerned.

So today, give thanks for the godly wisdom that not only guides your steps but also enriches your life. God wants so much for you, my friend! So choose to seek Him, obey His commands, and walk in His wisdom. Certainly, when you do you, will experience life at its most profound and very best.

Lord God, thank You so much for enriching my life with Your
wisdom in such a powerful way! Help me to walk in the center
of Your will so my life can be all You designed it to be.
Amen.

All-Around Well-Being

SCRIPTURE READING: PROVERBS 4; PHILIPPIANS 4:13; 3 JOHN 1:2

Turn your ear to my words . . .
for they are life to those who find them
and health to one's whole body.
PROVERBS 4:20, 22 NIV

In his third letter, the apostle John addresses a faithful layman named Gaius who was a great blessing to the local church. He fed and housed traveling pastors when they came through town, and he was generous with the time, money, and life God gave him. John's letter applauds Gaius' service, and he writes, "I pray that in all respects you may prosper and be in good health, just as your soul prospers" (v. 2). John's prayer recognizes that the Lord actually wants us to prosper in all three aspects of life—physically, financially, and spiritually.

We often think about the spiritual benefits of submitting to God, but we shouldn't miss the health and financial blessings that accompany walking with Him. When our focus is on keeping our relationship with God growing, it will make a tremendous difference in every aspect of our lives because the issues that arise will not seem so overwhelming. We will not attempt to assuage our troubles with wealth or drown them out with addictive behaviors that impact our well-being—tactics that always fail. Instead our focus is on the Father. And we know we "can do all things through Him who strengthens" us (Philippians 4:13).

So if you find yourself overcome with worry about health or financial matters, there may be some underlying fear or issue that is driving your concerns. Ask God to help you identify the source of your anxiety and what's causing your problems. Focus on your relationship with Him and allow Him to work in you. And as He does, the other areas of your life will be brought into a healthy balance. Wouldn't that be wonderful?

Father, I know that Your Word is life. Work in me, reveal
what is wrong, and bring all things into a healthy balance.
Amen.

The Boundaries of Love

SCRIPTURE READING: PROVERBS 5; GENESIS 2:24

Be exhilarated always with her love.
PROVERBS 5:19

Today's proverb calls husbands to always rejoice in the love of their wives. But there is a wider application. The blessing of wisdom is that we learn to love and appreciate whoever is in our lives in an appropriate manner. God calls everyone to a holy life guided by important principles because He wants us to enjoy all the blessings He has for us. That means He puts boundaries on sex—commanding that it be exclusively between a man and a woman who are married to each other (Genesis 2:24)—because He cares about what happens to us physically, emotionally, and spiritually. This may sound like an old-fashioned notion to some, but God commands it for your health and well-being, knowing that violating those boundaries can lead you to serious heartache.

However, no matter what sin you've committed or what behavior has trapped you, God is not your enemy and never will be. On the contrary, He is your biggest Advocate. Right now, you may be feeling somewhat ashamed or embarrassed because of the things you've done. You may be wondering if there's any turning back. Yes, there is! The fact that you're feeling guilt is evidence that the Holy Spirit is convicting you of your sin and drawing you back to the Lord. So don't be scared or disheartened. God's message to you is always that He loves you and that you're worth redeeming. So reject any immorality in your life and allow the Father to lead you in holiness and truth. He wants you to enjoy the purpose that He created you for, and He's committed to helping you find true love, joy, and fulfillment. And isn't that what you really want, after all?

Lord, I repent of the ways I have sinned against You. I
want to walk in holiness, Father, because I know that
You hold the keys to all my soul really longs for.
Amen.

The Mind of God

When you walk about, they will guide you;
when you sleep, they will watch over you;
and when you awake, they will talk to you.

PROVERBS 6:22

Friend, wouldn't it be wonderful to know exactly what your heavenly Father thinks of the challenges confronting you today? Of course, discerning God's infinite mind is contingent upon the instruction of the Holy Spirit, but how do you receive His guidance? You know that the Lord imparts His wisdom through His glorious Word. But do you realize that when you read Scripture, you are receiving His very thoughts into your own mind?

Through the Bible, you discover how the Father solves problems, works in and through people, moves on behalf of those who trust Him, responds in different situations, and interacts with all of creation. It is an awesome guidebook that teaches you the ways and character of the living Lord. You learn who He is and how much He loves you. And when you read Scripture, you are doing no less than sitting and listening to Almighty God. The Holy Spirit's role is to illumine the Word, so you can understand and obey it. And you will come to know the mind of Christ about your circumstances as you allow the Spirit of God to interpret His Word to you.

The Holy Spirit is a marvelous Teacher. And if you are a Christian, He indwells you and works tirelessly to empower you and impart His life and wisdom to you. So if you need to know God's viewpoint of what's going on in your life, spend time in His Word, listening to the Holy Spirit. And don't doubt that He will talk to you—because He certainly will (James 1:5–6). In fact, it's what He longs to do (Hosea 5:15).

Dear Lord, how I long to know Your thoughts about my
situation. Speak to me through Your Word, Father. Don't let
me miss Your instruction and guidance. In You I trust.
Amen.

NOVEMBER 7

Life Through Truth

SCRIPTURE READING: PROVERBS 7; PSALM 139:14;
PROVERBS 16:3; MATTHEW 10:42; ROMANS 8:17; 12:2; EPHESIANS 5:1;
PHILIPPIANS 4:13; 2 TIMOTHY 1:8–10; JAMES 1:17

That they may keep you . . .
PROVERBS 7:5

Do you feel good about yourself? How you feel about yourself affects how you respond to God and others. You'll either feel recurring pain because of your faults and failures, or your life will be characterized by peace and joy because you feel secure in your relationship with the Lord. Friend, if you're allowing ugly messages such as, "I can't do anything right" or "I'm a worthless nobody," to torment you, you're not only hurting yourself—you're also sinning against God. You must change what think about yourself and allow the Lord to transform your mind through His Word (Romans 12:2). Embrace these principles:

- I can do all things through Christ who strengthens me (Philippians 4:13).
- I am God's beloved child (Ephesians 5:1).
- I will never lose the rewards the Father has stored up for me (Matthew 10:42).
- The Lord gives me good gifts out of His unconditional love for me (James 1:17).
- I belong to God's family and I am a coheir with Christ (Romans 8:17).
- Christ died for me so I will live for Him (2 Timothy 1:8–10).

God's messages of love will diffuse the insecurity you feel and help you to have the confidence you need to face anything that comes along. So dig deep into the Word. Certainly, His truth will keep you, encourage you, and guide you in the way you should go.

Lord, thank You for Your wonderful Word! Replace the lies
I've believed with Your truth that I may enjoy the life You envision for me.
Amen.

You Are Blessed

SCRIPTURE READING: PROVERBS 8; JOHN 14:2–3; ROMANS 5:1; 8; 15:7;
1 CORINTHIANS 15:50–58; 2 CORINTHIANS 5:18–19; EPHESIANS 2:10

Riches and honor are with me,
enduring wealth and righteousness.
PROVERBS 8:18

Do you realize all that is available to you because of Jesus? Through Him, God has blessed you with riches so remarkable that it's worth taking a quick inventory of what they are. Of course, He has redeemed you, buying you back from the penalty of sin and forgiving your every transgression. The Savior has justified you, declaring you righteous (Romans 5:1), and has reconciled you, bringing you back into an intimate relationship with Himself (2 Corinthians 5:18–19). Likewise He has sanctified you, setting you apart as His own and conforming you to His image (Romans 8:29)

But the Father has also included you in His great, eternal plan. Imagine that—the God and Creator of the universe wanted you to be a part of His indescribable blueprint for the future. The Lord has envisioned all of your wonderful potential and is planning great things for you to achieve so you can share in His victories (Ephesians 2:10).

Furthermore, God has placed you into a union with Himself that can never be broken by anything in this world or beyond (Romans 8:38–39). And one day, He will glorify you—giving you His immortal, incorruptible nature (1 Corinthians 15:50–58). With this in mind, He is building an eternal home in heaven for you (John 14:2–3). And as a member of His family, you will enjoying an incredible inheritance and rewards that are beyond what you can imagine.

Did you realize that all of that is part of what you received when Jesus became your Savior? Today, meditate on each individual blessing and thank God for blessing you so lavishly.

Lord Jesus, there are so many things to thank You for! I
am so grateful that You looked upon my lowly estate and
saved me. I worship Your holy and precious name!
Amen.

The Blessing of Obedience

SCRIPTURE READING: PROVERBS 9; LUKE 5:1–11

By me your days will be multiplied,
and years of life will be added to you.
PROVERBS 9:11

While obedience may seem difficult at times, the joy that comes from obeying God is both tremendously fulfilling and fruitful. For example, in Luke 5:1–11, Peter was caught off guard by Jesus' request. Peter had fished all night and caught nothing, but the Lord Jesus suggested that he go back out on the Sea of Galilee for one more try. It seemed ridiculous to the seasoned fisherman. Most commercial fishing was done at night in order to avoid the heat of the day. Additionally, he and his crew were exhausted from a difficult and unproductive night. It is understandable why he was resistant to Jesus' request.

Likewise, there will be times when God asks you to do something that doesn't make sense from your perspective. You may be tired. Perhaps you've been down that road before and experienced defeat. You wonder why you should waste your life on another failure. However, you must have the same response as Peter: "I will do as You say" (v. 5). Because Jesus is God, you must submit to whatever He asks of you because, believe it or not, He really does know better than you do.

At some point each one of us has been guilty of telling God why His method will not work. However, Peter made the right choice, and this one decision changed his life forever. He sailed His boat back out into the deep waters of Galilee and dropped his nets—only to draw back such a "great quantity of fish . . . their nets began to break!" (v. 6). So obey the Lord and be prepared for a miraculous blessing. He will multiply your effectiveness and the impact of your life in ways you've never imagined.

Lord, I don't understand Your direction, but I will obey You—
confident that You always lead me in the best way possible.
Amen.

Remember Him

SCRIPTURE READING: PROVERBS 10; ISAIAH 9:6; MATTHEW 1:23; 9:15;
JOHN 6:35; 8:12; 10:11–14; ROMANS 11:26; EPHESIANS 2:20; 1 TIMOTHY 2:5;
HEBREWS 4:14–16; 7:25; REVELATION 1:4–5; 5:5; 19:11–16; 21:6

The memory of the righteous is blessed.
PROVERBS 10:7

There have been many courageous warriors, brilliant minds, and inspiring world leaders throughout the ages. Yet all the brightest minds, all the mighty men of the centuries, all the notable accomplishments of good men everywhere can never invoke the praise and admiration of Jesus Christ, our Lord, Savior, and coming King. Just think about some of the names He is called in Scripture.

Jesus is *Immanuel, God with us* (Matthew 1:23); the *Lion of Judah* and the *Root of David* (Revelation 5:5); the *Wonderful Counselor, Mighty God, Eternal Father,* and *Prince of Peace* (Isaiah 9:6). He is our *Great High Priest* (Hebrews 4:14–16), *Good Shepherd* (John 10:11–14), *Bridegroom* (Matthew 9:15), *Deliverer* (Romans 11:26), *Mediator* (1 Timothy 2:5), and *Intercessor* (Hebrews 7:25). He is the *Chief Cornerstone* (Ephesians 2:20), the *Light of the World* (John 8:12), and the *Bread of Life* (John 6:35). He is the One who is and who was and who is to come, the *Faithful Witness,* and the *Firstborn of the Dead* (Revelation 1:4–5). Jesus is the *Beginning* and the *End* (Revelation 21:6); the *Resurrection and Life* (John 11:25); *Faithful and True,* the *Word of God,* our unconquerable *King of kings* and *Lord of Lords* (Revelation 19:11–16).

What a wonderful Savior we serve! So meditate on the wonder of His Person, the strength of His love, the depth of His wisdom, and the invincibility of His power. Jesus is worthy of all your praise. No mortal can compare with Him. So think about who He really is and worship Him. Surely in doing so, you will be blessed.

Dearest Lord Jesus, I praise Your holy, magnificent,
and indomitable name! To You be all honor
and glory now and forevermore.
Amen.

Forsake Fear and Embrace Blessing

SCRIPTURE READING: PROVERBS 11; GENESIS 3:8–10; ISAIAH 41:10

Through knowledge the righteous will be delivered.
PROVERBS 11:9

There is no doubt that the Lord has something special planned for your life. But the question is, Are you ready to receive it? Although you may desire to experience the wonderful things the Father has in store for you, one of the most subtle inhibitors of His blessings is anxiety. Of course, your fears may have many sources: things you've learned, guilt, shame, doubt, and insecurity, among many others. But the origin of fear is actually sin.

In Genesis 3:8–10, we read the story of how Adam and Eve experienced anxiety for the first time after they ate from the forbidden tree and felt shame before God. Since that time, the enemy has used the emotion of fear to entangle believers in bondage. Essentially, we often miss God's blessings because we are too afraid to step out in faith and receive them. Instead, we're enslaved by the what-ifs: *What if I fail? What if people laugh at me? What if no one loves or respects me?*

Yet God has a response for all our apprehensions: Trust Me. For us to do this, three things are necessary. *First,* we must identify our fears. *Second,* we must ask God to reveal their source. *Third,* we must stand on the promises of His Word to overcome them.

Friend, in Isaiah 41:10 the Father says, "Do not fear, for I am with you; do not anxiously look about you, for I am your God. I will strengthen you, surely I will help you, surely I will uphold you with My righteous right hand." So don't live in fear. Instead, accept God's guarantee to help you regardless of what challenges arise. Step out from the shadows of fear today and reach for His strong hand. The blessings that result just might surprise you!

Lord, You know my fears. Set me free from them, Father,
so I can enjoy the life You've planned for me.
Amen.

The Way to Victory

The righteous will escape from trouble.
PROVERBS 12:13

Are you facing a devastating trial today? Do you lie awake at night, wondering, *Father, what am I going to do? I don't know how to go on.* Are the pain and emptiness caused by your problems overpowering you? During those times, a person can feel very lonely and helpless. We feel no one understands what we're experiencing. The pain goes so deep and the insecurities can be so overwhelming that we doubt anyone has ever felt as insignificant or low as we do. Yet we're not alone. We never really are.

Neither was Daniel. He had been wrongly accused (Daniel 6). His enemies had tricked King Darius into punishing him for worshipping God, and the sentence was death by lions. But despite his terrible circumstances, Daniel kept his eyes fixed upon the Lord and was miraculously saved.

The same could be true for you. Like Daniel, if you want to win the battles you experience, you must fight them on your knees alone with God. Do not argue or stand up for yourself. Remain faithful to Him, and He will protect you. Keep your eyes on the Father, rather than on whatever situation may arise, and He will lead you to victory.

So today, take some time to read the story of Daniel 6 and then cling to your heavenly Father. Fight this battle on your knees—not with your weapons, strategies, or resources but with faith in God. Entrust Him with your doubts and difficulties. Invite the Lord to be your Redeemer, Defender, General, Lion Tamer, and Protector. It's not only the best way to win; it's the most wonderful, eternal path to triumph every single time.

Lord, I don't know what to do, but my eyes are on You.
Provide a way of escape and lead me on the path to victory.
I know that those who trust in You are never disappointed.
Amen.

NOVEMBER 13

Blessed Assurance

SCRIPTURE READING: PROVERBS 13; ROMANS 15:13

The life of the godly is full of light and joy.
PROVERBS 13:9 NLT

When we know with certainty that God is in control, that He loves us beyond measure, and that He is at work in our lives, we have the genuine capacity to praise and thank Him even in the midst of the most dire and discouraging times. And our praise and thanksgiving inspire very real and enduring feelings of joy and peace within us.

Consider for a moment what it is that causes us frustration and anxiety. When we look at our circumstances apart from the Father's divine power, wisdom, love, and help, we can do nothing else but measure them against our own capacity to overcome them. It is no wonder we feel hopeless and fearful when challenges arise! From our limited perspective, all we can see is that life is out of control and marked by meaningless chaos. What a terrible way to live!

But when we realize that nothing touches our lives without permission from God, that He works all things together for our good, and that He is truly in control, it changes everything. This truth not only gives meaning to our struggles, but it also alerts us to the fact that the Father has a greater plan for our lives that He is preparing us for. What an awesome assurance to know that our God is sufficient in all times, for every circumstance we face, and that He is leading us to become more than conquerors. Truly, the One who guards us is the enduring source of all our gladness and confidence. So today and always, "May the God of hope fill you with all joy and peace in believing, so that you will abound in hope by the power of the Holy Spirit" (Romans 15:13).

Lord, I praise You for being the sovereign King of all
that exists—good, all-powerful, unfathomably wise,
and loving in how You lead all Your children.
Amen.

Watch Your Mouth

SCRIPTURE READING: PROVERBS 14; MATTHEW 12:34;
EPHESIANS 4:29; 5:4; HEBREWS 13:15

The lips of the wise will protect them.
PROVERBS 14:3

There is nothing that can get us into more trouble more quickly than our mouths. We can be amazed at the things we say. And Jesus made this stark indictment: "The mouth speaks out of that which fills the heart" (Matthew 12:34). If we're honest, we would probably admit that we don't always like what we hear when we listen to our own words.

Many people, including those who work in churches and ministries, face a battle with their tongues. We struggle to speak what edifies and glorifies God with our words. Ephesians 4:29 instructs, "Let no unwholesome word proceed from your mouth, but only such a word as is good for edification according to the need of the moment, so that it will give grace to those who hear." But that is easier said than done. And the prevailing culture of negativity leaves little room for us to encourage others. In fact, sometimes it seems like the world rewards those who are critical and faultfinding.

But as followers of Christ, we're called to be different. We are to speak in a way that gives grace to those who hear. We cannot edify others or lead them to Jesus when we're talking as does the world—with questionable language and coarse jesting (Ephesians 5:4).

Therefore, listen to what you say and make sure that you are devoted to Christ with what's flowing forth from you. If your words are ungodly or unedifying, examine your heart and repent of whatever God shows you. And do as Hebrews 13:15 admonishes: "Continually offer up a sacrifice of praise to God, that is, the fruit of lips that give thanks to His name." Because in that way you guard not only yourself but also all who hear you.

Father, reveal what is in my heart. Help me to edify
others and glorify You with everything I say.
Amen.

Cheer Up

SCRIPTURE READING: PROVERBS 15; EXODUS 14:14; JOSHUA 1:1–10

A joyful heart makes a cheerful face,
but when the heart is sad, the spirit is broken.
PROVERBS 15:15

Most of us, at one time or another, have found ourselves in need of a good, inspiring pep talk. Perhaps we have lost something important to us, or maybe we felt downtrodden and needed a friend to encourage us. Whatever the situation, it was helpful to have someone comfort us in our concern, inspire us to action, and lead us to victory.

This was certainly the case for Joshua as he considered entering the Promised Land (Joshua 1:1–10). You can probably imagine how desperate Joshua felt. Still reeling from the death of his friend and mentor, Moses, the heavy mantle of leadership had fallen on his shoulders. Stretched out before him were the seemingly insurmountable obstacles of conquering a land full of hostile forces with a people ill equipped for the fight. How could he possibly snatch victory from those overwhelming jaws of certain defeat?

Rather than leaving Joshua to his own devices, God provided the necessary instruction. He told him to get up and get moving, and that He would clear the path. "Be strong and courageous," He declared. "Do not tremble or be dismayed, for the Lord your God is with you wherever you go" (Joshua 1:9).

Friend, God is giving you this same pep talk today. So be of good cheer and let your broken spirit be comforted. Regardless of your troubling circumstances, take courage in His promise that He is with you "wherever you go." Because certainly as He did with Moses and Joshua, "The Lord will fight for you; you need only to be still" (Exodus 14:14 NIV).

Father, thank You for encouraging my spirit and infusing my heart
with Your joy. Lead me as You did Joshua and give me hope.
Amen.

The Rewards of Obedience

SCRIPTURE READING: PROVERBS 16; HEBREWS 11:27

When a man's ways are pleasing to the LORD,
He makes even his enemies to be at peace with him.
PROVERBS 16:7

What a beautiful promise from today's proverb—one that many of us long for. However, this is what we must understand: Just as the natural laws of life dictate that what goes up must, at some point, come down, there are also spiritual laws that have rewards and consequences that are even more certain. We must take God's Word seriously.

For instance, when a person chooses to base his or her life on the wisdom of Scripture, he or she will have blessings that cannot be known otherwise. Not every gift will be financial, of course—some are much more valuable than that. A person who obeys the Word of God will have the blessings of peace, security that does not waver with circumstances, unshakable joy, and favor from the Father. That doesn't mean there won't be adversity, enemies, and losses. But we'll be able to endure, "as seeing Him who is unseen" (Hebrews 11:27). However, just as sure is that a person who spends his or her lifetime disobeying God will reap devastating consequences.

While the Lord is gracious and forgiving, He does—in His kindness—honor His Word in all circumstances to show He is holy, just, and trustworthy. Therefore, it's crucial to have a balanced view of God, who does not give us commands to obey so that we'll feel punished, or so that He can accuse us when we make mistakes. On the contrary, it's His protective love—His heart as our Father—that sets the boundaries for us so we'll experience the joy, peace, and abundant life He created us to enjoy. So obey Him and rejoice in the blessings He gives you.

Lord, I know that many of the issues I'm facing are
because I haven't taken Your Word seriously. Please
forgive me and lead me in the way I should go.
Amen.

Honor the Lord in Adversity

SCRIPTURE READING: PROVERBS 17; JOB 42:2

A wise servant will . . . share an inheritance.

PROVERBS 17:2 NKJV

Even when you are living life in the center of God's will, there will be times of heartache and difficulty. Joseph loved the Lord and obeyed Him, yet he found himself being sold into Egyptian bondage. David was the anointed king over Israel; however, he waited years to take the throne. Trouble filled both of these men's lives. Later, Joseph was wrongly accused by Potiphar's wife and put into prison. David's life became a nightmare as King Saul hunted and sought to kill him.

In difficult times, the blessings of wisdom and the keys to victory are found in learning how to live with an eternal perspective and honor the Father regardless of what happens. David and Joseph trusted God's promises and waited for the Lord's deliverance even though it took years for them to come to fruition. But it just goes to show that no purpose of God's can be thwarted (Job 42:2). It is always wise to trust in Him.

The same is true for you. So today consider: How committed are you to God's plan? Are you willing to wait for His timing in order to achieve the goals He has placed before you? The Father will use your trials to prepare you for greater blessings. Joseph submitted himself to the Lord, and God used him to save the nation of Israel from starvation. David weathered the adversity and became one of Israel's greatest kings and the forefather of the Messiah. Likewise, the Father has a greater plan for your life than what you can perceive from your human viewpoint. So let Him have all of you. Hold nothing back from Him, and you will experience the good hand of the Lord guiding you through every trial and fulfilling every promise.

*Lord, I trust You to lead me. It is so hard to wait
and even more difficult as trials arise. But I will
honor You with love, obedience, and devotion.
Amen.*

Overcoming Hindrances to Praise

SCRIPTURE READING: PROVERBS 18; PSALM 22:3;
ISAIAH 41:10; JOHN 4:5–42; ROMANS 12:2

He will be satisfied with the product of his lips.
PROVERBS 18:20

They say that praise is the overflow of the human heart, so why is it that we do not exalt God more often? Take, for example, the story of Jesus' encounter with the Samaritan woman (John 4:5–42). This woman was simply conducting her daily chores when she was unexpectedly approached by the Messiah. We can only imagine her surprise when Jesus confirmed His identity. Yet instead of praising Him, she went in to the city and asked, "Come, see a man who told me all the things that I have done; this is not the Christ, is it?" (v. 29).

We can learn something from this event. In order to rejoice at the Lord's intervention in our lives, we must be prepared to receive it. *First,* we must know the truth. A primary reason for our lack of praise is ignorance of God's Word and how to apply His principles. When we realize how the Father is answering our prayers and fulfilling His promises, we will naturally be filled with praise. *Second,* we must watch for His intervention with the right spirit. This requires submission to the Lord Jesus and consistent repentance of all known sin. This also involves the renewing of our minds so we won't be held in bondage to false beliefs but can know God's will (Romans 12:2). *Finally,* we must rid ourselves of fear. It is necessary to move beyond worrying about whether or not our heavenly Father accepts and cares for our deepest needs. He does. We should never be afraid, because He is most definitely with us (Isaiah 41:10).

Friend, is something preventing you from worshipping God today? If so, ask Him to reveal the issue to you and respond in faith to whatever He commands. Then let Him be enthroned upon your praises (Psalm 22:3).

Lord, You are my God! Free me so I may
praise You wholeheartedly.
Amen.

The Love of Wisdom

SCRIPTURE READING: PROVERBS 19; MATTHEW 7:7–11;
JOHN 17:26; EPHESIANS 3:14–19; HEBREWS 13:5

He who gets wisdom loves his own soul;
PROVERBS 19:8

Have you ever noticed how Jesus closes His great prayer to the Father at the end of John 17? He prays: "That the love with which You loved Me may be in them, and I in them" (v. 26). This is one of the clearest passages about how deeply and limitlessly God loves us. In fact, this form of love is even greater than the unconditional love we experience and understand, because our finite minds cannot comprehend the breadth, length, height, and depth of it (Ephesians 3:14–19). Jesus, in effect, says that just as the Father loves Him, the Father loves us as well!

One of the ways the Lord expresses His Fatherhood to us is through this unconditional love. He also expresses it through His desire to communicate with us, through meeting all of our needs and through the truth that He is always with us (Matthew 7:7–11). In Hebrews 13:5, He says, "I will never desert you nor will I ever forsake you," and because He is omnipotent, omniscient, and omnipresent, He is the only One who can successfully keep this pledge. God not only promises always to guide us on the right path and to right conduct; He also disciplines us when needed. This is an expression of His love as well, because He sees how we are falling short of the wonderful freedom and life He's planned for us and sets out to make it right.

And so you can see that when you fear and obey the Lord—which is the very definition of wisdom—you love your own soul because you are opening yourself to His love. What greater gift could anyone hope for?

Father, thank You for Your astounding love to me.
I worship You and long to know You more.
Amen.

338   BLESSINGS OF WISDOM

NOVEMBER 20

Fruitful in Every Season

SCRIPTURE READING: PROVERBS 20; PSALM 1:1–3

The glory of young men is their strength,
and the honor of old men is their gray hair.
PROVERBS 20:29

G od has so formed your life that you can be fruitful and blessed re-gardless of the stage you're experiencing—whether in childhood, adolescence, early adulthood, midlife, or the golden years. Psalm 1:1–3, promises, "Blessed is the man [whose] . . . delight is in the law of the Lord, and in His law he meditates day and night. He will be like a tree firmly planted by streams of water, which yields its fruit in its season and its leaf does not wither; and in whatever he does, he prospers."

In other words, the deeper you take root in your relationship with the Lord—increasing your intimacy with Him and steadfastly obey-ing His call—the greater access you will have to His eternal nature and boundless resources, which are what make your life truly impact-ful. You stay productive with continuing worth and influence in eter-nity. The cares that would normally wear you down and age your soul actually serve to renew and free you from all the things that enslave and discourage you (Romans 8:20–25). In fact, you become more lov-ing, joyful, peaceful, patient, kind, gentle, steadfast, temperate, faithful, eternal, and of greater value to everyone who comes into contact with you (Galatians 5:22–23).

Is this what you're longing for? Because whether you're searching for a new beginning, wondering if there is more to this life, or hoping to leave a lasting legacy, only God can satisfy your needs or give your life meaning. And when you seek Him, you will not only find answers to all your yearnings, but you will stay fruitful in a way beyond your imagina-tion, regardless of whether you're eight, eighteen, or eighty.

Lord, thank You for having good purposes for me
regardless of my age, challenges, physical capabilities,
or stage of life. To You be all the glory forever!
Amen.

Receiving God's Blessings

SCRIPTURE READING: PROVERBS 21; NUMBERS 13–14; PSALM 34:9–10

There is precious treasure and
oil in the dwelling of the wise.
PROVERBS 21:20

None of us wants to miss the blessings the Lord has planned for us. Naturally, we want to receive every one of the gifts He desires to give us. However, because of the choices we make, we often forfeit the good things He has planned. For example, the nation of Israel wandered in the desert for an additional forty years because they refused to obey God and enter the Promised Land. Though the Israelites were on the brink of tremendous blessing, the leaders were too afraid of the challenges before them. So they turned away from the outpouring of God's goodness for themselves and for the nation through their unbelief (Numbers 13–14).

The Christian life is one of surrender and obedience, not independence and rebellion. To live such a life means we bring our choices to the Lord and are prepared to accept His direction. Remember, God always leads us in the best way because of His perfect character, wisdom, and power. So we must learn to listen to Him and not proceed until He directs us in the way we should go.

So friend, open God's Word and allow His Spirit to speak to you as you bow before Him in prayer. Keep your focus on Him regardless of the circumstances that arise. And always do as He says. Because as Psalm 34:9–10 NLT admonishes, "Fear the Lord, you His godly people, for those who fear Him will have all they need. Even strong young lions sometimes go hungry, but those who trust in the Lord will lack no good thing."

Lord, I thank You that every good and perfect gift is from Your
hand. Help me to walk in all Your ways so I may please You and
experience all the good blessings You've planned for my life.
Amen.

Counteracting Pride

SCRIPTURE READING: PROVERBS 22; ACTS 17:26

The rich and the poor have a common bond,
the LORD is the maker of them all.
PROVERBS 22:2

None of us likes being told we're prideful, and usually we're the last to realize when arrogance characterizes our lives. Pride often begins with low self-worth and then spins into a vicious cycle. We feel insecure when we're communicating with others, and we worry that they'll either realize we're not as great as we think we are or they'll somehow gain an advantage over us. So we minimize the other person—pointing out our superiority in intelligence, wealth, beauty, social status, race, or what have you.

Yet this is ignoring the truth that "He made from one man every nation of mankind to live on all the face of the earth, having determined their appointed times and the boundaries of their habitation" (Acts 17:26). God is no respecter of persons—He loves us all with an everlasting love. The very person you are disparaging is an individual Jesus died on the cross to save—just like you. So the Father hates any pride He finds in your heart, because at its core, it means that you refuse to acknowledge all He has done for you as your Creator and Savior.

So how do you counteract pride in your heart? First Thessalonians 5:18 instructs, "In everything give thanks." Instead of complaining about the negative aspects of your life, express gratitude to God for all the blessings He has given you—even the trials. Praise Him for all the good He has done in your life and the wonderful plans He has for you. When you start giving Him the glory, you'll realize how deeply blessed you really are and that it's all come from His loving hand. And you'll want everyone you meet to experience those same blessings.

Father, I do give You thanks! Forgive me for any way I've been prideful.
I bless Your name for having mercy on me and providing for me.
Amen.

Your Defender

SCRIPTURE READING: PROVERBS 23; ISAIAH 54:17

Their Redeemer is strong;
He will plead their case against you.
PROVERBS 23:11

No matter how weak and insignificant you feel today, remember that God is with you. Insecurity hurts all of us at one point or another. This is especially true when you're obeying the Lord and conflicts with others arise. They may criticize you and pressure you to stray from His path, which can make you doubt what is true and what God has promised you. You wonder why He would allow such opposition when you're being obedient and faithful. But to protect yourself, you must put those negative thoughts behind you and continually pursue a close relationship with Him. God will give you hope and encouragement to sustain you, no matter what you're going through.

The Lord promises in Isaiah 54:17, "No weapon that is formed against you will prosper; and every tongue that accuses you in judgment you will condemn. This is the heritage of the servants of the Lord, and their vindication is from Me." Always remember that the enemy is intent on keeping you on shaky ground, feeling like a failure and utterly discouraged. If Satan can paralyze you with insecurity, then he can get you to start thinking that God isn't being fair or that He isn't helping you as He should. The next thing you know, instead of obeying God's will and leading people to Him, you're spreading your bitterness and insecurity to others. It's a terrible cycle, and the enemy knows exactly how to keep it moving toward destruction.

Thankfully, you don't have fall victim to the enemy's tactics. You can decide to focus your entire attention on God's will and count on Him to vindicate you. So today, trust Him with the conflicts before you and praise Him for being your wise and matchless Defender.

Lord, You are my Mighty Warrior! Thank You for using
this conflict so I can learn to love and trust You more.
Amen.

Eternity in Your Heart

SCRIPTURE READING: PROVERBS 24; JOHN 14:2–3;
1 JOHN 2:17; REVELATION 18:14

There will be a future, and your hope will not be cut off.
PROVERBS 24:14

A great deal of what the Father is teaching you is meant to ready you for eternity. Remember, in John 17:3, Jesus tells you, "This is eternal life, that they may know You, the only true God, and Jesus Christ whom You have sent." So the Lord's primary goal is to bring you deeper into an intimate relationship with Him—a relationship that will persist even after this world passes away.

The problem is that there are still earthly strongholds in you, ways you pull away from the Father in order to chase fleshly, and therefore unhelpful, goals (Revelation 18:14). Of course, in your sight all you pursue may appear good and right. However, God sees farther down the road than you do—much farther—and He wants to save you from the things that will ultimately cause you pain. This is the reason for many of the trials and difficulties you face today—the Father is refocusing your life on things that will count in eternity (1 John 2:17).

You see, your planning is short term, meant to comfort you in this life. But the Lord doesn't want you to get to heaven and have regrets that you wasted your life here on temporary issues. Therefore, He always has His eternal kingdom in view—how you will live and what rewards you'll possess after this world is gone. So the Father teaches you how to bear "fruit that will last" (John 15:16 NIV). In that way, He prepares you for what's ahead so you'll be able to enjoy fully all the benefits of everlasting life with Him—a life of praise to Him, illuminated by His glory.

Father, thank You for thinking of my joy in eternity!
Surely all You do is good, and I look forward
to praising You forever and ever.
Amen.

NOVEMBER 25

The Power of Praise

<small>SCRIPTURE READING: PROVERBS 25; ACTS 16:16–34</small>

*Like apples of gold in settings of silver
is a word spoken in right circumstances.*
PROVERBS 25:11

Do you praise God only when things are going well? Many of us make this mistake. We must learn to worship and thanks Him during bad times as well. In fact, we will never know the true power of our praise until we learn its value in our trials (Acts 16:16–34). For example, praise:

- focuses your attention on the Lord rather than on the challenge
- reminds you of God's perfect sovereignty and love
- prepares the way for the Father to release His awesome power in your life
- allows you to recognize the good ways the Lord is working in your situation
- magnifies the presence of God and the fact that you're not alone
- gives a powerful witness to the lost by exalting the name of the Lord
- fills your heart with the joy and strength of the Lord

When the circumstances in your life seem insurmountable, you can either dive into the depths of despair or look up and rejoice in the Lord. You can blame others and become angry at God, or you can cry out to the One who is capable of turning your sorrow into joy. Praise God, not only for what He is planning for your future but also for what you can learn from your present situation.

*Father, I do indeed praise You! Nothing I desire compares
with You, and nothing I will ever face will confound
You. Thank You for loving and protecting me.
Amen.*

Even the Curses

SCRIPTURE READING: PROVERBS 26;
LAMENTATIONS 3:33; 2 CORINTHIANS 12:7–10

A curse without cause does not alight.
PROVERBS 26:2

When facing adversity or challenges, most Christians immediately ask, "Why is this happening to me?" Of course, we know the Father is wise in how He is molding our lives and does not owe us any explanations. But it's also prudent to consider our ways in the day of adversity. This is necessary because, as today's proverb tells us, "An undeserved curse will not land on its intended victim" (Proverbs 26:2 NLT). Likewise, we know that God "does not enjoy hurting people or causing them sorrow" (Lamentations 3:33 NLT). This means that if He has allowed trouble to touch our lives, there might be something particular He is dealing with.

For example, in 2 Corinthians 12:7, Paul states, "Because of the surpassing greatness of the revelations, for this reason, to keep me from exalting myself, there was given me a thorn in the flesh, a messenger of Satan to torment me—to keep me from exalting myself!" Paul understood what it was that the Lord was addressing in his life—the universal human temptation to think too highly of oneself. And because of that, Paul was able to submit to the Lord's provision of adversity with joy.

The same is true for you. Once you identify what the Lord is targeting in your life, you'll be able to welcome His discipline, knowing He has allowed it for your good. Of course, that doesn't mean that the trial will automatically end or get easier. But like Paul, you'll be able to endure, understanding that God's grace is sufficient for you and that His mighty resurrection power is being perfected in you through your weaknesses and trials (2 Corinthians 12:9–10).

Father, I thank You that even the curses and trials are ministers
You work through for my good! Only a truly almighty, wise,
and loving God could do that! I praise Your holy name!
Amen.

NOVEMBER 27

Express Your Love

SCRIPTURE READING: PROVERBS 27; DEUTERONOMY 6:5–6; 1 JOHN 4:8

He who cares for his master will be honored.
PROVERBS 27:18

Is your relationship with the heavenly Father one of duty or delight—debt or devotion? God, who is love, desires that your fellowship with Him be motivated by your personal, growing, and demonstrable affection for Him (1 John 4:8). This is why He proclaimed, "You shall love the Lord your God with all your heart and with all your soul and with all your might. These words, which I am commanding you today, shall be on your heart" (Deuteronomy 6:5–6). Your heavenly Father is a Person, and He wants a relationship with you! Although He could have existed forever without creating mankind, He made you for Himself and gave His Son so you could be reconciled to Him forever.

As His child, you are free to love Him for who He is, for what He has done, and for all He will do for you. And each day is an opportunity to express your gratefulness for and devotion to Jesus. Therefore, do so! *First*, you can express your love for Him with your words. There is no such thing as true intimacy in a marriage without verbal interaction, encouragement, and praise. Likewise, God wants to hear you proclaim His excellencies and your care for Him. So tell Him why you're grateful for Him. *Second*, demonstrate your love for the Lord by cheerful obedience. Work heartily at the tasks He gives you, honoring Christ as your Master. Serve others with compassion and understanding as His ambassador on earth.

Friend, the more you know Jesus, the more you will care for Him. And the more you love Him, the more passionately you'll want to honor Him. It is a divine circle of devotion filled with incredible blessings. So don't hold back; express your wholehearted love for Him today.

Lord, how I love You! May the words of my mouth and the works of my hands demonstrate how deeply I delight in You.
Amen.

Obedience and Blessings

SCRIPTURE READING: PROVERBS 28; JEREMIAH 7:23

A faithful man will abound with blessings.
Proverbs 28:20

Do you believe that you will be rewarded for your Christ-honoring behavior? Do you trust that if you obey God, He will really bless you? It's true that as believers, we are called to "store up for [ourselves] treasures in heaven, where neither moth nor rust destroys" (Matthew 6:20). Many of our rewards will come in eternity. However, we are also promised that the way we live will make a difference here on earth (Jeremiah 7:23).

One way to think about it is to realize that a blessing is *any expression of His goodness and love toward us.* We typically limit our concept of rewards to things like answered prayers, supernatural provision, and other positive events. But sometimes the Father blesses us in the midst of difficulty with things like inner strength, new insight into our circumstances or His character, the peace that transcends understanding, or greater spiritual maturity. He may also realign our focus so we can see His perspective, empower us to achieve God-sized tasks, or give us greater influence with those around us.

Friend, when you obey God, you will be greatly enriched in one way or another, because there is no such thing as submitting to Him without your soul benefiting from it. Some kind of blessing will always follow your obedience. So if the Lord has called you to do something specific for His kingdom, remember that He never makes insignificant requests. Obey Him and keep watch for the marvelous ways He expresses His goodness and love toward you.

Lord, open my eyes to the less obvious ways You are blessing me
and expressing Your love and goodness toward me. Enable me
to grow spiritually so that I will value the things You value.
Amen.

Justice Is Coming

SCRIPTURE READING: PROVERBS 29; EXODUS 14:14;
PSALM 37:5–6; ROMANS 8:37; 1 JOHN 5:4–5

The king gives stability to the land by justice.

PROVERBS 29:4

As you go about your daily routine, do you sometimes feel as though the world is winning? From the irritations and conflicts of your personal circumstances to bad news in your community and throughout the world, it's easy to become discouraged and focused on the negative. Likewise, the victory over sin and death that Christ won on the cross can seem remote from daily application. Why would God allow such chaos and such evil people to triumph?

However, never lose sight of this truth: "Whatever is born of God overcomes the world; and this is the victory that has overcome the world—our faith. Who is the one who overcomes the world, but he who believes that Jesus is the Son of God?" (1 John 5:4–5). Friend, this is the blessing of wisdom—the assurance that you are more than a conqueror through Jesus Christ (Romans 8:37). Does this mean that you will feel successful in every encounter and conflict? No. Sometimes it may feel as if evil is prevailing. God may allow you to go through times when His truth working within you is obscured to another's eyes. However, the Lord God is just and will work everything out in His time. One day everyone "will give account to Him who is ready to judge the living and the dead" (1 Peter 4:5). Your job is to trust Him for the outcome.

Ultimately, the victory is yours because of the God who loves you. In the meantime, however, cling to this promise: "Commit everything you do to the Lord. Trust Him, and He will help you. He will make your innocence radiate like the dawn, and the justice of your cause will shine like the noonday sun" (Psalm 37:5–6 NLT). Certainly, He will fight for you as you trust in Him (Exodus 14:14).

Lord, You are the ultimate Judge, and You will set everything
right in Your time. Thank You for leading me to victory.
Amen.

Go Deeper

SCRIPTURE READING: PROVERBS 30

Neither have I learned wisdom, nor do I have
the knowledge of the Holy One.
PROVERBS 30:3

The Christian life has the potential of being a profoundly satisfying and joyful existence. Unfortunately, many of God's people never experience all that He has for them. Why? Because they never take the time to learn how to walk with the One who knows and loves them best. They know something about the Lord, but they never develop a personal relationship with the Savior or experienced the fulfillment that comes from knowing Him on an intimate level. This lack of closeness halts spiritual growth because it is an essential requirement for becoming all we were created to be. If we don't know God, we can never become more like Him.

For many, developing this intimate relationship with the Lord is a challenge because of the control we're called to relinquish. We must not only make the choice to seek the Father and love Him above all else, but we also must come to a point where we desire His love more than anything else this world can offer. True intimacy begins with that choice, and it only grows as we surrender our will to Him. This is because walking with the Lord means being in tune with His heart and placing His priorities above our own.

Our world is crying out for meaning and fulfillment, and far too often, people are looking for this in all the wrong places. But Jesus is the only One who can truly satisfy the deepest longing of your heart. So your journey to life at its very best requires an act of your will to know, trust, and obey the Lord. Friend, don't miss out. The Father is waiting to lead you along the most wonderful path—one you will never regret traveling. So submit to Him and experience all He has for you.

Lord, break down whatever is standing between me
knowing You as profoundly as possible and walking in
Your will. I submit myself to You wholeheartedly.
Amen.

God with Us

As you near the end of the year, you can do so with the understanding that the Lord God is with you and that He will never fail or forsake you. No matter what situation arises or where you may find yourself, you can face whatever comes with the knowledge that His presence and unfailing wisdom will guide you every step of the way.

Prophecy Fulfilled

SCRIPTURE READING: PROVERBS 1; MATTHEW 13:17

Understand . . . the words of the wise.
PROVERBS 1:6

Do you trust God to answer your prayers? Surely there are requests you've presented to the Father, burdens on your heart that make you desperate for His intervention. And if there's anything that can steal your peace, it's when the blessings you ask the Father for are delayed and seem impossible to attain. The months and years pass, and you wonder if He will ever come through for you.

But there is something very meaningful and instructive in waiting for the desires of your heart to come to fruition, painful though it sometimes may be. In doing so, you must set your heart to believe that God will indeed answer you. Think of the thousands of years people were waiting for the Messiah to come—hearing the prophesies, though they did not understand them completely. As Jesus said, "Many prophets and righteous men desired to see what you see, and did not see it" (Matthew 13:17). But God made infinite preparations and fulfilled countless details in arranging for the special night when He would take the form of man—changing the course of human history and the eternal destinies of all of us who are believers. And today we see that Christmas is undeniable evidence that no matter how long the delay, the Lord *always* keeps His promises—but also that He does so in a way we may never be able to predict.

So take heart! It may appear from all outward circumstances that God's plan for you has fallen apart. But friend, the Lord delights in situations that are unworkable from a human standpoint because when He answers, you have no doubt whatsoever that it is God Himself who has come to your aid and provided your salvation.

Lord, help me to always remember that Your pattern is to build faith in You before You fulfill Your promises. Thank You for always helping me at exactly the right moment.
Amen.

Truly Know Him

SCRIPTURE READING: PROVERBS 2; EXODUS 33:13, 15

My child, listen to what I say, and treasure my commands.
PROVERBS 2:1 NLT

There is a big difference between the relationships you have with those who demonstrate unconditional love and those who show you that they care only when you do what they require. The former truly love you for who you are; the latter have only a self-centered interest in you. This is also true of your relationship with God. If you seek Him only when you need something, your relationship with Him will be one-sided and hindered in its growth.

Moses understood this, which is why he was committed to spending time with God—listening to Him, fellowshipping with Him, and meditating on His truth. He wanted his relationship with the Lord to be growing, vibrant, and complete. How do we know this about Moses? Because he said, "Let me know Your ways that I may know You, so that I may find favor in Your sight . . . If Your presence does not go with us, do not lead us up from here" (Exodus 33:13, 15). Moses wanted to experience God's presence and favor even more than he wanted to enter the Promised Land! He understood that an intimate relationship with the Father would always be more fulfilling than anything else the world could offer. So if the Lord wasn't part of the things he wanted—if they weren't His best for Moses' life—they weren't worth having.

Friend, do you long for more from your relationship with the Lord? Remember that your love for the Savior will grow when you take the time to be with Him. Of course, there is risk involved with intimacy. But whenever you are tempted to hold back, remember God gave all He had so that you could know Him and so He could demonstrate His unconditional love toward you.

Lord, I want to know You as Moses did—with profound fellowship and intimacy. Reveal Yourself to me. My heart is open to You.
Amen.

A Gift from the Foundation

SCRIPTURE READING: PROVERBS 3; JOHN 1; MATTHEW 1:22–23

> *By wisdom the LORD laid the earth's foundations,*
> *by understanding he set the heavens in place.*
>
> PROVERBS 3:19 NIV

Have you ever wondered why the prophets and even Jesus' enemies gave so much attention to His birth? It's because when God does something so incredible, it's worth noting. You see, Jesus' story really begins far before His birth. John 1:1 tells us, "In the beginning was the Word, and the Word was with God, and the Word was God." Jesus was not created like you and I were; He is the uncreated, eternal God—without beginning or end. And because of that extraordinary eternity-altering moment when "the Word became flesh, and dwelt among us, and we saw His glory" (John 1:14), human eyes were finally able to behold the exalted Lord of all creation.

This was not the mere birth of a baby. It was the absolute shaking of the spiritual and physical realms when God Himself was incarnated, becoming one of us in order to carry out all the promises He'd given through the ages. Matthew affirms, "All this took place to fulfill what was spoken by the Lord through the prophet: 'Behold, the virgin shall be with child and shall bear a Son, and they shall call His name Immanuel,' which translated means, 'God with us' " (Matthew 1:22–23). This is the foundation upon which every bit of our hope and joy rests. It is the truth that God is with us.

So this Christmas, focus on the gift that was planned for you from the foundation of the world. The Lord God is with you! Focus on His presence no matter where you are or what happens. Because if you do, you will not only rediscover the absolute wonder of Christmas, you will also see how Jesus meets your every need.

> *Oh, Lord Jesus! Thank You for being with me through*
> *whatever I experience. Help me to understand the*
> *profound and wonderful fullness of Christmas!*
> *Amen.*

All Things

SCRIPTURE READING: PROVERBS 4; JEREMIAH 33:3; ROMANS 8:28–39

The beginning of wisdom is this: Get wisdom.
Though it cost all you have, get understanding.
PROVERBS 4:7 NIV

The tragedies we read about in the news are enough to cause us to ask, *Is God really in everything?* It's a question that cannot be ignored when we watch defenseless people become victims to violent storms, earthquakes, volcanic eruptions, wildfires, avalanches, and other terrestrial disasters. And it's an inquiry we'll most likely make when we ourselves experience unexpected losses. Left unanswered, our hearts can become calloused and hardened, unwilling to fully trust the Lord. And it will not only inhibit our witness to unbelievers, but will ultimately hinder our intimacy with Jesus.

But as you consider your life today, know this: The Lord is indeed in everything. Romans 8:28 says, "God causes *all things* to work together for good to those who love God, to those who are called according to His purpose." However, in order to understand what this means, we need to understand what it does *not* mean. This does not signify that the Lord instigates the evil in the world. Rather, He will permit it only if there is some divine, eternal purpose He can achieve through it. You may not be able to see what His reason is, but you can fully trust that if you will continue following Him in faith, eventually you'll see some worthwhile good come from your suffering.

But don't miss the main point—God can work through *all things* that happen to you for your good and His glory. There's nothing you can experience that He won't use to teach you something important. Therefore, meditate on Romans 8:28–39 today and take your questions to the Lord. He wants to give meaning to your life, so allow Him to reveal His great purposes to You (Jeremiah 33:3).

Lord, You know the struggles that burden my heart.
Help me to understand all You wish to teach me.
Amen.

Closed Doors

SCRIPTURE READING: PROVERBS 5

Listen to me and do not depart from the words of my mouth.
PROVERBS 5:7

Disappointments can be hard to bear. One minute life can appear to be on track for what we hope and dream. The next moment our way is blocked, seemingly without remedy. How do we respond when faced with closed doors?

If our hearts are set on a certain course of action, we may push ahead anyway, refusing to believe God would close the door for a time or a purpose we cannot see. We move forward by manipulating people or circumstances, ensuring we get what we want. Sadly, we find ourselves outside of the Father's plan, with great heartbreak. Another way we may respond to a blocked path is to become upset that the Lord isn't bowing to our will. In fact, we can become so angry that He isn't doing things our way that we give up on Him and walk away. Again, we reject the safety and security of His perfect will and find only devastation.

On the other hand, the godly response is to wait and trust. When the Lord blocks our way, we are to have faith in Him, taking time to assess the situation and pray for guidance. We thank God for closing doors that are not in His will and ask the Spirit to increase our sensitivity to the open doors He has for us—acknowledge that as God, He knows what's best and is providing it.

Friend, are you facing closed doors today? Listen to God and don't depart from the path He has for you. In other words, pray, wait, trust, and obey. Praise Him even when you don't understand the obstacles on your path and remain faithful to whatever He calls you to do. Because in this way, you'll always be sure to experience the very best of what He's planned for you.

Lord God, thank You for the doors You close.
Lead me in Your perfect will to the doors
You would have me walk through.
Amen.

DECEMBER 6

Your Father's Provision

SCRIPTURE READING: PROVERBS 6; ROMANS 5:8; 8:15

Observe the commandment of your father.
PROVERBS 6:20

Have you ever considered the fact that from the beginning of time, the Father was preparing His perfect plan and diligently orchestrating all the details of it so that you could become His child? This is why He sent Jesus on His incredible mission. Completely God and fully Man, Christ left His home in heaven to be the final lamb—the perfect sacrifice that would totally satisfy God's requirement of the shedding of blood for the remission of sins. And Jesus' obedience unto death opened the way for you to join His family.

Because of Jesus, you've been given the privilege of being adopted as a child of God and to be a coheir with Christ. Think about that for a moment. The God of the universe, the Creator of everything and everyone, the infinite King of kings and Lord of lords, who is all-powerful and all-knowing, went to such great lengths to have a relationship with you. And He did so despite of all of your faults, failings, and fears (Romans 5:8). Additionally, this new relationship you have with Him is very special. Romans 8:15 affirms, "You have not received a spirit of slavery leading to fear again, but you have received a spirit of adoption as sons." Adoption was a very serious matter in ancient times. A parent might be able to renounce a natural child, but by law, one who had been adopted would belong to the family forever. This is why we never have to fear—our relationship with the Father is permanent.

Therefore, friend, never fear approaching your loving heavenly Father for guidance. You can trust in His sure care, protection, and provision. Because the One who saves you will surely do anything for you, so you can always trust the manner in which He directs you.

Father, thank You for adopting me, loving me, and providing
so much for me. I know I can trust You to lead me.
Amen.

The Prison of Busyness

SCRIPTURE READING: PROVERBS 7; ROMANS 6:5–11

Her feet do not remain at home.
PROVERBS 7:11

What does freedom mean to you? Although many people have different definitions of true liberty, the one thing almost everyone can agree upon is that it is extremely costly. In a national and political sense, freedom often requires the lives of brave men and women to achieve it, maintain it, and defend it. The same is true in the spiritual sense, though nothing has ever been as costly as what Christ paid for your liberty from sin on the cross (Romans 6:5–11).

Unfortunately, there will always be opponents who will challenge the existence of freedom. Perhaps the worst adversary you will face is the enemy of your soul, who does whatever he can to keep you from experiencing the abundant life God has for you. The strategies and tactics he uses are extremely destructive, one of the most devastating being trapping you in a perpetual state of busyness—giving you no time to sit still and interact with God. You fill your days with activity rather than following the Father's will and learning His ways. In that manner, the enemy weakens your defenses, keeps you exhausted, and blinds you to the sin keeping you captive.

Friend, that's not the extraordinary life the Father created you to enjoy. I realize that everything you are doing may seem right and good, but the very best thing you can do is stop and focus on God. It takes discipline, but when you keep your eyes on the Lord and your feet are firmly planted on the pathway of His will, you'll experience a far more fulfilling life—the abundant life of freedom you were made for. So today, stop the running and allow the Father to lead you to liberty.

*Father, I confess that sometimes I stay busy because I
am afraid to face You. Please forgive me. I surrender
myself to You, trusting You to lead me to liberty.
Amen.*

Hail the Incarnate Deity

SCRIPTURE READING: PROVERBS 8; EXODUS 3:14; JOHN 1; 8:5–7;
10:30; 15:26; COLOSSIANS 1:15–16; REVELATION 19–20

When He established the heavens, I was there.
PROVERBS 8:27

Jesus is often referred to as Savior, Messiah, Christ, and High Priest, just to name a few titles. The most important and accurate description of Jesus, though, is one that we don't often understand: Jesus is God.

Of course, we say, "Jesus is Lord," but what exactly does that mean? If Christ were not deity, then it would be blasphemous to ascribe total lordship and sovereignty to Him. In fact, in John 8:57–58, Jesus shocked the Jews by saying, "Before Abraham was born, I am." "I AM," of course, is the divine name that the Father communicated to Moses (Exodus 3:14), and by using this expression, Jesus claimed to be God. And in John 10:30, He asserts, "I and the Father are one."

And true to form, Scripture clearly shows that Christ is, in fact, fully God and utterly worthy of all honor, glory, power, and praise. In John 1:1–5, we see that Jesus is not only present at creation, but that everything in the universe came into being through His wisdom and power and exists for His pleasure (Colossians 1:15–16). And in Revelation 19–20, we see that one day He will come again as the reigning Lord of all creation to judge the living and the dead.

Friend, if you trust in God's holy Word, then you must recognize the true nature of the One who gave so much for you. This makes His atoning sacrifice and the promise of His presence even more wonderful. The One who created and saved you and is always with you—there's nothing He can't handle. So praise Him today for how much He loves and cares for you.

Lord Jesus, I praise Your holy name! You formed
the heavens and the earth and to have You as my
Defender is more wonderful than I can express.
Amen.

Be Filled

SCRIPTURE READING: PROVERBS 9; PSALM 42:2; MATTHEW 5:6

"Come, eat."
PROVERBS 9:5

Have you ever found yourself thirsting for the Lord? Do you understand what David felt as he wrote, "My soul thirsts for God" in Psalm 42:2? Or what Jesus meant when He said, "Blessed are those who hunger and thirst for righteousness, for they shall be satisfied" (Matthew 5:6)? In reality, each of us will long for many things in our lives. Studies show that, aside from the basic needs of food and water, all humans share love, acceptance, respect, and security as essential requirements for the well-being of their souls.

It is not uncommon for people to spend years searching for someone or something that will satisfy their needs. What they fail to realize is that God is the only source of ultimate satisfaction. In Him are the worth, confidence, joy, and peace for which they long. The same is true for us. We may have a lot of things in life, but they can never fulfill the deepest yearnings within us. What really matters is that we have God—the Creator who knows our limitations, faults, and failings, yet continues to love and accept us unconditionally. He also knows exactly how to answer those profound needs within us to a depth and degree that nothing in this world can match.

Friend, the more you hunger and thirst for God, the more of Himself He will reveal to you. And the more He reveals, the more you will love and trust Him, finding true contentment in your soul. So stop chasing things that don't satisfy. "Taste and see that the Lord is good; how blessed is the man who takes refuge in Him!" (Psalm 34:8). Because when you do, you will experience greater levels of joy, peace, worth, acceptance, respect, and security than you ever have before.

Father, Your love is sweetness to my soul and fulfillment of all
I yearn for. Fill me to overflowing with Your presence.
Amen.

Everlasting Timing

The righteous has an everlasting foundation.
PROVERBS 10:25

Do you realize that God is the Lord of time? That He exists outside of it and rules over every moment? In Isaiah 46:10, He tells us, "I make known the end from the beginning" (NIV). Yet because God rules over all time, He sees the strategic value of using it wisely in your life. As Isaiah 30:18 instructs, "The Lord longs to be gracious to you, and therefore He waits on high to have compassion on you."

For example, if you're playing an instrument in a symphony, you must know when to play and when to pause to create a moving and impactful experience. It is no different in your relationship with God. As the all-wise Master Conductor of your life, He works through timing for maximum effect to accomplish His eternal purposes in your character and circumstances.

So today you may be waiting on something that is extremely important. As time passes, your faith is stretched, your doubts surface, and you have to decide what you really believe. The Father uses this opportunity to address strongholds in your life and teach you to keep your eyes on Him. He also works through this waiting time to put everything into place in fulfillment of His promises to you.

But the point is that your hope cannot be based on what happens today, tomorrow, next month, or even next year—they don't make anything happen. Rather, your trust must be in the Lord, who is from everlasting to everlasting, who wisely leads you, and who accomplishes all things for you (Psalm 57:2). Your moments are under His watchful care, as meticulously directed and treasured as the rest of the workings of creation. So you can and should trust Him with your timing.

Father, I will wait for You—the God of all creation,
the Lord of time, and the Master Conductor of my life.
Amen.

DECEMBER 11

Heard and Answered

SCRIPTURE READING: PROVERBS 11; HEBREWS 11:6; JAMES 1:5–6

He who earnestly seeks good finds favor.
PROVERBS 11:27

Perhaps you've imagined the billions of prayers that reach the ears of God each day: petitions for healing, help, favor, and honor. If so, then maybe you wonder if the Lord really hears you, especially when you're not as faithful as you know you should be. When you lift your personal requests to the Father, do you trust that He is listening and will respond?

Friend, without a doubt, the Father will answer you. If you are faced with a difficult choice or challenge, the Lord promises to provide the wisdom you need to make the correct decision. James wrote, "If any of you lacks wisdom, let him ask of God, who gives to all generously and without reproach, and it will be given to him. But he must ask in faith without any doubting" (James 1:5–6). This is where your trust in God enters in. You must believe that if you go to the Lord with even the smallest detail, He will hear your prayer and answer it. Of course, he does not say you will automatically receive exactly what you ask for, in the exact moment you request it. The key is to pray with undivided trust. The Father always answers your cries, but His solutions and timelines may be different from yours.

Your responsibility is to rid your mind of doubt. Remember, Hebrews 11:6 says, "He who comes to God must believe that He is and *that* He is a rewarder of those who seek Him." You are guaranteed the Lord will fulfill His promises—but you must believe Him. So examine your level of faith the next time that you have a need in your life. And as you take your request to God, have full confidence that you're not only heard—you also will be answered.

Lord, I do believe You exist and will answer my prayers.
Thank You for hearing and loving me, Father.
Amen.

Think Peace

SCRIPTURE READING: PROVERBS 12; MATTHEW 5:5–9; PHILIPPIANS 4:8

Those who promote peace have joy.
PROVERBS 12:20 NIV

Thinking God's way does not come easily to us because it is often contrary to the world's perspective. The world says, "Fight for your rights, don't let anyone push you around." But Jesus teaches that it is actually the merciful, the meek, and the peacemakers who are successful and valued in God's kingdom (Matthew 5:5–9). The world holds material prosperity and personal comfort as the ultimate measures of achievement. But throughout Scripture we find that true success is when we become more like Jesus and faithfully follow His plan—promoting peace with the Father and unity with our brothers and sisters in Christ.

Of course, our minds direct how we respond in different situations based on our values and priorities. So our responsibility as Christ followers is to feed our minds with a steady diet of God's Word. Only scriptural truth can counter the continuous stream of ungodly, hostile, and destructive information that enters our thinking. Another responsibility is to screen what we allow to enter our minds. The Bible gives us the standard by which to evaluate the acceptability of ideas and attitudes we encounter: "Whatever is true, whatever is honorable, whatever is right, whatever is pure, whatever is lovely, whatever is of good repute, if there is any excellence and if anything worthy of praise, dwell on these things" (Philippians 4:8).

So promote peace in your own soul and with others by meditating on Scripture, applying it to your life, and following God's standard for your thinking. You will not only live in a way that pleases the Father but you will also influence others to have a relationship with Him. That is real success and the true path to joy.

*Lord Jesus, I want to be a peacemaker—reflecting You
in all my words and actions. I want to become more like You
and faithfully follow Your plan. Lead me through Your Word.
Amen.*

Realizable Desires

Desire realized is sweet to the soul.
PROVERBS 13:19

Is there some prayer that you have been longing for God to answer? There is nothing wrong or sinful with asking God for blessings. In fact, the Father takes joy in meeting the desires that fit His will for your life. Psalm 37:4 says, "Delight yourself in the Lord; and He will give you the desires of your heart." This is a wonderful promise, which most of us have claimed at one point or another. But when is it appropriate for us to claim it?

Right away we see that Psalm 37:4 is a conditional promise. The requirement given is that God must rule our hearts and be the focus of our lives. We find our joy in Him. We love Him and enjoy spending time in His presence—reading His Word, worshipping at His throne, and seeking Him in prayer. He is our strength and comfort in times of adversity. In other words, the Father satisfies our needs, and our relationship with Him is the source of our profound contentment, peace, hope, and gladness. If Jesus is all that to us, that eliminates many of the desires we would normally request, doesn't it? We wouldn't need to ask for anything that would usually give us a sense of self-worth, identity, belonging, competence, honor, or security because we would find all those things in Him.

Therefore, friend, test your motives for your requests and wait on God to fulfill your heart's desires. The Father loves to bless you. But if that longing replaces Him in any way, satiates the needs only He can satisfy, or becomes an idol in your life, He will not compete with it. And if you refuse to wait for Him to provide, then you will undoubtedly miss His very best and the sweet blessings of the soul He has for you.

Lord, I delight myself in You and wait for Your perfect
provision. May You always be my all-in-all.
Amen.

The Power of His Peace

SCRIPTURE READING: PROVERBS 14; ISAIAH 26:3; JOHN 14:27

A tranquil heart is life to the body.
PROVERBS 14:30

Conflict is part of living. However, a common problem today is that most people don't know how to deal with it, nor do they understand the source of real peace. As a result, we have become a medicated society—the common goal being to escape from conflict through addictive substances and behaviors.

This is ultimately because people tend to define peace as the absence of hostility and anxiety, but the biblical term actually refers to something far broader. Jesus used the Greek word *eirene*, which means "to bind together." Scripturally, this kind of peace involves a sense of wholeness or inner completeness that brings stability to a person's life, no matter what is taking place in that individual's circumstances. It is not a sense of serenity that comes today and goes tomorrow, but rather of prevailing—that is, undefeatable—tranquillity that nothing in this world can overcome (John 14:27).

Of course, the key to this enduring peace is found in a relationship with Jesus—the Prince of Peace. If you want tranquillity that is everlasting, you need to work on your intimacy with Christ and pursue oneness with Him. His peace is free, a gift available to every one of His children—but it can be embraced only as we walk closely with Him.

Friend, if you will focus your attention on the Son of God, He will give you perfect peace (Isaiah 26:3). That does not mean you'll be immune to trials, challenges, or losses, or that circumstances will never again throw you off balance. Rather, it means that regardless of what you endure, you'll be able to face it with the Lord's prevailing peace, which will always be adequate to carry you through anything He allows you to experience.

Lord Jesus, thank You for giving me Your peace— the
tranquillity of heart that transcends understanding.
Help me always to walk in oneness with You.
Amen.

DECEMBER 15

Proclaim the Good News

SCRIPTURE READING: PROVERBS 15; LUKE 2:8–20

Bright eyes cheer the heart;
good news strengthens the bones.
PROVERBS 15:30 HCSB

In Luke 2:8–20 we find the very first proclamation that the Messiah had come to earth. Interestingly, the people who were blessed to hear it weren't kings, priests, or prophets—they were shepherds. God sent this most wonderful birth announcement to ordinary people—men who didn't have wealth, power, or social standing to recommend them. In fact, by Jewish standards, shepherds were considered outcasts. They were spurned because of the work they did with sheep, which made them ceremonially unclean. These forgotten individuals may have wondered if their lives really counted for anything. Thankfully, God's resounding answer was "Yes!"

The Lord did not choose great speechmakers or monarchs to proclaim the Good News of Jesus Christ that night. He chose the shepherds. Why? Because they were people just like you and me. And when they heard the joyful tidings, they didn't worry about what people would think of them or how it would look. They just knew it would give the people hope to hear that the Messiah had finally arrived. So wherever they went with their flocks, they would tell the story about how the Savior had been born in Bethlehem.

Don't miss this message: It doesn't matter who we are. What God wants most from us is that we tell His Good News and praise His name. Those shepherds did not detract from the gospel because of their lowly estate; rather, they became *part of* the beautiful message that the Savior had come to reach *all of us* no matter how humble or lonely we are. And He declares that He is the One who gives us our hope, our identity, and our worth.

Father, I thank You for the privilege of proclaiming
the Good News of salvation through Jesus! Thank you that
a relationship with You is the only qualification I will ever need.
Amen.

Humbly Trust His Promises

SCRIPTURE READING: PROVERBS 16; 1 KINGS 8:56;
PSALM 84:11; MICAH 6:8; JAMES 4:10

*He who gives attention to the word will find good,
and blessed is he who trusts in the Lord.*

PROVERBS 16:20

God's promises never fail. When He tells us He will do something, we can count on it happening, even if it takes longer than we first imagined. This was certainly true with all the prophecies concerning the coming of the Messiah: "Not one word has failed of all His good promise" (1 Kings 8:56).

With this in mind, what's the key to overcoming difficult times? James explains: "Humble yourselves in the presence of the Lord, and He will exalt you" (James 4:10). You must be willing to die to your own hopes and dreams in order to have the fullness of life God has for you. For example, the Jews expected a military hero, not the Suffering Servant, because they did not understand the Lord's plan to provide for the redemption of the world. Likewise, you may have been overlooked, treated unfairly, or have had to wait a long time to see His promises come to fruition. Instead of allowing discouragement to overwhelm you or fighting against your circumstances, set your heart on being humble before God—trusting His purposes.

Micah 6:8 reminds you, "He has told you, O man, what is good; and what does the Lord require of you but to do justice, to love kindness, and to walk humbly with your God?" Why? Because humility transforms you into the image of Christ. It also empowers you so that you can stand firm whenever confusing situations arise or the enemy attacks. Living a life of humility may not be easy, but it certainly leads to God's richest blessings. Therefore, humble yourself so that you may experience all that He has for you. And remember, "No good thing does He withhold from those who walk uprightly" (Psalm 84:11).

*Father, I will trust in Your good promises.
You're God and I'm not. I will submit myself to You.
Amen.*

Envy

SCRIPTURE READING: PROVERBS 17

*Better is a dry morsel and quietness with it
than a house full of feasting with strife.*
PROVERBS 17:1

People will wait in line for weeks to buy the latest technological gadget that will quickly be obsolete. They'll get into a fight with a stranger at a store over toys that their children will forget about a couple of weeks after Christmas. They'll even spend their rent for an item that they "have to have," but they'll have trouble remembering to use once the next big thing comes along.

The enemy will tempt you by fixating your attention on something that you think you must possess and by convincing you that you'll never have true happiness without it. It usually involves a need in your life that the Lord is perfectly capable of satisfying. However, you try to fill the need with something or someone that is not God's will because you doubt either His ability to provide it for you (His sovereignty) or His motivation for withholding it from you (His love). You simply don't trust the Lord, and because of that, something that should have a very small place in your life becomes an enormous preoccupation for you.

Friend, it's human nature to want what someone else has, but you need to be honest with yourself. Have you been trying to fill a need in your heart with possessions rather than with God? Are you attracted to things and people that promise to bring you happiness but who never really satisfy you? Then you've fallen to the sin of envy and you must get right with God. Prayerfully ask the Father to reveal any need you're not trusting Him to fill, and repent. Then ask Him to teach you to look to Him for all of the desires of your heart and express your confidence that He can satisfy your soul like no one and nothing else can.

*Lord, I confess that I've looked for people and things to fill my
emptiness. Forgive me, Father, and satisfy my soul with Your presence.
Amen.*

DECEMBER 18

Seek Him

Scripture Reading: Proverbs 18; Psalm 46:1–2

The mind of the prudent acquires knowledge,
and the ear of the wise seeks knowledge.
PROVERBS 18:15

Are you are facing a stressful time? The holidays can be extremely tiring. And if you've received any news that troubles your heart, you may find yourself wondering how you will face another day. Of course, there is a way, but it has nothing to do with human ability. Instead, it has everything to do with God's sovereign strength.

When the pressures of your world mount, you will certainly be tempted to think that you have to work things out on your own. However, while God does want you actively involved in the problem-solving process, His greater desire is for you to call out to Him and declare your dependence on Him.

In Psalm 46:1–2, the psalmist writes, "God is our refuge and strength, a very present help in trouble. Therefore we will not fear, though the earth should change and though the mountains slip into the heart of the sea." These words portray a physical representation of the way we feel emotionally when trouble strikes and everything seems to be falling apart. Very few of us are prepared to handle a sudden sorrow or a trial that continues over a long period of time. Fear, frustration, and doubt can give way to a longing to escape—abandoning the problems and getting away from it all.

But how can you right your upside-down world in a positive way that builds you up instead of tears you down? Begin with God. Spend time with Him in prayer. You may think you can't afford to lose another minute, but you can't afford to miss the opportunity of allowing the Father to comfort you and provide the help you need. So go to Him and find the strength and wisdom you require to go on.

Lord, I need You. I need Your strength and wisdom for the
pressures I'm facing. I trust You to show me what to do.
Amen.

The Kindness of Freedom

SCRIPTURE READING: PROVERBS 19; HEBREWS 2:17–18

What is desirable in a man is his kindness.
PROVERBS 19:22

One of the gifts the Lord gives you as His child is that He removes the sinful things that no longer fit who you are as a believer. His desire is to maximize your potential by teaching you to live out the holiness He has given you. He wants you to become a reflection of His love, patience, kindness, gentleness, and hope to a lost world. This is because there's no power in the life of a believer who is not living a pure and obedient life. His light will not shine as brightly through you when your character is marred by sin.

Of course, Jesus understands the struggle you have with sin, to a deeper degree than any person could ever grasp. On the cross, He carried the sin of the whole world on His shoulders, and He felt the terrible weight of it. Why? Hebrews 2:17–18 reports, "He had to be made like His brethren"—like you—"in all things, so that He might become a merciful and faithful high priest in things pertaining to God, to make propitiation for the sins of the people. For since He Himself was tempted in that which He has suffered, He is able to come to the aid of those who are tempted." In other words, in His kindness toward you, He laid aside His divine place in heaven to identify with you.

Jesus' compassion moved Him to liberate you from the penalty and hold of sin. And friend, He turns and asks you to do likewise—to be merciful and kind to others by showing them to way to be free. So learn how blessed and fruitful it is to live in complete freedom as His child by obeying Him and loving others with His love.

Lord, thank You for setting me free from sin. Help me to show Your kindness to others so they can be free as well.
Amen.

What's in You

The spirit of man is the lamp of the Lord,
searching all the innermost parts of his being.
PROVERBS 20:27

God knows what is in you. He sees what makes you respond as you do, hurt as you do. And be assured, He understands it all far better than you could ever comprehend it. You have dreams and desires today. And it is Christmastime, so perhaps your prayers for them are a little more impassioned, somewhat more desperate. This is natural, of course. During such a hectic season, all of our activity makes us more tired and lonely, which means our defenses are down and our hearts are more vulnerable.

At such times you may feel isolated, abandoned, and misunderstood, but be assured, the Lord your God sees you, knows the pain you carry, and is well aware of the desires of your heart. Why doesn't He answer them? Because He is also cognizant of what you need to meet the real and profound needs within you—freedom from bondage, healing from wounds, strengthening of character, and deeper faith in Him. Those are the details He can see that you may not be aware of, but which will determine whether you can truly enjoy the blessings you cry out for. He searches your inmost parts to prepare and satisfy you fully.

Be assured, "The Lord longs to be gracious to you." However, this verse from Isaiah 30:18 continues by saying, "Therefore He waits on high to have compassion on you." The reason He hasn't answered certain prayers yet is out of *mercy* for you. So don't lose heart. Keep trusting in Him because He certainly knows what is absolutely best for you.

Father, this is a difficult season, and You know what my
heart longs for. I don't understand Your delays, but I thank
You for always leading me in the best way possible.
Amen.

The Heart of Caesar

SCRIPTURE READING: PROVERBS 21; MICAH 5:2; LUKE 2

*The king's heart is like channels of water in the hand
of the LORD; He turns it wherever He wishes.*
PROVERBS 21:1

Sometimes those in authority over us may seem unmovable and even somewhat beyond God's influence. Yet Luke 2 tells us of how Caesar Augustus made a decree that everyone in the inhabited earth was required to go back to his or her city of origin for a census. This didn't seem like the Lord had anything to do with it, and no doubt Caesar believed he'd made the decision on his own in order to tax the citizens.

But from eternity past, the Lord decided who the Roman emperor would be and when he would make the historic declaration that would mean that Joseph of Nazareth would take Mary to Bethlehem and ultimately give birth to Jesus there. This, of course, was in fulfillment of Micah 5:2, that the Messiah would be born in Bethlehem, the City of King David. God turned the heart of Caesar to make a decree that would ultimately show beyond a shadow of a doubt that Jesus was who He said He was—the Promised Messiah from the line of David.

Now maybe you are wondering, *What does this have to do with me?* Friend, the same God who engineered all of these amazing circumstances to provide for your salvation is *with you*, and His ability to help you is absolutely limitless. All things concerning your life—including the hearts of people in authority over you—are in His hand. You may not be able to influence the people who could change your circumstances, but He certainly can—and He will. So take heart today that He is directing your situation like a watercourse and is helping you mightily even when it may not seem like it.

*Lord, thank You, all hearts are in Your hands,
and the ways You help me are truly limitless.
Amen.*

DECEMBER 22

Mary's Honor

SCRIPTURE READING: PROVERBS 22; ROMANS 5:3–5; 1 PETER 5:6

The reward of humility and the fear of the
LORD are riches, honor and life.
PROVERBS 22:4

Being found with child without a husband most likely opened Mary to terrible ridicule from those who did not comprehend her awesome assignment. Jewish society treated unmarried pregnant women with terrible shame and scorn. In fact, girls in this condition were often punished with stoning until death. We might wonder, was it really necessary for Mary, such a humble and submissive servant of God, to face so much persecution when all she was doing was being obedient? Why did so much adversity have to follow her?

Yes, it was difficult, but the truth is that hardships can have a very positive influence on a person's life. In fact, in Romans 5:3–5, the apostle Paul writes, "We . . . exult in our tribulations, knowing that tribulation brings about perseverance; and perseverance, proven character; and proven character, hope; and hope does not disappoint, because the love of God has been poured out within our hearts through the Holy Spirit."

Certainly, as Mary raised Jesus, she would need perseverance, character, and hope—and to model those characteristics to Him. She had an astoundingly great privilege—to give birth to the Son of God. Anyone else might have become proud, ambitious, and conceited. But Mary knew that with this amazing honor came an equally immense responsibility. And throughout history, she's been venerated for her faith and sacrifice.

Likewise, you may be wondering about the trials God allows in your life and how He's directing you. But submit to Him as Mary did. Like her, "Humble yourselves under the mighty hand of God, that He may exalt you at the proper time" (1 Peter 5:6). Because that is certainly the path to true and lasting honor.

Lord, I humble myself before You and submit to Your great
plans, knowing Your purposes far exceed my own.
Amen.

The Eternal Internal Gift

SCRIPTURE READING: PROVERBS 23; MATTHEW 1:23;
28:20; JOHN 14:26; EPHESIANS 4:30

My inmost being will rejoice.
PROVERBS 23:16

As we know, the Lord Jesus is our beloved and faithful " 'Immanuel,' which translated means, 'God with us' " (Matthew 1:23). So as His crucifixion neared, He spent His last hours with the disciples explaining that the gift of the Holy Spirit, who would be the divine, enduring agent of the Lord's presence with them following Christ's death and ascension. The Holy Spirit is why Jesus could say, "I am with you always, even to the end of the age" (Matthew 28:20). No longer would they be separated from God in any way—not physically, spiritually, or relationally. His continuing Spirit would indwell them unto the day of redemption (Ephesians 4:30).

The same is true for you. You are never alone. You are never helpless. You are never comfortless. God is with you—the presence of His Holy Spirit within you is unconditional and unceasing. Once you are saved, His residence is absolutely permanent. There is never a moment when the Holy Spirit is not with you. And even better, He teaches you everything you need to know to do what is right so you can be pleasing to the Father and walk in His will (John 14:26).

Friend, the presence of the Holy Spirit is unconditional. Whether the joy of the Lord is overflowing in you or the depths of despair overwhelm you, He is there. So take comfort in knowing the great resource, power, wisdom, love, and security you have as a child of the living God. Through the Holy Spirit, the Father is intimately involved with every detail of your existence, His help is immediate, and everything you need for victory is available before you even ask.

*Lord Jesus, thank You for Your indwelling Spirit who always
leads, comforts, guides, and empowers me. To You be all the glory.
Amen.*

The Virgin Birth

SCRIPTURE READING: PROVERBS 24; ISAIAH
7:14; LUKE 1:30–35; ROMANS 5:12

By wisdom a house is built, and by understanding it is established.
PROVERBS 24:3

Isaiah 7:14 tells us, "The LORD Himself will give you a sign: Behold, a virgin will be with child and bear a son, and she will call His name Immanuel." Certainly, the virgin birth was necessary in order to fulfill Isaiah's prophecy and distinguish Jesus as the Messiah. But God had another important reason for the way He orchestrated Christ's unique birth.

Had Jesus' descent been through an earthly vessel, He, like us, would have been born in sin and therefore unable to save us. After all, God was clear: Sin entered the world through Adam and spread death to all mankind through his seed (Romans 5:12). With a normal birth, the seed of the sin nature comes through the father. Yet as we know, Jesus was miraculously conceived by the Holy Spirit (Luke 1:30–35)—not by a human father—so He did not receive the sin nature and lived a completely sinless life. That made Him the perfect substitutionary sacrifice for us—the only payment that would ever be completely sufficient.

This is why the virgin birth is absolutely central to our salvation and why the cross was acceptable to our heavenly Father. With great love and unfathomable wisdom, the Lord executed His extraordinary plan of salvation—holy God became a Man and lived a sinless life so He could bear our sins and rescue us from the deadly wages of our transgressions.

Friend, God knew exactly what it would take to forgive you of all your sins, and He gladly gave it. Therefore rejoice in His wonderful wisdom and provision today and glorify His holy name.

Lord Jesus, I rejoice in Your virgin birth and thank You for
living a sinless life and saving me. To You be all honor,
glory, power, and praise in this and very generation.
Amen.

Wise Men Seek Him

SCRIPTURE READING: PROVERBS 25; GENESIS 1:14

The glory of kings is to search out a matter.
PROVERBS 25:2

The Magi, also known as wise men, were a special elite class of advisers and leaders from the East, probably from somewhere in Mesopotamia near the city of Babylon. They were most likely astronomers who discovered an unusual star that indicated the birth of the long-expected Jewish king. But how did these men know about the Messiah? After all, they were from far-off pagan lands. Why would they even care?

The Book of Daniel helps us unravel this mystery, because there we find the ancient connection between the wise men of the Babylonian Empire and the prophesies of Israel. The Magi who visited Jesus were most likely descendants of those who learned from Daniel and other Jews about the God of Israel and the promised Messiah. Generations later, when the sign of the Jewish king finally appeared in the sky, the Magi would have recognized its significance. We don't usually think of stars as a means of divine guidance. But when God made the sun, moon, and stars, and placed them in the heavens, He designed them not only to provide light for the earth but also for another important purpose. He said, "Let them be for signs and for seasons and for days and years" (Genesis 1:14). Even these lights in the celestial expanse were part of the Lord's astounding plan to herald the Messiah, which He'd set in motion from the foundation of the earth.

The point is, God can be found if you will look for Him. The primary way, of course, is through His Word. But knowing Him more profoundly is the greatest gift you will receive this Christmas. So seek Him and enjoy discovering more of who He is.

God, how I long to know You better. You are my
greatest gift, Lord Jesus. Lead me to love You more
and walk in the center of Your path for my life.
Amen.

DECEMBER 26

Feeding the Fire of Your Faith

SCRIPTURE READING: PROVERBS 26; EXODUS 16:3; 2 CORINTHIANS 10:5

For lack of wood the fire goes out.
PROVERBS 26:20

There are certain thoughts and phrases that arise in your mind that begin your downhill slide to doubt and disbelief. You may not even realize they are there. For example, when the Israelites left Egypt and wandered in the wilderness, we know they made this terrible statement, "Would that we *had died* by the Lord's hand in the land of Egypt, when we sat by the pots of meat, when we ate bread to the full; for you have brought us out into this wilderness *to kill this whole assembly* with hunger" (Exodus 16:3).

Did they really prefer dying in Egypt? Did they genuinely believe Moses' goal was to kill them with hunger? How could they possibly come to such conclusions? We must understand that their reasoning did not begin at that point. More than likely, they began by thinking something as simple as, *I wonder when we're going to eat?* But imagine the difference if instead of being negative, they had focused on the Father's astounding provision on their behalf. How the God who parted the Red Sea, led them by a pillar of cloud by day and fire by night—how their wonderful Deliverer would certainly sustain them. No doubt that focused on His provision, they would have been filled with faith.

The same is true for you. Are your thoughts fanning the flames of your faith or drowning it with doubt? If unbelief characterizes what you think, then build up your mind with His truth. In doing so, you "demolish arguments and every pretension that sets itself up against the knowledge of God" (2 Corinthians 10:5 NIV) and ensure you're throwing wood on the right fire.

Lord, I confess that I have thoughts that drown out my faith.
Identify the strongholds of unbelief in my life and replace
them with Your truth so I may walk in Your victory.
Amen.

DECEMBER 27

Your Best Friend

SCRIPTURE READING: PROVERBS 27; JEREMIAH 31:1;
JOHN 15:13–14; HEBREWS 2:17–18; 7:25

Do not forsake your own friend.
PROVERBS 27:10

How many true friends do you have? How many people can you trust with the most profound issues of your heart? Often our lives are filled with acquaintances, people we have a passing association with. But we all know how rare it is to establish a deep, genuine, and unshakable friendship with another person.

Thankfully, in John 15:14, Jesus spoke to the disciples about the intimate friendship He offers to each person who believes in Him: "No longer do I call you slaves . . . but I have called you friends, for all things that I have heard from My Father I have made known to you." So how dedicated is He to your relationship? He said, "Greater love has no one than this, that one lay down his life for his friends" (v. 13). You are assured that Jesus is committed to you to the point of death. Therefore, you can know for certain that He is your truest friend. And as your Friend, He:

- accepts you completely.
- understands you fully (Hebrews 2:17–18).
- is eternally committed to you (Jeremiah 31:1).
- always lives to make intercession for you (Hebrews 7:25).

There will certainly be times when you feel that there's no one you can trust. In those moments of despair, remember your enduring ray of hope—the unconditional love and friendship of Jesus. He will never abandon or forsake you, and He will always understand whatever you feel in your heart. So turn to Him often and do not ignore the best Friend you will ever have. Because His is the one relationship you can enjoy that will never disappoint you.

Jesus, thank You for being the best Friend I will ever have! May our relationship continue to grow in love, depth, and confidence.
Amen.

Walk in Victory

SCRIPTURE READING: PROVERBS 28; EPHESIANS 1:19–20

When the righteous triumph, there is great glory.
PROVERBS 28:12

Jesus wants you to live in the victory of His presence today. Amid the uncertainties and pressures surrounding you, He is at your side to strengthen and encourage you. And when your eyes are fixed on Him rather than the world around you, you'll begin to see the triumph you can walk in every day of your life.

Instead of striving to live up to others' standards, the Holy Spirit will teach you to dwell on the things of God, which are pure and honoring to Christ. This does not mean that you'll never feel rejected, lonely, or defeated. Rather, it means that you can continue to walk in victory despite those feelings, because Jesus is your hope, goal, and example, and His Spirit lives in you, reminding you of all the promises He's made to you.

He is the Savior who bore the weight of all our sins and still remained victorious. He has faced the greatest enemies the soul will ever know—sin and death—and has triumphed over them through His glorious resurrection. And in Ephesians 1:19–20, we are assured that "the surpassing greatness of His power" is available to "us who believe"—the very same "working of the strength of His might which He brought about in Christ, when He raised Him from the dead." In other words, His resurrection power is available to you today!

Friend, God uses every frustration, fear, and feeling of hopelessness to remind you of your need for Him. And one day you'll see the brilliance of God's work and understand the purposes behind each of the trials you've experienced. Understand that today—realize that nothing you're facing is a mistake. The Lord is in control. So walk in the victory of knowing that your life is in God's hand and He's working everything out for your good.

Jesus, all Your ways are victorious! Thank You for
always leading me on the path to triumph!
Amen.

When You're Persecuted

SCRIPTURE READING: PROVERBS 29; MATTHEW 5:44; JOHN 15:19–20

The wicked despise the godly.
PROVERBS 29:27

If you've been a Christian for any length of time, you've probably noticed that not everybody is going to comprehend your desire to follow Jesus. In fact, very few people will, and there may be times you'll be misunderstood and mistreated—some will actively oppose you because of your commitment to Him. Jesus said it Himself, "I have chosen you out of the world. That is why the world hates you . . . If they persecuted me, they will persecute you also" (John 15:19–20).

Therefore, in order to withstand persecution, you must know with certainty that you're being harassed for the cause of Christ and not simply because of your own foolishness, error, or stubbornness. So ask yourself:

- Has the Lord really directed me to take the stance for which I'm being persecuted?
- Am I facing conflict for His name's sake or my reputation? Is this about the Kingdom of God or my personal career?
- Who will get the glory in victory?

If the person who is applauded for the triumph is anyone other than Jesus, it may be that you've taken a stand for the wrong thing. True persecution is always related to the Lord's work. As such, it has a spiritual root and can be won only through faith and obedience to the Savior.

As you follow Christ, your goal should be to see people freed from their sins, healed from their wounds, and filled with faith in Him, so they can escape the strongholds of the enemy. So when true persecution arises, get on your knees, pray for those who oppress you, and ask the Father how to walk in obedience so He'll get all the glory (Matthew 5:44). This is what Jesus did, and it's the path to true spiritual victory.

Jesus, I want to reflect You regardless of how others treat me. May
You be glorified and others saved even when I am persecuted.
Amen.

The Word of the Lion

SCRIPTURE READING: PROVERBS 30; ISAIAH 46:10; REVELATION 5

The lion which is mighty among beasts . . .
does not retreat before any.
PROVERBS 30:30

One of the most exciting things a believer can do is embrace the Word of God. If there is a problem, the Lord has a solution for you within its pages. If there is heartache or sorrow, the Holy Spirit will give you comfort and peace through its promises. And in times of insurmountable difficulty, Scripture reminds you of God's greatness and how nothing can stand against Him.

This is actually why reading the Book of Revelation is particularly exciting and a great blessing. It provides an eyewitness account of things to come and the ultimate fulfillment of God's eternal promises to the Body of Christ. When the Lion from the tribe of Judah—Jesus, our Messiah—returns, no one will be able to oppose Him (Revelation 5). His victory is sure—which means ours is as well. Sadly, for the men and women who turn from the Lord and refuse to accept Jesus as Savior, just the opposite is true. Their defeat is devastatingly certain.

While many of the events of the future remain a mystery to us, they are not to God. He declares, "the end from the beginning, and from ancient times things which have not been done, Saying, 'My purpose will be established, and I will accomplish all My good pleasure'" (Isaiah 46:10). And He reveals just what He knows you need to live triumphantly in this life. Your mission is to pick up His Word, read it daily, and believe Him. Saturate your heart with His principles. Then when trouble comes, you will have the strength of the Lion and His truth to stand on—and when you have those, you have an everlasting guarantee of ultimate victory.

Worthy are You, Lion of Judah, to receive power,
glory, honor, and blessing! Guide me daily
with Your Word of truth to triumph.
Amen.

A Future Worthy of Your Joy

SCRIPTURE READING: PROVERBS 31; JOHN 14:3; REVELATION 22:3

Strength and dignity are her clothing,
and she smiles at the future.
PROVERBS 31:25

Like the godly woman of Proverbs 31, you can smile with joy at the future. Why? Because as a Christian, you have the promise of a future home with Jesus in heaven forever. Jesus said, "When everything is ready, I will come and get you, so that you will always be with me where I am" (John 14:3 NLT). He has been preparing that special place for you for more than two thousand years, and one day soon, He will return to receive you to Himself so you can enjoy unending fellowship with Him.

Of course, most people want to know what they'll be doing in heaven. Revelation 22:3 says, "There will no longer be any curse; and the throne of God and of the Lamb will be in it, and His bond-servants will serve Him." This means that when we get to heaven, we will joyfully worship the Father with our gifts. Yes, there will be rest too—we will no longer suffer from trouble, heartache, toil, or temptation. But that doesn't mean we're going to sit down and do nothing. We will serve the living God forever. And the nature of our heavenly service will be influenced by the faithfulness we demonstrate right now. The way we carry out our responsibilities here on earth will affect the assignments we are given there.

So today, serve the Father wholeheartedly in whatever He gives you to do, always remembering that someday soon these burdens will be gone and you'll be able to enjoy Him forever. And smile with the joy at the future, knowing the good that is to come.

Lord, I end this year with joy because You are so faithful! All my
days are Yours and—even better—I will be with You for eternity!
So I rejoice and look forward to Your kingdom to come.
Amen.

About the Author

*D*r. *Charles F. Stanley* is a *New York Times* bestselling author who has written more than sixty books, with sales of more than ten million copies. He has been senior pastor of the First Baptist Church in Atlanta, Georgia, since 1971, and his outreach ministry—In Touch—reaches more than twenty-eight hundred radio and television outlets in more than fifty languages. Dr. Stanley was inducted into the National Religious Broadcasters (NRB) Hall of Fame in 1988. Dr. Stanley's goal is best represented by In Touch Ministries' mission statement: to lead people worldwide into a growing relationship with Jesus Christ and to strengthen the local church. This is because, as he says, "It is the Word of God and the work of God that changes people's lives."

Personal notes for your walk in wisdom with God . . .

Personal notes for your walk in wisdom with God . . .

Personal notes for your walk in wisdom with God . . .

Personal notes for your walk in wisdom with God . . .

_____

_____

_____

_____

_____

_____

_____

_____

_____

_____

_____

_____

_____

_____

_____

_____

_____

_____

_____

_____

_____

_____

_____

Personal notes for your walk in wisdom with God . . .

Start your day with the Lord.

Life can be hectic. There are schedules to juggle, deadlines to meet, and family activities to manage. But each morning comes with a new opportunity to draw closer to the Lord.

Start your day off right with an encouraging and uplifting devotion delivered straight to your inbox, ready for you as you prepare to take on the day. Subscribe for free at **intouch.org/subscriptions**.

ALSO BY
CHARLES F. STANLEY

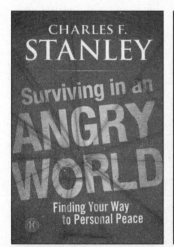

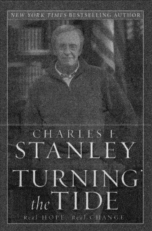

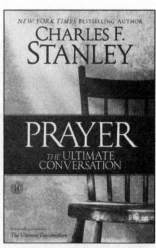

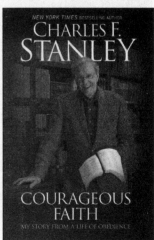

Available wherever books are sold or at SimonandSchuster.com